LIVING
WITH
CONTRADICTIONS

A Married Feminist

By the Same Author

THE GROWTH AND DEVELOPMENT OF MOTHERS

LIVING
WITH
CONTRADICTIONS

A Married Feminist

Angela Barron McBride

HARPER COLOPHON BOOKS
Harper & Row, Publishers
New York, Hagerstown, San Francisco, London

Grateful acknowledgment is made to the publishers for permission to reprint excerpts from the following:

Collected Poems of Elinor Wylie. Copyright 1932 by Alfred A. Knopf, Inc., and renewed 1960 by Edwina C. Rubenstein. Reprinted with permission from Alfred A. Knopf, Inc.

The House of Blue Leaves by John Guare. Copyright © 1968, 1971, 1972 by John Guare. Reprinted with permission from The Viking Press, Inc.

The Iceman Cometh, from *The Plays of Eugene O'Neill.* Copyright 1940, 1946 by Eugene O'Neill. Reprinted with permission from Random House, Inc.

"Our Lady of the Snows," from *The Five Nations,* Volume XXI, by Rudyard Kipling. Published by Doubleday and Company, Inc.

The Price, from *The Portable Arthur Miller,* edited by Harold Clurman. Copyright © 1968 by Arthur Miller and Ingebord M. Miller, Trustee. Reprinted with permission from The Viking Press, Inc.

"The Princess," from *The Poems and Plays of Alfred Lord Tennyson.* Published by Random House, Inc.

Saint Joan, by Bernard Shaw, from *The Bodley Head Bernard Shaw Collected Plays with Their Prefaces,* Volume VI, edited by Dan H. Laurence. Published 1973 by Max Reinhardt, The Bodley Head Limited. Reprinted with permission from The Society of Authors on behalf of the Bernard Shaw Estate.

A hardcover edition of this book is published under the title of *A Married Feminist.*

First HARPER COLOPHON edition published 1977
ISBN: 0–06–090556–5

79 80 81 10 9 8 7 6 5 4 3 2

To the sweet memory of my mother,
Mary Szczepanski Barron

CONTENTS

Part antebellum belle—
Crinolined voluptuary,
Dripping sweetness, weighed with perfume;
Ripe, then over-ripe.

Part space-age virago—
Suited animal energy,
Laughing, spoiling for new pleasures;
Strident, then silent.

Part changeless Madonna—
Draped in evergreen dreams of hope,
Giving all and more, nursing love;
Fertile, then barren.

No male Yahweh *(I am who am).*
The She God cries out, "I am who?"
But *I am. I am. Let me be.*

INTRODUCTION

I am a married feminist. What does that mean? Am I part of a new breed of women, or someone about to burst because of the contradictions in my person? There are weeks and months when I'm not sure which description best fits me, but such tensions are the essence of being a married feminist.

How do I explain my concept of married feminist? I am a woman who feels pulled in two directions—between traditional values and conventions on one hand, and a commitment to feminist ideology on the other. A woman who finds custom appealing and comforting, yet despises the patriarchal patterns that make women second-class citizens. I am a woman who wants a loving, long-term relationship with a man, but bitterly resents being considered only someone's other *half*. A woman who values family life, but deplores the sterile, functional view of man as head of the family and woman as its heart. A woman who regards men as attractive because they are the opposite sex, but who also believes marriage should go beyond sexual differences instead of being limited by them. A woman who feels children give her a stake in the future, yet doesn't want her own possibilities obliterated by the burdens of preparing children for life. A wife who wants to belong to one man, yet not be his private property. I am sensitive to the fact that *demanding* can make a woman look selfish, but I also know that being undemanding can deprive a woman of her sense of self. A married feminist wants roots, but she doesn't want to feel rooted.

The apparent contradictions felt by a married feminist are legion. I've listened to fashion plates sing the hedonistic pleasures of not being a mother, and felt like putting them over my knees and spanking them for their selfishness. I've heard gingham types say all they ever wanted out of life was to be a wife and mother, and felt choked by their smugness. I bristle when people spit out the word "feminist" as if it were a communicable disease; I protest when others sneer at marriage as if it were an outdated misery. I meet women with young children and I hesitate to ask if they also have jobs. I don't want to put them on the defensive and make them think I am subtly criticizing them for lack of ambition. But if I avoid the question and don't ask, I feel I'm just reinforcing the prevailing opinion that mothers should not work outside the home until their children are grown. I feel like a conservative when people talk about abortion as just another form of contraception, yet I feel radical in groups that advocate outlawing *all* abortion. I think a society that doesn't value children is degenerate, but one that forces a woman to breed is inhuman.

I coldly answer the census taker who asks the name of the head of the household, "There are *two* heads of this household; be sure to put down the names and occupations of both," but I wonder if I have made a dent in the bureaucratic consciousness. Maybe I've just encouraged the young and embarrassed male interviewer to look for a female who wouldn't protest when mortgage papers promote the image of "husband *et ux.*" I'm tired of being dismissed as *ux.*, but I'm also tired of fighting. I get very annoyed when some feminists criticize men for treating them as sex objects but continue to wear ultra-seductive clothes and teasing smiles. I get even more angry when reporters attend a feminist function and lace their coverage of events with descriptions of who's wearing what. I applaud doing away with a double standard for sexual behavior between the sexes, but I think indiscriminate coupling is also dehumanizing. Female macho just means you've subscribed to stag values. I think women need to be more than simply housewives, but I dislike feminist platforms that are just as rigid about what the appropriate life style should be as those who glorify the "little homemaker." People used to worry, "Is she still a *virgin?*"; now they exclaim, "She's *still* a virgin?" Neither view allows a woman to be her own person.

Press the button and I can feel guilty about anything. I feel guilty that I never seem to have the time to make an assortment of Christmas cookies from scratch, *and* I feel guilty about feeling guilty about that. As a married feminist I've doubled my interests, so on good days I feel especially vital, but on bad days I feel washed out. I not only attend meetings of the PTA *and* NOW (National Organization for Women), but can muster up twice as many feelings of inadequacy when I don't have time for either one. My traditional impulses lead me to imagine my daughters framed by tulle and flowers on their wedding days (if they choose to marry), yet I'm bothered by the connotations behind their father "giving them away." I beam when prominent men credit how important their wives have been to their success, yet I wish woman's acclaim wasn't so limited to reflected glory. When a woman friend asks me to donate a homemade pie to a bake sale, I feel torn between not wanting to turn this sister down and my realization that sisterhood will never get clout with puff pastry.

"Think clitoris"[1]* is sound advice after years of being told by Freud and his followers that women are frigid if they don't have vaginal orgasms, but I'm not convinced that sexual satisfaction is best achieved by greedily demanding *all* the clitoral orgasms

---

*Notes to the chapters begin on p. 219.

women now know they can theoretically have. I'm torn between wanting women to undertake jobs that were formerly the exclusive province of men, and fearing my husband may miss out on a good job because hiring a woman is the fashionable thing to do. I'm for childbirth being treated by insurance companies and employers as no more or less debilitating than any other condition that requires hospitalization and convalescence, yet I think the new mother should enjoy some privileged status in society so she can have the time to adjust to the emotional and physical demands of her new responsibilities. But so also should the new father.

I want discrimination to evaporate without it also meaning the end of being discriminating. I strive to be an understanding person (it's a mark of maturity), but regularly choose not to understand when a man complains that child care and housework aren't very compatible with allegiance to an employer. Conceding that change isn't easy to effect so often leads to "interim" concessions by women, and no change in the status quo. A woman and a man should be able to decide for themselves whether they want strict equality to be the rule in their relationship or prefer instead conventional role divisions, yet I so believe in parity that I find it difficult to be truly open-minded. It's not easy to have opinions and avoid being opinionated, but I try. I want to dissociate myself from an androgynous world view that implies a homogeneity akin to the sort you find in plastic flowers. And androgyny[2] that suggests a full range of experience being open to both sexes strikes me as too spicy to be labeled unisex.

Because I have been affected by Freud's emphasis on the male sex as primal, I howl with delight at the embryologists' news that the penis is an exaggerated clitoris, the scrotum is derived from the labia, and the original libido is clearly feminine, not masculine.[3] But does that information have any practical value, except in a sexist shouting match? I agree with Naomi Weisstein when she says, "We must construct a women's culture with its own character, its fighting humor, its defiant celebration of our worth."[4] I see some of this already in the domestic humor of Erma Bombeck and Peg Bracken. I like jewelry, bubble bath, and beautiful clothes, but I don't want to be assessed as a decorated side of beef when I walk by construction workers. I subscribe to *Ms.* magazine *and* the *Ladies' Home Journal.* I admire Simone de Beauvoir *and* Julia Child. I agree with Shulamith Firestone when she makes a case for feminist revolution[5] *and* Midge Decter when she casts a critical glance at some of the implications of "women's liberation."[6] But there are points where I disagree with both of them.

I enjoy reading the "women's" section of the newspaper—I can always use an extra recipe—but I am disgusted when news editors relegate serious discussion of day care and the achievements of women scientists to these pages. I like fine crystal and silver serving dishes, but I don't want to devote my life to their upkeep. I need to work, to have my own savings account, yet I know that getting a job is not an automatic guarantee of happiness. I want my daughters to know that girls can be physicians and not only nurses. Yet I don't want them to denigrate nursing. I am a nurse, and I know firsthand that nursing isn't watered-down doctoring, but an important profession with its own body of knowledge. I need to be needed by my husband and children, but I don't want to consecrate myself to their needs and find myself a shred of doormat a few years from now. I think there must be some psychological differences between the sexes because the realization that you're female and not male (and vice versa) must shape personality in some discernible fashion,[7] but I hesitate to acknowledge any distinctions for fear of being immediately defined by what I can't do rather than what I can do. I'm for human liberation, not just women's liberation, but I know that you invariably take the steam out of women's unique grievances by casting them in general terms. I want different possibilities than my mother had, but I don't want my life style to seem a hostile repudiation of hers.

Part of me finds my fifteen-year-old dream—about not having

a date for the upcoming prom—ludicrous in a feminist head. But the nightmare of loneliness is real, and is always erased by waking up and touching my husband. Why does my unconscious need to reenact this melodrama? To remind myself that marriage saved me from being without a partner? Will the dream come again and again until I exorcise prom hysteria from my still adolescent soul? Are my emotions the expression of eternal verities, what Erik Erikson calls woman's "fear of being left empty, and more simply, that of being left"?[8] Or is my need to be chosen by a man, to be found lovable, a statement of my own lack of confidence, my self-hate at being a member of the second sex? These ruminations, too, are a function of being a married feminist.

For many women the present time is characterized by tensions between the traditional and the feminist points of view. The tensions permeate every aspect of a woman's life, if she is at all aware of both streams of thought. For the first time in decades the subject has become a "hot" one as a whole new literature has developed critiquing the role of women, their rights and responsibilities, discussing the relationship between the sexes in the family, on the job, before the law, and in just about every segment of human experience. Novels, poetry, magazines, theoretical writings on the topic abound. Some of the writing puts the importance of women into historical perspective, some is sardonic, some is a tiresome rehash of what Betty Friedan said better more than ten years ago, some presents heartbreaking analysis of the most intimate emotions, some is angry rhetoric advocating revolution, some is cool reason spelling out needed reform.

One thing is definite: media coverage of the vast, amorphous women's liberation movement has left few women (or men) untouched by the need to reconsider in a new light exactly who they are and what they want. But the turmoil of ideas and opinions has also created much sadness and unease. Many women regret their failure to have had certain feminist insights twenty years earlier, others may feel guilty because they are traditional enough not to want to get a job, still others wish that "barefoot and pregnant" *were* the answer, yet are painfully aware that it is not. Most of all, many women have come to feel they are nothing more than a walking, talking mass of contradictions, suspended somewhere between the past and the future, trying not to repudiate themselves as they repudiate old beliefs.

It's to all these swirling and diverse feelings that I want to address myself in this book. As I explore the basic units of a woman's life—her relationship to her own body, to her parents, to her husband and children, to the home, religion, a job—I hope to present a thorough sense of how disconnected one can feel as a married feminist. At the same time, I want to demonstrate that many personal areas of strain simply mirror the conflicting values in the women's liberation movement. For example, many feminists are caught between wanting women to gain access to previously male-only options, while at the same time do not want to impugn what has been woman's traditional domain. The individual woman may be similarly caught between wanting new possibilities for herself, yet not wanting to sacrifice the comforts of home and family which she has always thought herself entitled to. In this book, I have looked at new things to be angry with, at those I find comforting, at sexism in others and in myself, and at how disturbing and yet invigorating being a married feminist is.

The chapters are part anecdote and part analysis. Since conflict and resolution are hard to talk about in the abstract, I seesawed back and forth between concrete examples of what it's like to be a married feminist and general philosophizing about that condition. The diary-like material in each chapter captures my own ongoing struggle with the issues, and the reflective portion was shaped by my professional background as a psychiatric nurse and developmental psychologist. This method is particularly appropriate, I think, for discussing feelings that too often get dismissed as personal idiosyncrasy when they actually are manifestations of broad social realities. I'm convinced, for example, that many of the dilemmas and pulls I've experienced are not unique to my own situation (otherwise I wouldn't have written this book), but are the inevitable by-products of growing up in a tradition that viewed woman as man's gracious helpmate rather than as a complete person in her own right.

I've deliberately tried to avoid what might be construed as a confessional tone because I don't want disclosure to become an end in itself.[9] I have, however, tried to use disclosure as a way of dramatically presenting some aspect of experience. By deliberately recounting anecdotes that highlight a particular problem and then critically examining them for what they imply about female psychology, I think women can fashion new objectivity from subjectivity. I also believe it's important to realize that resolving conflict requires that we name, and attempt to understand, what it is that troubles us. You have to scrutinize the personal out loud before you can hear what's going on inside of you and do something about it.

Though in using the phrase "married feminist" I mainly refer to women, it need not be totally inapplicable to men. (In fact, I assume throughout the book that the female married feminist winds up being married to a male one.) Men are also being pulled today between traditional values and a commitment to feminist ideology. Sometimes the pulls are the same, sometimes different. I can't speculate about what men are going through, except in a general way. Also, women have been subsumed under the heading "man" for so long that I'm sensitive to the dangers of doing the reverse; I'd rather let men speak for themselves. Nor do you have to be married to feel like a married feminist. Not only are many of the basic conflicts the same, but single women are directly affected by role expectations for married women since marriage is the norm in our society.

Generally, I use the term "traditional" to mean the view of woman as having primary or complete responsibility for child rearing, housekeeping, cooking, shopping, and visiting the sick— a *Kinder-Küche-Kirche* mentality best expressed in the proverb "It's a man's world; woman's place is in the home." This view expects woman to cultivate her sex appeal and manners, be soft-spoken and uncompetitive, build up her man's ego, and work only at jobs that are extensions of the fundamental domestic–nurturing role. For me personally, "traditional" also means growing up in the very Catholic "Little Poland" section of Baltimore, becoming a nurse, marrying and bearing two children. The first twenty-one years of my life were shaped by religious and ethnic values that encouraged devotion to home and family, and being a "good girl." There will of necessity be a middle-class bias in the presentation because I am most conversant with those values, but then most Americans have been influenced by middle-class attitudes even if they're too poor to actualize them or rich enough to snub them.

I use the term "feminist" rather loosely too. I take it simply to refer to a person who strongly supports the rights of women and egalitarian relationships between the sexes. I recognize, however, that within the women's liberation movement there are many variations on this theme—reformers protesting against subjection, socialists linking women's exploitation to a Marxist analysis of private property, and radical feminists who look to Science to tame Nature and usher in an era of artificial reproduction, relieving women of their biological chores altogether.

Perhaps it would be wise to end these preliminary remarks by making clear that the expression "married feminist" isn't meant to suggest that the roles represented by those two words will be depicted as living in easy harmony by the end of this book. I chose the phrase as a shorthand way of conceptualizing the day-to-day conflicts so many women now feel. These conflicts may ultimately be incapable of fixed resolution, who knows? Not that I don't desperately want to make peace between the warring factions. (Peacemaking has always been a very feminine thing to do!) Better to have the differences and tensions out. Now is the time for every woman to figure out for herself whether she can bring together her own opposing views, live with her own split personality. Time enough later on for history to fit the pieces into some whole we can all understand. Let us journey boldly into the eye of the storm, into ourselves.

1

THE BODY

To men a man is but a mind.
Who cares what face he carries
*   or what form he wears?*
But woman's body is the woman.

Ambrose Bierce
The Devil's Dictionary
(1906)

Woman *is* her body. Descartes' mind/body problems were nothing compared to those a woman faces every day. She knows that mental health requires coming to terms with her own body, yet the bones and flesh resist assimilation. She fights the endless series of judgments. The woman wants to protest, "I'm not just a body; I'm *me*. I have a mind and soul too." But philosophers, lords and courtesans speak from the grave: "Silence gives the proper grace to women." "Women are only children of a larger growth." "A man must know how to defy opinion, a woman how to submit to it." What kind of advice is this which comes to us across the centuries? Submit? *Submit!* "Anatomy is destiny," intones the Greek chorus, Sigmund Freud conducting. The 1923 lament of Elinor Wylie still has much meaning: "I am, being woman, hard beset."[1]

The first dilemma a woman experiences is coming to terms with her own body. Historically, woman has been regarded as destined to delight the eyes, gratify the senses, and produce children, but relatively little importance was ever attached to her muscular strength, wit, intelligence, and creativity. While not many today would wholeheartedly agree with the sentiment expressed in the old German proverb "A woman has the form of an angel and the mind of an ass," that image would probably still hold more appeal for the traditionalist than the converse—a woman with the form of an ass and the mind of an angel. Though a modern female Faust might still make a pact with Satan for beauty rather than brains, her feminist sister would no doubt prefer brains because they last longer, or, better yet, tell the devil that she prefers a package deal. (It's noteworthy that the misogynist isn't even willing to admit beauty belongs to women. Schopenhauer held the opinion that "it is only the man whose intellect is clouded by his sexual impulses that could give the name of *the fair sex* to that undersized, narrow-shouldered, broad-hipped, and short-legged race: for the whole beauty of the sex is bound up with this impulse. Instead of calling them beautiful, there would be more warrant for describing women as the unaesthetic sex.")[2] But short of supernatural intervention, it's never been easy for woman to be a whole person. Taught to be alluring, a woman is neutered into a sex object; encouraged to be fertile, she is reduced to the status of a brood mare; pushed to underplay her intelligence, she is castigated for her lack of genius.

I don't remember a time after puberty when I didn't feel imprisoned by my body. I was locked inside it and couldn't get out. Yet much of this trapped feeling results from the ways in which a patriarchal society has written biology to serve its own ends. Freud went so far as to describe the vagina as "an asylum for the penis."[3] A woman's body doesn't even belong to her! There's something ludicrous about terming woman's breasts a secondary sexual characteristic, even if they're not part of the genitals proper. And there's something even more ludicrous about calling an organ unique to the female a "little penis," but that's how the clitoris has been represented. What's more, even its excitability is supposed to have "a male character."[4]

Masochism is widely believed to be normal to women. One theorist goes so far as to say women seek pain in moments of stress and uncertainty: "Pain provides them with a definite relief for a surplus of varying tensions arising from fleeting and undefined stimuli for which controlled localized discharge is not always available."[5] How convenient. If a woman's body gives her pain, she can be reassured that her discomfort is *normal!* Even the fact that females, on the average, are physiologically more mature from birth through adolescence[6] has been used against them—"The nobler and more perfect a thing is, the later and slower it is in arriving at maturity"[7]—when it could obviously be used to make quite the opposite point.

In a brilliant and witty essay entitled "Society Writes Biology," Ruth Herschberger points out how the male cell is usually presumed to act with a teleological sense of destiny, while the female only reacts. The word "vestigial" is often applied to any organ in the female which is similar to an organ in the male. Always the female part is a diminished male organ! Even the conditions of female embryonic development are described as negative rather than positive because emphasis is repeatedly placed on the absence of male hormones rather than the presence of female hormones.[8] In the final irony, the sperm has been portrayed as the purposeful agent in reproduction, while the ovum is presumed to have direction and purpose only after union with the sperm.

This version of fertilization has been in vogue off and on since Aristotle's time. Not only did that noted philosopher think women did not suffer from baldness because they never used the contents of their heads,[9] but he described reproduction in terms of the male who generates and the female from whom he generates. The woman's contribution was merely a kind of raw material, while the man, by giving the principle of life or soul, contributed the essential generative agency.[10] Thomas Aquinas was also a believer in Aristotelian biology:

> As regards the individual nature, woman is defective and misbegotten, for the active force in the male seed tends to the production of a perfect likeness in the masculine sex; while the production of woman comes from a defect in the active force or from

some material indisposition, or even from some external influence.[11]

Defective and misbegotten are labels not easily shrugged off.

Such value-laden descriptions of biological functioning have treated the female as inferior from the beginning. Religion too has described woman's body in a pejorative way, viewing it as one big occasion of sin: thinking of a woman, you have *impure* thoughts; touching her, you feel *dirty* stirrings. Genesis emphasizes how shameful the body is and clearly states that childbirth must be painful, as punishment for Eve's disobedience. So from earliest times, woman's body was meant to be a source of distress to her. The self-image of the women subjected to the menstrual taboos and purification rituals described in Leviticus must have been riddled with a sense of gross inferiority. And we've inherited much of this sense of inferiority, whether we're always aware of it or not.

My body has always been my ball and chain. Though I felt weighted down by it, I've never actually wanted to be a boy. I just wanted to be free of the preoccupation a woman has with her form and its imperfections. I wanted to be more than a body, but I've never been able to shake the self-consciousness that is a feature of always being on display (and women always are). I know any obsession I've had with appearance has certainly not been unique to me. From earliest childhood a girl in America is told her "face is her fortune" in some way or another. If you want to ingratiate yourself with new parents you say their baby boy looks big and strong, or their girl baby looks like she'll grow up to be a real beauty. Popular music, romantic fiction, cartoons, jokes— everything seems to encourage this view, although with our increased awareness of it today, perhaps the emphasis has lessened. But I wonder . . .

One of my first memories is of getting a smallpox vaccination. "When you grow up, you'll be glad I didn't make a big round mark on your arm," the pediatrician told me. "I vaccinate the boys on the arm, but girls on the leg because I don't want their arms to look ugly sixteen years from now in a bathing suit." I was grateful for his thoughtfulness, yet distinctly remember I began to worry then that moles and freckles (which I already possessed) would also disfigure me. At the time, I felt branded by his needle and I still do. Burned into my flesh was this warning: "You're different; you're a girl." I've also hated bathing suits since then. . . . On the whole, I found my little-girl body quite compact. I felt sorry for boys who had to walk with an appendage dangling from their torsos, and dreaded the day when my breasts would pop out, because I didn't want to list like a ship with too much cargo. But in those days, pondering what the difference between the shape of a boy's bicycle and that of a girl's really meant was the closest I came to contemplating eternal sexual verities. . . . One Easter, I painted my lips with red jelly beans and while I was admiring my movie-star mouth, my father walked in. With an anger I didn't understand, he hollered at me to wash that junk off my face. He muttered something about looking like one of the girls on the block, but it was years before I realized what "The Block" was (Baltimore's infamous area of stripjoints, which my policeman father patrolled).

I spent large portions of the first decade of life with raw knees. I was always falling down, then getting sermons on my lack of coordination. Yet no one thought to retire my dresses as play clothes so I could wear out the knees of dungarees instead of my own. . . . I spent hours rummaging through my mother's drawers, dabbing her cologne behind my ears, putting on her rhinestone earrings, reading anniversary cards my father had given her, sifting through the hodgepodge in her pocketbooks. I was hunting for clues about what it was to be a woman. I was searching for some secret I knew she had, but wouldn't willingly share with me. . . . One of the worst insults you could pay a girl then was to say she had muscles. A friend once said he could feel my arm muscles and I started to cry. Who would ever want a girl with developed biceps? . . . Sometimes my mother would sign my straight-A report card and remind me, "Remember, it may not be how smart you

*are but how dumb the rest are." I knew she was trying to keep me
from getting a swelled head (modesty is becoming in a girl), but
getting my head together was a much bigger problem than the one
she was worried about.*

*I'm tempted to say my body has always been a source of distress,
but that's not true. I remember the thrill of swooping down a
pavement incline on my tricycle, or pumping my swing so high I
felt I could touch the treetops, or running down a hill convinced
I would be able to fly if I got a fast enough start. My body stopped
being my friend around puberty when my parents started alluding
more and more (or so I thought at the time) to what a beautiful
baby I had been with my sausage curls and full pink cheeks, as if
to say, "But look at you now!" Their memories of a little girl that
was gone forever plus the onset of menses when I was only a lumpy
ten made me an unwilling candidate for womanhood. . . . When
I was nine, my mother noticed that I was getting hair under my
arms and bulges under my shirt, so she decided to read me the first
of a Catholic three-book series (supposedly for girls twelve, fourteen, and sixteen) on becoming a woman. Sitting red-faced in a
green rocking chair, she read me this pamphlet on the sacred
mysteries of menstruation. It was a shock to know that this sort of
thing happened to women, but it did explain all those little machines in ladies' rooms that obviously didn't dispense candy. What
she said struck me as a pastiche of "This shows you're now a
woman—it's connected with having babies—even the Blessed
Mother menstruated—remember to be modest in front of men."
I remember thinking that it was dumb for anyone to imply that I
would go prancing around without my clothes. There was also an
undertone to what she was saying which I couldn't name, but I
knew it was more important than her script.*

*Several months later, my underpants were spotted. I had always
thought of blood as bright red and this was mahogany-colored
(when blood is oxidized by the air it turns brown, which I didn't
know at the time), so I didn't know whether I should conclude that
this was the looked-for mark of femaleness. Since this trickle was*

over in two days, I decided to pretend it hadn't happened. It was hard to think that those stains signified maturity. My mother noticed the marked underwear the next time she did laundry and confirmed that my suspicions were correct. She handed me a cotton pad anchored on a sanitary *(the word still sounds dirty) belt to use "next month." It looked just like a slingshot and made me think of that line about the slings and arrows of outrageous fortune. To this day, I'm struck by how much I needed her to tell me that I had actually menstruated for the first time, rather than my being able to tell her. Denial was operating full force. Fifth grade wasn't the same after that; I felt curiously removed from the rest of the girls who were uninitiated and the boys who looked so carefree. . . . After that, I spent what seemed like years trying to decipher the full meaning of "Modess because . . ." only to conclude that the eternally begowned girl above the words knew something I didn't know. I also put in a good deal of time trying to figure out how I was going to buy sanitary pads—sold then in a plain brown wrapper much the way some pornographic material is now packaged—without anyone noticing my purchase. There was something very hilarious about buying the biggest box of Kotex because it was the most economical, then sashaying past the knowing cashier trying to look as casual as possible with a two-foot box.*

Soon after I started menstruating, my breasts started exuding a yellow substance which stuck to my undershirts and made my skin raw. It was obvious to me that I had cancer and was fated to die young. It was my grim secret and I wasn't about to tell anyone, because it was such an embarrassing disease to have. No male doctor was going to examine my cracked nipples. During that week of private torment, I played the part of languishing Camille to the hilt. I knew that once I was in my grave, everyone would regret how she or he had mistreated me, but no one seemed to notice the fear and horror behind my brave smiles. My mother, once again, noticed the soiled underwear and took me to the doctor, who explained that my new hormones were just revving up and they had inadvertently stimulated my milk glands; things would be back to normal in just a few weeks. "Milk in my breasts!" Cancer was somehow more romantic, even though I didn't want to die. . . . *My mother gave me the other two sex-education pamphlets to read by myself when I was about twelve. They emphasized that you get babies when a man touches you intimately, which led me to avoid as many of my father's kisses as I could for the next two years. I didn't really think that kissing was what the books had in mind when they referred to the "marital act," but I wasn't about to take any chances. . . . My mother had almost died giving birth to me. That was a fact everyone in the family knew. She and the other relatives would talk of their pregnancies and deliveries in loud, excited whispers, and my eavesdropping convinced me that becoming a nun was the most sensible thing a woman could do.*

From an early age, I became addicted to sneaking a peek at my reflection in a store window, a passing car, or someone's eyeglasses. No narcissist, still I was always checking to see if I had disappeared, and I never ceased to be surprised that my image looked so unfamiliar. I hated photographs of myself because the flat cardboard figure labeled "me" could not be denied the way you could disown your distorted reflection in a toaster. So many of my friends were similarly obsessed with their appearance that I began to wonder if we would ever be excited by a man's body. We were so much our own love/hate objects. . . . I remember my girlhood as a time when I was so busy trying to be a "good sport" that I didn't have much time for sports. I was so afraid of running and looking silly, of my backside wobbling or my breasts bobbing, that I was reluctant to do anything athletic if there was anyone else around. And there always seemed to be somebody around. The little girl in the Walt Disney movie Return to Witch Mountain *describes her principal sports interest as "spectator," and that would have been a fairly good description of me. What began as self-consciousness ended with my taking perverse pride in being a professional spectator, a people watcher rather than a doer. There was some sense in which I felt destined to always be a "forever ender" (which I frequently was at recess time), someone who always keeps twirling the rope but doesn't jump in herself.*

I've always wanted to be older (until recently) because I felt I

*would be better able to meet the demands of age than of youth.
A young woman is supposed to have a good sense of rhythm, be
able to carry a tune, be soft, cheerful, pretty, graceful, bubbly.
These are qualities you either have or you don't; I've always preferred those you could develop over time if you had enough brains
and determination. . . . So I often used to wish I could turn into
a disembodied spirit and float around oblivious to the impression
my form was making on anyone. Maybe that's why I've always had
a yen for science-fiction stories about people of the future who,
finding their bodies too much of an encumbrance for their expanded intellects, shuck their skin and bone shells and assume
humanoid forms only when they're encountering some inferior
people who would be frightened by their true radiance. But such
tales usually end with the reminder that such people would inevitably lose their ability to feel and to love, to weep and to laugh. I
agree that would be a high price, one I would be unwilling to pay.
Anyway, it's not my body I really want to get rid of, but the feeling
that it's always getting in the way of my really being* me.

　"*Eyes are the gateway to the soul,*" *I once heard someone say,
and thereafter spent a large amount of time opening mine wide,
curling my eyelashes and flicking them with mascara in the hope
that someone would take a good look and see me as I saw myself.
. . . To be a good dancer, a woman should be able to follow the
man's every step; she should be light as a feather. Alas, no partner
ever mistook me for anything but a person. The more I tried to
dissolve into the other person, the more leaden my feet became.
. . . I remember dating an engineer in college who proceeded to
hum, once when we were taking a walk, a song that was popular
at the time about the girl that you marry being pink and soft as a
nursery and someone you can carry. I didn't know if he was trying
to tell me he was interested in me or trying to warn me that I'd
better get in shape so the man who might want to sweep me over
his threshold wouldn't be ruptured in the process. Compliments
and criticisms always seem to be woven together into the fabric of
a woman's life, so I don't think my reaction was anything more*

than garden-variety paranoia. . . . I grew up wondering whether I had a face that would launch a thousand anything. But then I would console myself that I would never turn out to be so stupid as to start a war. Poor beautiful Helen of Troy, how many regrets did she have? . . . I've always wanted to be a femme fatale, *yet secretly knew that would be fatal. It would kill me.*

In high school, I overheard two of my male cousins talking about our family, specifically the eight of us who were first cousins on my mother's side. After sharing some gossip, they concluded: "This family has everything; Audrey has the looks, Angela the brains." I'll never forget how neutered I felt. I understood what they were saying. Audrey had just been named prom queen; I had just won a scholarship to college. Both were accomplishments to make a family proud. I was pleased that others saw me as intelligent, but my pleasure paled as the implicit insult sank in: "You're not pretty, you're not pretty, you're not pretty—ha, ha, ha-ha-ha." And I wasn't pretty the way Audrey was. She had a Veronica Lake hairdo, heavily lashed eyes, a hint of glamorous wickedness in her laugh, and a figure that really looked good in clothes. She was popular, droll, youthful. I had permanented brown hair, a "good little girl" smile, a matronly shape, and, worst of all, I always looked sensible. I was earnest, moody, and felt old before my time. I was already a failure! Brains were small comfort on dateless evenings. Living by your wits was what you had to do if no man wanted to take care of you. Yet I could already see that being beautiful had its dangers too. Either you were dismissed as "just another pretty face" or reminded that Nature bestows a good mind on females who don't have any other assets. Whatever you were, as a girl, it wasn't good enough.

Psychologist Don Hamachek seems to think that girls have an easier time at adolescence than boys:

Girls are expected to do little else with their bodies except adorn them and make them as attractive as possible. Boys, on the other hand, are expected to do something with their bodies and are judged more on that basis. Another way of stating it, I suppose, would be to suggest that when it comes to the physical side of the self, at least, girls tend to be judged more in terms of how they look and boys more in terms of how they perform.[12]

Since girls have greater flexibility for altering their looks—"Even a somewhat unattractive girl can look attractive with the aid of proper dress, padding, and cosmetics"—than boys have for changing their performance, they presumably have the advantage. Some advantage! He sounds like Thackeray on women: "To be beautiful is enough!"[13] But it's never *enough*, and practically impossible to hold on to as you grow old. As Joyce Maynard said in her chronicle of growing up in the sixties, *Looking Back*, "I don't know a single girl who's really satisfied with how she looks."[14] There's something uncontestable about being able to do twenty push-ups, even if your friend can do thirty, but how do you measure your aquiline nose against one cute as a button? The unattractive girl knows that the finest dress can disguise just so much, padding can float away while you're swimming, and mascara can drip so you look more like a vampire than a vamp. Even if you know how to transform yourself by the clever use of artifice, it's still an artificial accomplishment, not real. You live in dread of being discovered to be a phony, and that's worse than not performing up to snuff. If you're not attractive, it's *you* who are repudiated and not just whether you can catch a ball, which is only an aspect of you, not all of you.

I've always thought it unfair that a man can be bowlegged and knock-kneed, but any asymmetry is soon overlooked if he's clever or kind. A paunchy man can be described as cuddly or comfortable, but not a paunchy woman. For women, there are very exact standards of beauty—which, alas, always seem to be changing. First Venus de Milo's shape was perfection, later, her proportions were declared overly ample. Curly hair was in, then straight, then back to frizz. Pale skin, tanned skin; beauty spots, no spots. Dye, cut, wave, strap, shave, bleach, cream, file—the beat goes on, and soon you feel beaten. But all those fashion-magazine standards do not transform their disciples into paragons of loveliness. What they actually do is standardize women, homogenize their unique appeal. The model is selected because she represents some version of perfection, only to be used as a backdrop for a manufacturer's product. Through his love, Pygmalion gave life to his statue, but these days you fall in love with the woman who looks like a mannequin. Every woman has her own brand of attractiveness. But you have to be sure enough of yourself to believe it's other people's (not your) problem if they can't see your specialness.

I'm traditional enough to have beamed at the success of my ruse when a college boyfriend was surprised that I had been named to the dean's list—"You don't look like a brain"—yet a part of me always wondered if beauty by itself wasn't rather useless. I discounted as emptyheaded those girls who were forever primping, yet continued to ask, "Mirror, mirror, on the wall, who's the fairest of them all?" I agreed with my grandmother when she said "Pretty is as pretty does," but I kept thinking you had to be pretty before you could even do something. I wanted to be transformed into a perfumed, fragile flower, yet I knew deep down that the vacuous beauty was scorned by men as well as women. What conflict! Which will it be—useless or useful, loved or respected, being or doing, heart or mind, Mary or Martha, lover or worker, whore or mother?

Which will it be? Which will it be? The question hounds women from cradle to grave. Life, of course, doesn't really allow such either/or choices, and there's the rub. Classically, the heart is supposed to rule woman's body, but her mind can never be excised. Instead, something approaching a "normal schizophrenia" takes over. If I'm the heart and he's the mind, if I'm the body and he's the soul, then I must be two different people occupying the same form. The outside part of me doesn't want to perspire, but the inside part knows the only way you can be as cool as a cucumber is to be a vegetable. Outside, I have long polished nails, mounds of curly hair, and a tight dress, but the inside me knows it's a put-on. The outside me offers you warmth and approval, but the inside me never ceases to be critical. I want everyone to like me, but I know you can't please everyone all the time and please yourself.

When I was growing up, the conflicts seemed endless. I was supposed to be attractive and remain virginal. I wasn't supposed to run after men, but was expected to catch a husband. I was supposed to get good grades, but make it appear effortless. I was supposed to go hiking if a handsome man asked me to, but be disinterested in any sort of exercise program which might give me the staying power for a long hike.

The conflicts vary from person to person, but all females experience them in some way. And different women devise different resolutions to the conflicts they perceive about their bodies. My own way of handling these contradictions and pressures was to become overweight. Obesity has never been treated as a fundamental feminist issue, but I'm convinced that it is. For one thing, being big can inspire respect; as "The Bitch Manifesto" says, "Large bitches have a good deal less difficulty being taken seriously than small women."[15] And most of all, I wanted to be taken seriously.

Though I now think that becoming fat was my personal response to being female, it of course was never a conscious decision. As a little girl, maybe I just took the jingle too literally: "What are little girls made of? Sugar and spice, and everything nice." Eat fluff to be fluff. If I'm going to be sweet, I need to eat sweets. If I'm going to be soft, I have to look soft. If I'm going to be good, don't I have to eat goodies? If I'm going to be receptive, why not become a receptacle? I hoped things would "go better with Coke." The skin is the partition between the person and the environment. And I wanted some insulation, to hide under a plump comforter, to spin my own cocoon. No gilded cage for me; I would make my own.

It's true that more women than men are overweight.[16] Toddler girls have traditionally been expected to be as chubby as cherubs. Though the adolescent may prize being Twiggy thin, the Kewpie-doll shape remains the norm for the very young. But if you're fat in the first few years, you will have extra fat cells for the rest of your life. So many women are obese today simply because "baby fat" was encouraged during these crucial years.

Poverty forces a cheap, starch-filled diet, and there are more poor women than men. Those over sixty-five, so often pictured in the larger dress sizes, are the single poorest group in the United States.[17] The expensive recreational activities that the rich rely on to burn off extra calories are not available to lower-class women, who have the highest incidence of obesity.[18] Overeating is closely associated with depression, and more women than men are troubled by depression.[19] There is some evidence that obesity may have a stabilizing effect in a precarious overall adjustment and that depression may even be successfully masked as long as the excess weight persists.[20] Maureen in Joyce Carol Oates' novel *Them* tries to escape her home's poverty by selling her body, and is discovered by her stepfather, who gives her a severe beating. She then withdraws to her bed and spends months stuffing her face, her sensuous body bloated but *compliant.* When she recovers from the depression, she reverts to being thin.[21]

More women than men are victims of the "night-eating syndrome," characterized by eating little or nothing in the morning, then eating to excess at night, with accompanying insomnia. Perhaps this is a response to years of worrying about being alone, without a date at night; they may get in the habit of feeling unsatisfied whenever they're a stay-at-home, hence eat to relieve it. Or nighttime eating may be a defense against sexual activity, woman's nighttime duty in some homes.[22] Too little exercise encourages the accumulation of calories, and women participate less than men in sports, discouraged by writers like George Gilder, who declares: "When intruding on the male athletic arena, women may serve only to detract from its symbolic and ritual content and thus its value in male socialization."[23] In many ethnic cultures, it's important for a man to have a plump wife as living proof of his prosperity. The oldest existing statue, the Paleolithic "Venus of Wilendorf," is a representation of a very obese (fertile) woman with large breasts and a massive abdomen. Fatness, honor, and creativity linked together.

Though obesity may, as one gets older, be more the result of a bad habit than a defense mechanism, many women begin to overeat so they won't be eaten up. Margaret Atwood writes of some of these feelings in her novel *The Edible Woman;* feeling consumed as a person by her fiancé, the heroine bakes a cake in the shape of a woman, then invites him to eat the frosted version of herself.[24] "Sweetie." "Sugar plum." "Pumpkin." "Honey." "Sugar bun." "Dumpling." "Cookie." "Candy." These are our names. We are appraised as firm, ripe, juicy, tasty morsels. We're supposed to be the passive sex, and fat is saturated passivity.

Physical expansion also may reflect the desire to be big and powerful, to be impressive. Some women don't want to be small and weak—"just a girl," or "the little woman." Certain women eat to take the edge off their rage, to get enough energy to live through another day of struggling with the contradictions of being female. We eat because we are fed up. Psychiatrists agree that "obese people *always* have great problems with their angry feelings."[25] Since anger represents a threat in dependency relationships, it's often hidden under a thick veneer of compliancy. *Weight Watchers* magazine makes clear that the successful dieter will become more assertive as the pounds melt and the anger emerges.[26] It is assumed that fat people are placid, jovial, easygoing, generous, nurturing, and less dangerous than those with a lean and hungry look. Since these are qualities women are supposed to possess, no wonder so many women eat themselves into the shape—if not the state—of soft, genial, unthreatening mama.

The study of female obesity is revealing for what it implies about rejection of traditional female postures. Considerable research supports the notion that obesity in women is a manifestation of sexual conflict and a response to role stereotype. Dr. Hilde Bruch, a noted authority on the emotional aspects of eating disorders, has perceived that some fat girls have difficulty dieting because giving up the large size seems to mean the end of any possibility of being a different sex. She has also conducted tests in which overweight women stressed strength, responsibility, and generosity as their major interpersonal traits; they did not list those having to do with passivity, docility, and modesty.[27] Perhaps these women wanted to reject those qualities which would reduce them to doll-like figures. One of her patients associated dieting with being unimportant: "Mother was always so careful about what she ate. When she gained one or two pounds she would go on a diet. That proved to me 'people with nothing else to do, they can keep on dieting.' *I* had more important things to do, I am like my father. I always thought of mother as useless and unimportant." Another woman verbalized similar feelings: "I hate the small chattering magpie kind of woman, so small—such small souls."[28] Apparently, such women want to prove they have the same appetites that men have.

Robert Suczek examined the personalities of three hundred obese women and described them as "distinguished by an extreme emphasis on psychologic strength, hypernormality, narcissistic pride; and by a denial of weakness. These attitudes would appear to be reinforced by the maintenance of an unusual body size."[29] He concluded that the obese woman's very dimensions reflect her need for strength and massiveness in order to deny an image of woman that she considers basically weak, inadequate, and helpless. Such an attitude was summed up by one woman who said, "Being a woman means doing things as a minor study. Being big is my real aspiration. That means not to be a woman but be somewhat more than a man—a hero."[30] While there are repeated references in the psychoanalytic literature to the large body being equated with the phallus, most big women do not want to be men, but want to be what the Greeks called the "third sex," both

woman *and* man. Such women often have ultrafeminine exteriors
—a mass of jewelry and perfumed curves—but want to be valued
for their inner strengths and intellectual accomplishments.

One implication of these research findings is that conventional
weight-control groups which emphasize losing weight so you can
wear a bikini aren't going to be effective for women who may have
unconsciously repudiated such images. A consciousness-raising
group may be the treatment of choice when these women become
concerned about the health implications of their girth.

We yearn for the compliment "You are gorgeous," yet we are
afraid it is also the crowning lie. Can such compliments be
trusted? After all, beauty itself cannot be trusted because age
destroys the most beautiful body, and a woman wants proof that
her lover's affection will survive the ravages of time. It can be
comforting to dismiss the appraisals by putting off any final decision. "When I get thin, I'll be a knockout!" This way there's still
the promise of someday being a perfect beauty.

I grew up petrified that I would not be desirable or voluptuous,
but I was even more scared that I *would be.* I wanted to be
ravishing and not be ravished. I detected the same ambivalence
in my parents. They wanted me to be pretty, but they also mentioned all the troubles of having a comely daughter: waiting up
to make sure she returns home from dates safely; worrying about
her virtue, rape, the dangers of pregnancy and venereal disease.
I was scared of my body, my sexuality, and so were they. So I
stayed plump. That way they wouldn't have to worry; that way
I wouldn't have to worry. I hid my sensuous self under the protection of looking half-pregnant; I looked comfortable rather than
erotic. I knew the man who would love chubby me could be
trusted because he, by definition, had to be someone who wanted
me to be *more* than the fashion magazines expected a woman to
be. He would love me enough to see through to the real me—
strong, smart, lovable.

I have taken considerable space to analyze obesity as a manifestation of sexual role conflict because I can speak from personal

experience and because it is a very common problem. But being overweight is only *one* way of responding to the dictum "Woman's body is the woman." By rejecting full breasts and fleshy thighs, the very thin woman may also be saying no to what is expected of her. Anorexia nervosa, a relatively rare disease most often afflicting pubescent girls, is the flip side of obesity. Characterized by self-starvation, it has long been regarded by medical authorities as prompted by rejection of the female role, especially pregnancy; its onset typically occurs around the time of menarche. By becoming thin just when they would be developing curves, these girls deny their physical destiny and often are successful at delaying menarche because their bodies suffer the consequences of malnutrition.

In the professional journals anorexic girls are described as having grown up with fantasies about being young princes or pageboys who walk with a striding gait. Puberty put an abrupt end to such self-deception, so they responded to their budding bodies by trying to starve the female out of themselves. The mothers of daughters so afflicted, interestingly enough, are often women with frustrated ambitions, who are subservient to their husbands in many ways, yet do not respect them.[31] Presumably, they are women who themselves would have preferred the role of heir apparent to that of consort. Anorexia nervosa is a bizarre example of what can happen if the commonplace recommendation that reducing will make you beautiful and happy is carried to extremes. But the dieting isn't just supposed to make you beautiful, it's supposed to make you more like a boy. In fact, the unisex look, with its emphasis on flatness, aimed at putting women into men's clothes so they could be as active as men.

So the stout and the lean may both feel ambivalent about being a woman—the former may want to be as strong and powerful as a man and still look like a bountiful mother, the latter may want to be as cocky and active as a boy and still look like a sleek siren. Dr. Hilde Bruch says a number of women describe themselves as being a "dual person," torn between wanting to be attractive and having those qualities of generosity that so often are linked with being plump. Such individuals rate the fat self (perceived perhaps to be more womanly) as basically more considerate and kind than the slender half, and cannot understand why society continues to heap praise on the thin one, whose preoccupation with looks makes her rather selfish.[32]

The traditional progress from maiden to matron can also make a woman feel like a split personality. A young woman is expected to be svelte, fashionable, party-minded, bewitching, even a little ruthless in order to get a man, but when she becomes a wife and mother she is expected to be solid, gentle, nurturant, and domestic. There was a time when women were expected to put on pounds right after marriage to show how contented their new state in life made them feel. (Some thought this weight gain meant the woman was "letting herself go," while others wondered if men didn't want their wives to look a little dumpy so they wouldn't have to worry so much about being cuckolded.) This metamorphosis has even assumed mythic proportions in the black and Italian cultures: the feline black woman becomes "big Mammy"; the Sophia Loren shape spaghetties itself into "Mama Mia." How many women tell of weighing 110 pounds on their wedding day, then complain that marriage and childbirth enveloped them in fat? They usually feel partly to blame for their girth, but it's not unusual to hear, "Look what those babies did to me." This yearning for the thinner self may be a disguised repudiation of married life.

By now, the uneasy relationship between woman and her body should be more than obvious. If she is especially attractive, she may revel in her body's beauty, but she may also find herself typed as the empty-headed Playboy bunny or narcissistic monster so often portrayed in the movies. If her intelligence and vigor are valued, she may take pride in her strength of character, but she may feel that she has to wear drab clothes, ignore hairy underarms, and disdain makeup in order to project this image. (Disguising one's sex, either through donning mannish suits or developing the reedy look of a scholar or the titanic "battle ax" look, was half expected in the business world until recently. A body that was flamboyantly female was not taken seriously. To avoid comments —"How does it feel to have a sexy lady boss; do you take dictation after hours, heh, heh?" . . . "Wonder if his wife likes him having such a well-stacked blonde as a business associate?"—it seemed wise to appear unalluring, if just to separate yourself from having the supposed matrimonial ambitions of the secretarial pool.)

The culturally induced dilemma between the two roles, mother and vamp, may seem an insoluble problem. It's easy to understand women's envy of men. Men seem so much more at home with their bodies. They use their bodies to do things and aren't so preoccupied with them as the be-all and end-all of their existence. It's easy to understand, too, why feminists are tempted to deny women the function of their bodies as bearers of children, calling for test-tube babies, yet also want to glorify and champion that same body. There has been much preoccupation with wanting to denounce the body as if it were *the* enemy. And this is dangerous.

You can't repudiate your body without killing some part of yourself in the process. Woman isn't *just* a body, but woman *is* her body in the final analysis. Our minds, our souls, are shaped by our senses. We may rail against the many abuses engendered by the dogma "Anatomy is destiny," but we cannot liberate our sensuality if we ignore the body as the instrument for perceiving pleasure and pain. We must not allow ourselves to be deprived of self, like the woman who, asked by a marriage counselor which part of her body she liked most, couldn't think of any part she liked at all, but finally cried out, "I think I like my hands because they work for other people."[33] Our bodies are *not* the enemy, but many of the prevailing stereotypes, the erroneous association of certain personality traits with a certain physical shape, keep us from taking pride in our bodies. As women, we must strive to combat the conventional thinking which condemns us to a preoccupation with appearance and drives us to such self-defeating stratagems as overeating or starving ourselves.

The helping professions are prime offenders in reinforcing role stereotypes. For example, here is Dr. Rudolf Ekstein, a psychotherapist, who is using a puppet to help a disturbed adolescent girl talk about her feelings; but notice how he uses this device to reinforce traditional views of what it means to be female:

Therapist: Because you know what I think, Lizzie [puppet], between me and you, we want to make a high school girl out of her. Or are we wrong?
Patient (talking through the puppet): No, no, we should make a high school girl out of her, yes.
T: She's pretty enough to be a high school girl.
P: Oh yes, sure she is, of course.
T: But don't tell her too often, because, you know, if we tell her too often that she's pretty, she would just be full of vanity, you know.
P: Oh! No, never!
T: We want her to be a modest girl even though we know she's pretty.

Beauty is an important issue in a teenager's life, but larding a discussion of that issue with how important modesty is and the evils of vanity may have the net effect of making the patient even more insecure about her body. The therapist described this session with his patient as "a rather charming hour with Teresa . . ."[34] Charming?!

For too long, women have thought their only alternative was to change their body when they wanted to convey a different image. That constant search for the "new you" has got to end. You are you whether you put on a few pounds or take off a few. All those magical transformations promised by a flick of mascara or a super-firm girdle had the effect of preventing us from really learning how to control our own bodies or shape our own destiny. If we think facelifts and contact lenses will dispel our tensions about ourselves, we're not likely to strive for the physical mastery that yoga, calisthenics, or sports offer—true tension relievers. Instead of getting worked up about how we look, we have to work out in gyms. Not having confidence in our bodies is one reason we haven't had confidence in ourselves.[35] Every woman has the possibility of developing her body so that it reaches its genetic potential, and every woman also has the right to develop her mind and personality along the lines she wishes.

Traditionally, a woman was supposed to realize her body's full potential only when it was affirmed by a man. In fact, I've found that a long-term, loving relationship with a man *has* helped me come to terms with some of my self-hate, some of my fear of not being desirable. When a man you care for finds you sexually attractive *and* also values what you think and what you do, you feel less trapped by your body. His pleasure in you really does enable you to find added pleasure in yourself. (There are, of course, other ways to resolve self-hate: reflection, psychotherapy, a long-term relationship with another woman, achieving career success, to name a few.) But let me not be misunderstood: the feminist part of me shudders at any suggestion that a man's approval can save you; that's too much like the old rhetoric. Yet the married me knows that another's affirmation of your worth helps you see yourself with new eyes, just as you can help a man see himself with new eyes. You can come to value each other and yourselves in a way that increases over time as the sense of partnership binds you to each other. If the relationship between the woman and man places a high premium on loving with your *whole* person, that feeling that you want to melt into another person can signal the melting of the barriers we all erect between the life of the body and that of the mind. On the other hand, regarding your own body as an enemy and the underestimation of woman's worth prevalent in our society can be formidable obstacles to a coming together of equals.

Self-hate, directly attributed to the exigencies of being born one sex rather than the other, isn't likely to disappear, however, just because a man desires your body. Your uncertainties are bound to color your relationship with him. If you grew up embarrassed by your body's functioning, you may wonder if living with a man means you'll always have to run the water while urinating or ruthlessly aerosol away all toilet smells so he won't know how disgusting your body can be. If you think a man loves you mainly for your looks, the future threatens the steady erosion of your figure—and your happiness. Even if you resolve these comparatively superficial doubts, your feelings about bodily inferiority may cause you to engage in all sorts of competitions with him: "I'll show him, I can do anything he can do. Maybe I'm even better than a man." And if you both survive these competitive feelings and each learn to relax and appreciate the unique talents and features the other possesses, you may still find yourself playing games: "Do you ever wonder if I'm the best you could have done? . . . Am I really all you ever wanted in a woman?"

Men, of course, have parallel feelings. They also want to know "whether you will love me no matter what." The boy who grew up hearing "You're not going to let a *girl* beat you" will also have to work through competitive feelings when he has a wife. Talking about all the good-looking women he once dated may be one way of reassuring himself that he is attractive; piling up unnecessary hours on the job may be his way of feeling important. Men, too, worry: "Have I been *man* enough for her?"

The games may never end completely; the feeling of being vulnerable just because you're a woman may never disappear, but over time there's got to be the possibility of someday being *whole*. Knowing that your feelings of uncertainty and confusion are shared by many women and have been encouraged by our culture should help you in finding your own way out of the dilemma.

2

THE PARENTS

As is the mother,
so is her daughter.

Ezekiel 16:44

I am continually preoccupied by memories of what it was like to be a daughter and the expectations my parents had of me. They swirl about me, alternately comforting and stinging. My mother died just a few weeks ago. Her heart gave out at sixty-four. She was so much the embodiment of the gracious, patient, self-sac-rificing, conciliatory woman; I regard it as somehow fitting that she died when she didn't have any more heart left. I touched her dead form—dressed in the soft blue outfit she had thoughtfully set aside with matching undergarments and rosary beads in her closet for this very occasion—and realized more fully than ever before just how much I am daughter before anything else.

Daughter. The word conjures up memories of sachet hearts and patent-leather pumps, sitting on my mother's cushiony lap, being tucked in tightly by my father each night. But the word also means not being born a son and wondering if your birth was a disappointment. It means being expected to behave in a predeter-mined way because you're a girl. It means wanting to be just like your mother and wanting to be your own person.

The day after my mother's funeral was spent going through her

things. I found an old loose-leaf notebook in which I had pasted
greeting cards received during my early years. There was a lacy
card from my parents wishing me a happy eighth birthday: "Every
birthday finds you sweeter." One for my eleventh Christmas
pictured a little girl in a red gown with a locket around her neck.
It said:

> Just having a wonderful daughter like you
> Who's always so sweet and so dear
> A daughter who's always so lovable, too,
> And thoughtful each day through the year,
> Means a lot more than words ever could say
> And it always adds happiness, too,
> To all of the joys of a glad Christmas Day
> To have a dear daughter like you.

Sweet, dear, lovable, thoughtful—I wondered if I had ever really
met those specifications. Had they been disappointed? I certainly
was daughter enough not to want to disappoint them.

The card's bright colors blurred as tears came to my eyes and
I remembered the birth of my second daughter, who was born
near 1 A.M.—early enough for me to get some sleep that night,
but too late to call my parents right away and tell them of her
arrival. Since there was a phone next to my hospital bed, I decided
to deliver the message myself (my husband had done it the first
time around) as soon as the hour was decent. I knew they would
be relieved to know all had gone well. My mother answered after
the first ring and my father got on the extension right away when
she yelled out who was calling. I felt like Walter Cronkite about
to give an important bulletin. I said, "It's a girl. She's a really big
one, too. I like her already because the labor was only four hours
long." I don't remember what my mother said—something like
"Isn't that wonderful"—but my father said in a joking voice,
"Two girls—well, your husband wasn't any more of a man than
I was." My mother rather emphatically said the most important

thing was that we were both all right and he agreed, realizing from her tone that he had said the wrong thing. I hung up the phone, my blood turned to ice water. I felt sorry for myself and even more so for my father. I hadn't realized how much he had wanted a grandson. How much of a disappointment had my birth been? How typically female to feel tormented both by not being feminine enough to suit your parents and by the realization that they might have preferred a son in the first place.

Such musings aren't limited to someone with my experiences. It's hard for most women to admit, but girls and boys are not simply seen as different; traditionally sons have been preferred to daughters. Certainly a family may very much want to have a daughter *after* having had a son, but few parents want just daughters. What family doesn't have an uncle or cousin who wisecracks "There's always next time" if the firstborn is a daughter? (And if a daughter is desired, it may be because the parents really want a doll to dress up rather than a person who will grow and develop a mind of her own.) Frequently, parents aren't upset by the first child being a daughter because they want one of each and accept their firstborn as special without regard to sex, but a second daughter may feel the full force of their disappointment (especially if they believe in zero population growth and see this second child as having been their final opportunity for a son). Simone de Beauvoir remembers this being the case when her sister was born: "Her birth had been a disappointment, because the whole family had been hoping for a boy; certainly no one ever held it against her for being a girl, but it is perhaps not altogether without significance that her cradle was the center of regretful comment."[1]

Though you might think such preferences are beginning to change, I remember reading a couple of articles, right after alkaline and acid douches were reported to have some effect on controlling the sex of the child conceived, in which the experts warned that such interference with nature was ominous because the number of girl babies born would dip drastically. Lawrence

Galton has written that in the future parents will have much more effective methods of choosing the sex of their children, but emphasizes that such selection procedures would mean a preponderance of males in the population because parents prefer boys.[2]

The preference for sons goes back a long way. Today, we may no longer consider the mother doubly unclean after bearing a daughter as they did in the Book of Leviticus, but I know of mothers who have begged forgiveness from their husbands for not giving them sons. (According to Mosaic law, a mother of a son was considered unclean for seven days and had to spend thirty-three more in becoming purified of her blood; but if she gave birth to a daughter she was thought unclean for *fourteen* days and had to spend *sixty-six* more in becoming purified.)[3]

Anyone who reads the Bible can't help being impressed with the value put on sons. So many of the early stories center around the desire for a son. (Jacob marries Laban's two daughters, Leah and Rachel. He loves Rachel more than her sister, but he becomes impatient when Rachel remains barren after Leah has presented him with four sons. When Rachel sees her sister is winning favor, she gives Jacob her maid, Bilhah, in marriage. Bilhah bears him two sons, which Rachel claims as her own, so Leah strikes back by giving Jacob her maid, Zilpah, in marriage. Zilpah has two sons and Leah says, "What happiness! Women will call me happy." And so it goes. Rachel finally bears two sons of her own, and Leah has two more.[4] Daughters are seen either as potential mothers of sons or as troublemakers bound to be ravished. Eve's daughters are never named, and their existence is noted only in passing. There is a tradition that maintains each of her sons was conveniently born with a twin sister so he would have a built-in, anonymous mate.)[5] The notion that sons are the only children who matter has scarcely changed much over the centuries. From Adam to Jacob to Henry VIII to the present Shah of Iran to a woman's own mother and father, sons are special and few daughters ever forget it.

Though girls are no longer left on mountaintops, men still

define their manliness in terms of fathering sons, while women still feel that a good wife gives her husband a replica of himself. And even if your own parents don't say such things within earshot, they may express these feelings in other ways. In her bestseller, *Laughing All the Way*, Barbara Howar describes the sense, which she shared with her two sisters, of being a failure from the start: "Certainly we girls accepted with sympathy and understanding Daddy's disappointment that not one of us was a boy and tried very hard to help him make the best of a bad situation."[6] Margaret Mead remembers her father saying, "It's a pity you aren't a boy, you'd have gone far."[7] And Lois Gould, in her novel *Necessary Objects*, has this to say about the retailing czar Amos Lowen: "Anyway, as it turned out, he'd wanted daughters all along—or so he said. A houseful of useless daughters. Most people didn't believe it, but Amos could persuade them it was true. Daughters were proof that he could afford anything, even an overstock of children purely for decoration."[8]

The effect of these attitudes on a daughter can be great. Being female can be very pleasurable, but women understandably resent being dubbed second-best right from the start. The child who begins life as a bit of a disappointment (even if everyone is too polite to mention it) is doomed to feel less sure of herself than the child who enters life as the heir apparent. There's often a very different psychology operating from the moment the genitals clear the birth canal: sons are full of promise until they do something to *lose* your affection; daughters are disappointing until they do something to *win* your favor. You don't have to be a card-carrying psychiatrist to appreciate how destructive to personal growth being loved by default can be. If the Bible, the basis of Western values, distinguishes between the "sons of *God*" and the "daughters of *men*,"[9] why shouldn't your own parents see you as one step down the evolutionary ladder?

Women have been for centuries the invisible sex—disenfranchised, undereducated, barred from priesthood, hidden behind veils, denied succession to a crown or property by Salic law. Vita

Sackville-West may have been an acclaimed author, but she was denied inheritance of her ancestral home, magnificent Knole, because she was not her father's son. While few lose such a dazzling birthright, all women know what it is like to have fewer rights than their male counterparts.

It's difficult to talk about these injustices without feeling overwhelmed by them. How is it possible to overcome this legacy inherited from the Bible, history, literature, custom, and law? A part of me wants to make a list of grievances. Another part of me wants to shout, "Don't exaggerate, don't get bogged down in unbecoming self-pity." Modern parents love their daughters as much as their sons, don't they? Why confuse the ignorance of centuries past with the here and now? A growing number of parents are even beginning to prefer daughters. Only a few months ago someone said to me, "You should be thankful you have daughters; they're so much less trouble than sons, so much easier to raise." But does being seen as more obedient or more manageable mean they are valued equally? I'm not sure it does . . .

If I had been a boy, my name would have been John, after my father. I've always wondered what this shadowy John would have been like. Knowing the name of my alter ego made it easier for me to visualize him as a six-footer (like my father), not given to worrying about what other people thought of him. He would have learned to ride a two-wheel bike and to roller-skate, though my parents thought both activities were too dangerous for me to learn, since we lived in a congested part of the city. He would have been able to get a summer job with the grounds crew at the local park and cultivate a golden tan as he worked stripped to the waist.
. . . My parents related to each other, as did just about all their friends and relatives, along traditional lines. They quite literally met the specifications of a line by Tennyson—"Man for the sword and for the needle she"—in a poem lauding how right it is for man to command and be the head, and woman to obey and be the

heart. [10] *Though my mother had been a seamstress, my father earned all the money once there were children. Daily contact with murderers, rapists, and burglars naturally made him worried about his family's safety, but I often wondered if he would have been quite so protective if he had had two sons instead of two daughters. If I had been a boy, my father would certainly not have come to get me at midnight and walk me home—at the age of thirty-one —after visiting a cousin who lived only two blocks away. But it's overly simplistic to imply that my father's surveillance was meant to stifle. Though I would otherwise have had more opportunity to share the camaraderie of the bus, my father regularly drove me to and from my ghetto-located high school because he equated father- liness with fatherly eye and because chauffeuring was his way of communicating with me. He didn't know how to make small talk, so ferrying became his way of getting close. However, I didn't see his behavior as the overture it was. All I knew was that I wanted to come and go as I pleased.*

You could name what my father did: making money, painting, gardening, car maintenance, roof work, etc. My mother's job was undefined; she seemed to fill in all the spaces and just do whatever else needed doing. I remember her endlessly mending—socks, coats, and people. She always seemed to be cleaning, cooking, washing. I admired her industry and dedication. But somewhere along the way, I resolved never to learn how to sew because I didn't want to be a dumping place for raveled seams and missing buttons. I decided I wanted to focus on accomplishments you could name, because there was never an end to filling in all the spaces. . . . My mother was someone you could always count on to listen, to be sympathetic and tactful. She was the mediary between my father and my sister and me. When he groused about our using a five-cent stamp when a four-cent one would have been sufficient, she re- minded us how grateful we should be that he provided us with fine things other children didn't have. When he got annoyed at her or us for something he himself had mismanaged, she explained that he was feeling tense because of the pressures of his job and we should be understanding. We all communicated, even loved each other, through *my mother.*

My father's uncle was the pastor of our church and was regarded by many as the patriarch of the Polish community. He asked my mother to do his weekly laundry after someone else no longer could, and she felt complimented. She considered it an honor that he trusted her with his personal things. She darned the holes made by his carelessness with cigar ashes and put Roman collars on all his new shirts, even ironed his bathing suit. This wasn't salaried work, though my great-uncle was generous with his presents at holiday time. I could see that she genuinely liked pleasing him, but I knew I could never do all that work without pay. For all her efforts, she still was in the position of having to be grateful to him when he gave her a gift, even when she thought it was her due. . . . Conversations with my father sometimes seemed limited to only two themes. Through college he asked, "So how are your marks?" and afterwards it was, "Are you dating anyone in particular?" These very questions pinpoint a common dilemma for women: parents almost universally expect that the same daughter, encouraged by them to excel in school, will be able one day to put aside these interests and accomplishments and devote herself exclusively and happily to home and family.

My parents lived with my mother's mother for thirty of their thirty-six years together. Busia, as we called her, was a very strong personality. She had had the guts to emigrate from Poland when she was only thirteen, and arranged her passage without telling her parents of her intentions. In the summer she held court daily on the stoop in front of our house. Busia was opinionated, colorful, and no gourmet cook (she put gobs of birthday-cake icing between two slices of bread and called it a sandwich, and made baloney soup). My mother, on the other hand, was refined, someone you would paint in pastels and who had taken a tea-serving course in night school so she would know how to set an attractive table. I'm very much a combination of the two of them: I want to be a lady like my mother, yet I want to make my own rules when they serve my best interests. . . . My mother would go shopping and cut the price tags off her purchases as soon as she got home so my father wouldn't know exactly how much things cost. She invariably told him that she'd been lucky enough to get a number of things "on sale." How could he argue frugality against such a display of wifely cunning? I vowed that I would never resort to such subterfuge if I married. Why should a man be protected from knowing the high cost of living? Why should a woman regularly have to defend her right to buy what she needed? There's something about designating the man as the earner and the woman as the spender that transforms her into a spendthrift no matter now penny-pinching she is.

I used to be angry that my mother was such a patsy. Anytime anyone asked a favor, she didn't know how to say no. She told me that when she first learned how to sew, Busia would commit her to making dresses for her friends at cost, without asking her beforehand if she would do it. Since she was raised to be a dutiful daughter and loved her mother very much, she did the work uncomplainingly. When I listened to her tell of Busia's outrageous behavior, I would get so angry. Sometimes I had—and still have—the fantasy that I was acting out my mother's anger. Yet I myself conned her into sewing for me. I'd buy an intricate pattern and very expensive material, and tell her I planned to learn how to sew. One look at the directions and the fabric, and she would tell me to start on something easier and cheaper (which I never did). She would then go ahead and make the dress for me. The finished product would be lovely, but I would be ashamed of my tactics. I resented it whenever she was oppressed, yet I oppressed her myself. We played a game with each other, but I don't know its name.

In school, I remember the nuns emphasizing over and over how we should strive to honor our parents and take care of them as unselfishly as Ruth did in the Old Testament. [11] *They always managed to convey the impression that a son's responsibility was met with a check. Taking care of ailing parents—shopping, laundry, visiting, nursing, meal preparation—was the daughter's province. To the son was entrusted care of the family name; to the daughter was entrusted care of the family. I wanted to grow up to be generous, but discharging an obligation with cash seemed so much easier and cleaner than getting stuck with the daily chores where your performance was likely to be criticized—you could buy the wrong thing, not put enough starch in a collar, make a stew too salty. . . . I once overheard an aunt tell my mother, "A son is a son till he finds a wife, but a daughter is a daughter all your life." I was pleased to be portrayed as a lifelong comfort, but I also worried that my parents would never let go of me, never let me strike out on my own.*

If my father was off on payday, he would go to the police station to pick up his check and sometimes take me with him. It thrilled me to be so close to danger, and I loved to hear my father joke with his colleagues. Obviously, they liked and admired him. I began to think of becoming a policewoman, but my father said all they ever did was frisk female prisoners and serve as crossing guards. That didn't sound at all exciting. But my father did say that he had always wanted to be a surgeon and regretted not getting an education because his father died so early, leaving him at sixteen the eldest of seven. His love of the medical profession resulted in his encouraging me to study nursing. My career choice was sealed when he said many policemen married nurses they had met in the emergency room. . . . My father took great pride in his ability as provider. He would tease my mother, "Mary, you were smart to marry me. I'm a really good meal ticket." My mother invariably answered, "John, you're the greatest." Their exchange was as stylized as the movements in a waltz. Years later, when her health had deteriorated, he would try to perk up her spirits by kidding her that she had to get better because she wouldn't want him to succumb to one of those widows who buzz around new widowers. She would retort, "I don't care if you remarry, but don't let her get the money we saved for our daughters." "Well, I earned it," he would respond. "Well, I scrimped to save it," she would retort. She was mistaken. She had earned *it, too.*

I couldn't understand why, just because I was a girl, I was supposed to like knitting and babysitting, or be the one to "clear the table" and "help out in the kitchen" after every family gathering. I didn't understand why the saloons in our working-class neighborhood—and there were many of them—had side entrances for ladies, or why a tipsy woman was scorned so much more than a man who went on a Friday-night binge. Living in a rowhouse provided me with ample opportunity to hear the arguments of other families, but I didn't understand why the curses of a man were deemed "just anger," while an angry woman was condescendingly called a harpy. . . . It was obvious to me that head-of-household status belonged to the man. Men were deferred to and fussed over. But many of the women of my acquaintance boasted they were smarter than their husbands because they could persuade them to do what they wanted while making it look like the man's idea. Since so many of the men were inclined to be monosyllabic, the women did seem brighter. The fact that men were so easily manipulated by flattery made me feel that I belonged to the superior sex. But did I? Gradually, I came to believe that a man had to be my better to be my equal. If he was already a member of the privileged species and thereby had a built-in lead, then how could I respect him if he was only as good as I was or even less talented? With so much advantage, I expected more from men than women. Needless to say, I was continually being disappointed. [12]

Charm bracelets were the rage when I was in my teens. They personified in my mind what it was to grow up female. Every noteworthy event was commemorated with a silver or gold graven image, and the jingle-jangle became an end in itself. We weren't putting notches in our belts to commemorate our victories as much as collecting effigies to prove we were really living. The more clatter your bracelet made, the more important you must be. . . . Once I hit puberty, I began to keep a diary. In it I could be honest and admit that I didn't just want to affirm a man's accomplishments the way my mother did, but have my own—maybe even be rich and famous—that I wished my father would just once say I was pretty, that I wanted to travel all over the world but hated to go anywhere by myself. The entries were haphazard; so many days were glossed over because nothing much happened. My diary was loaded with feelings, but relatively few concrete events. One theme that ran throughout was that I couldn't imagine ever being on the other side of twenty-one.

My mother loved to read. She directed me to the section of the library she had devoured as a child—the shelves of fairy tales. I read them as case histories, as assurance that the prince always comes in the end. But I wondered if he would really come for me. If he didn't, I didn't know what I would do. "Once upon a time . . . they lived happily ever after" was a bond between us. Our love for ice cream was another bond. When my father worked the four-to-twelve shift, I often would go to the confectionery across the street and get snowballs or popsicles, and we three females would savor our icy treats. Because ice cream is a sort of frozen mother's milk, maybe that's why those languid afternoons comforted us so.

My parents believed in education as the ladder to success. Especially since my father felt frustrated by his lack of schooling, he urged my sister and me to get the one thing no one could ever take away from us. We were encouraged to aim high, yet acquire skills that would be of use in married life. But wanting educated daughters was very much of a novelty in our neighborhood, where mine was the first generation even to consider college a possibility. I listened to what seemed like endless choruses of "People think we're nuts for giving a girl an education. They say, 'What's the use? She'll just go off and leave you. Why give her fancy ideas?'" No doubt about it: my parents were torn between wanting us to have every advantage and wanting us to keep close to their hearth. It tore me to see them so torn. . . . They had a friend who engraved silver flatware; he convinced them to invest in twenty-four place settings of one of his patterns. Eight were destined for each daughter at the time of marriage, so from an early age I knew mine would be a stainless-steel life until a husband came my way. The needle seemed stuck on the ditty, "Marry your son, when you will; your daughter when you can."

I remember my father telling my mother about a friend of his who got his long-awaited son, but he was born a mongoloid: "So he got his son, but look where it got him. I haven't done so badly with my girls." Better a healthy daughter than a defective son? Some choice! . . . I wanted my first child to be a son because I had always wanted an older brother. My husband wanted a daughter; he got his wish on Father's Day, and I remember feeling jealous of their already special relationship. I wanted our second child to be a boy because I liked our first daughter so much that I didn't see how I could love another one with the same intensity. I wanted sons for rather traditional reasons, got daughters, and now can't imagine myself with sons, because having daughters helped me love my own femaleness. . . . My father talked of many things the night of my mother's funeral. At one point he said to my sister, "You especially thought we were disappointed that you weren't a boy. Well, I guess we did want one of each at first. But your mother and I were glad that we had the two of you." Whether they always were of that opinion no longer mattered; suddenly the circle had closed.

I've reached some closure. I was baptized Mary Angela and was "little Mary" long after I towered over my petite mother. But I've evolved from "little Mary" to Mary Angela to Angela. I'm finally my own person.

So many of my recollections dovetail with current insights in psychology and the experience of others. My impression that daughters are expected to be more dutiful than successful is confirmed by the very title of Simone de Beauvoir's autobiographical exploration of her early years, *Memoirs of a Dutiful Daughter*, and a magazine-article description of First Lady Betty Ford as first dutiful daughter, then good wife and loving mother.[13] In a moving article entitled "Woman in the Middle," Florence Rush recalls her early preparation for a life of caring: "At age four, when I saw my mother scrubbing the kitchen floor, I said, 'Mommy, why do you work so hard for everyone?' My mother remembered the words well and told them to me very often. She was grateful to have a daughter who could really feel for her. She often commented that a boy is wonderful but a girl really cares." Much later, when her own children were grown, Ms. Rush spent two years singlehandedly attending to the needs of her dying father and had these observations to offer about being a daughter:

> Anyway, my father died and left all his money to my brother . . . At my father's funeral, my mother's widowed state was much discussed but was not of great concern because she had a daughter to care for her . . . if I owed her for the rest of her life, I would not finish paying my dues until I was fifty-five. During this period, I noticed that my husband was never plagued by similar problems. His mother lived with and was supported by an unmarried sister. When, at my suggestion, my husband sent a check to help with the burden of support his mother returned the money. She would take help from her daughter but not from her son.[14]

The compliment "You really care; only you understand" bolsters the ego only to sap it of self-worth at a later time when the woman finds she can never care enough or be fully understanding. Duty is important in a civilized society, but it can foster feelings of guilt because we can never meet all the expectations someone else has of us.

Some degree of guilt keeps our moral sensibilities from atrophying; too much, and it's hard to find pleasure in anything. Forbearance, compassion, and tenderheartedness are good qualities and should be encouraged in everyone, male and female. But a balance between what we need and what others need is essential. And women have all too frequently been expected to do the sacrificing for the sake of others. Being long-suffering may be virtuous, but it can also be destructive. Meekness may encourage the selfish. The self-effacing can give rise to a tyrant, willing victims in their degradation. A proper sense of self and a healthy dose of self-assertion should be expected of daughters as much as sons. Dependence, however, is foisted on girls from the start. When mothers in one study were asked at what age they would allow their children to cross the streets alone, play unsupervised with scissors, or stay away from home for several hours without specifying exactly where they were, those with girls consistently responded with later ages than mothers of boys.[15]

The dilemma I felt between being expected to excel in school and yet put aside ambition once Prince Charming came along was part of what Beauvoir terms the contradiction between a woman's status as a real human being and her vocation as a female, between her original claim to be subject, free and active, and the social pressure to be object, submissive and passive.[16] As a result, a woman may be as fearful of success as of failure: she is afraid that achievement may mean she is too aggressive to be truly feminine.[17] That women expect to defer to men was borne out in a study of 460 Caucasian women of middle-class, urban backgrounds from New York City, Lima, and Buenos Aires in which the participants thought men wanted them to be listeners rather than leaders, and to stay in the background. The subjects from all three nations believed that a man desires a woman who will make more concessions to him than he to her. What's more, they also were convinced that women who deviated from this norm would be disapproved of by other women.[18] Certainly as a child I got the impression that girls who retained their tomboy independence after puberty couldn't expect sympathy from either sex.

Mary Jane Moffat comments on why many women keep diaries:

> Dissatisfaction with the way love and work have been defined for the female is the unconscious impulse that prompts many to pour out their feelings on paper and to acquire the habit of personal accounting on some more or less regular basis. The form has been an important outlet for women partly because it is an analogue to their lives: emotional, fragmentary, interrupted, modest, not to be

taken seriously, private, restricted, daily, trivial, formless, concerned with self, as endless as their tasks.[19]

To Anaïs Nin, her diary was the one place where she could be herself: "Playing so many roles, dutiful daughter, devoted sister, mistress, protector, my father's new found illusion, Henry's needed, all-purpose friend, I had to find one place of truth, one dialogue without falsity."[20] But diary-keeping is not a solution. The solution to role dissatisfaction is to make what is female synonymous with what is human. But until now, even the concepts of psychotherapists on what qualities constitute a healthy mature adult differ significantly from those for a healthy mature woman.[21]

My girlish preoccupation with fairy-tale thinking is typical of someone who feels that being chosen rather than choosing is her destiny. Girls don't feel the same way about the future that boys do. When Peace Corps volunteers—almost by definition a spunky lot—described their plans over the next five years and at the age of forty, the females differed most from the males in their ability to describe life at forty. While their portrayals were as complex and full of detail as their male counterparts', they differed in the degree to which the future was seen as demanding a continuing response to challenge, and in the extent to which they depicted themselves as the primary agents of major decisions to be made.[22] When navy personnel of both sexes, between the ages eighteen and twenty-two, were tested as to their future orientation, the females were more inclined to think in terms of "I wish I knew" and the males in terms of "I will live to be."[23] "I Wish I Knew" could easily have been the theme song of my daughter years.

I identified with my mother, her ideals and her grievances. But I also absorbed my father's. The proverb "Like mother, like daughter" is supposed to sum up a girl's prospects, but that rule just isn't psychologically true. A daughter's self-esteem is determined in large measure by whether she has a close, warm relationship with her father. There is considerable support for the notion that the father exerts a stronger influence than the mother in general sex-typing. Children do pay special attention to the behavior of same-sex models, but they also identify with the person in power.[24] So while convention has it that a daughter walks in her mother's footsteps, there isn't a traditional daughter alive who hasn't developed a dual self-concept.[25]

I know I am hot-tempered like my father, but still I believe it's important to remember relatives' birthdays with cards the way my mother always did. My interest in world affairs comes from her, but I learned from my father how to unwind with gardening. His pride in his paycheck made me want always to have one of my own. Her pride in a tastefully furnished home gave me a yen for interior decorating. His ambition left me with a taste for recognition; her social ambitions made me want to have as many friends as she did. But I'm not just something they concocted by each giving me a complement of genes. There are opinions they held in common which I have rejected. There are qualities I've taken on from Busia, who taught me what it was to be an unconventional woman.

And my parents didn't stay the same over the years. By the time I was a grown woman, my father had ceased to have rigid ideas about what constituted men's and women's work; my mother no longer soaked up his resentments like a sponge, but dished out her own. He became the romantic as she became more hard-nosed. (Bernice Neugarten, who is famous for her study of personality throughout the life cycle, regards such shifts away from traditional sexual roles as typical of the second half of life: "Men seem to become more receptive to affiliative and nurturant promptings; women, more responsive toward and less guilty about aggressive and egocentric impulses."[26] Her perceptions suggest that even individuals who want nothing to do with the current women's movement become dissatisfied with sex-role stereotype the longer they live.) I absorbed many of my parents' values, but they listened to my criticisms of their way of life. They acted, I reacted; I acted, they reacted.

A woman's earliest self-identity is shaped in childhood, but it need not be her last. The most destructive part of being a dutiful daughter is not in meeting the needs of others, but translating "dutiful" to mean unquestioning and thereby getting stuck with a static self-image that limits meeting your own needs. Many women continue to refer to themselves as "girls" (and are so frequently described that way) long after it's biologically true. This is symptomatic of the kind of low self-esteem which makes a woman feel she must be what others say she should be, rather than taking the initiative to be her own person. If they liked their mothers and admired their fathers, women have customarily seen being personally likable as crucial. Marrying a man like father became the goal of their adult years rather than considering how they might integrate the strengths of both parents in their own person.

Historically, the progress from daughter to wife has allowed women little opportunity for self-definition (even the detour along the way for some job experience frequently has taken place in a setting selected for the quality of the bachelors). Women have regularly been encouraged to defer categorical tastes and opinions until they marry so they can adapt their interests to match those of the unmet mate. "Something in the young woman's identity must keep itself open for the peculiarities of the man to be joined and of the children to be brought up,"[27] writes Erik Erikson, though he also thinks that much of a young woman's identity is already determined by her brand of attractiveness and in the selectivity of her search for the man by whom she wishes to be sought. Women have not been encouraged to leave dependence behind as they strive for self-sufficiency. Too much self-assertion was considered a liability in the quest for a husband. Besides going from the "protection" of one man to another, the roles of both daughter and wife required that she be pleasing, solicitous, and unassuming. Though masculinity is earned, femininity has required only conformity. Full maturity for anyone, however, is achieved by realizing that you have choices to make.

If you grew up suffocated by your second-class status as a daughter, you need to explore how you came to feel that way and get clear about what you would want to be instead. There is a time for respecting the opinions of your parents and a time for seizing responsibility for your own life. I think the woman who respects both the traditional and the feminist ways would want to approach adulthood convinced that she can be like her mother *and* her father, not repudiating them, but going beyond them to shape her own special destiny.

3

THE HUSBAND

Ice cream, soda, ginger ale, pop.
Tell me the name of my sweetheart.
A B C D,
Does he love me?
Yes, no, maybe so; yes, no, maybe so.
What will he be?
Rich man, poor man, beggar man, thief;
Doctor, lawyer, Indian chief.
What will I be married in?
Silk, satin, calico, rags.
What will my ring have?
Diamonds, rubies, emeralds, glass.
Where will we live?
Little house, big house, pig pen, barn.
How many children will I have?
One—two—three—four—etc.

Jump-rope Rhyme

There was a time when I wanted to be married much, much more than I wanted to be a feminist. At recess I lustily chanted the above rhyme purporting to prophesy whom one would marry. My favorite pencil game consisted of listing five boy's names, five letters of the alphabet, five occupations, five months of the year, etc., and then eliminating ("My mother said to pick the very best one, and you are not it") all but one item from each category until I knew the first name of my husband-to-be, the first initial of his last name, his job, the season when we would marry, and many other vital statistics. I didn't put much stock in these predictions, but they reassured me that there *would* be a husband in my future. Who he was mattered less than that he was waiting in the wings.

I wanted to get married so no one would ever call me a prunish spinster. I wanted to get married because everyone who was anyone did it. I wanted to get married because my parents would then have to see me as a grown-up. I wanted to get married because I yearned for a sex life—and a person from my background didn't have one without the priest's benediction. I wanted to get married because I didn't want to grow old by myself. My view of marriage was traditional: a gold band being slipped on my ring finger, the organ blaring out the processional, "and they lived happily ever after."

Not that some feminist doubts didn't prick my consciousness, though I would have been reluctant to label them as such at the time, because feminists weren't supposed to be the marrying type. Growing up, I gave considerable thought to why brides got a special blessing at the Nuptial Mass. I tentatively decided it was because theirs was seen as the really tough role, demanding all sorts of extra grace. I wondered why women cried at weddings. Tears of joy and remembered pleasures, or of bittersweet memories and dreams gone sour? I relished the attention the bride received, but it was depressing to think that everything after the wedding day was downhill (certainly less happy, since you'd already lived through "the happiest day of your life"). I despised the Polish custom of ceremoniously replacing the wedding veil during the reception with a handkerchief-like piece of lace to show that the bride was now a matron. The orange blossoms and filmy yards of tulle were so romantic, and the skimpy replacement made most brides suddenly look older and plainer.

My mother was always reserved about discussing love and marriage. Her only advice was that it was better for a woman to marry someone who loved her more than she loved him because a woman could always learn to love someone who was good to her. She wanted me to remember that a man usually loves as much at the beginning as he ever will; some will love less as soon as the woman becomes the wife. From her point of view, you either had the advantage or were taken advantage of. Grim advice, I thought. Learning to love someone who is good to you sounded like something you'd say to a dog about to switch masters. How unromantic! Yet she was right. Long before talk of marriage contracts, I could see that you got the best terms you could *before* signing on the dotted line, not afterward. If two became one and that *one* was the husband, then you had to make sure that he would truly cherish you, not just swallow you up. My distrust of men was building and would continue to do so as I found my mother's caution confirmed by the cynicism and condescension of some male psychoanalysts:

> One has to admit in all fairness that woman, in her relations with man, is at a serious disadvantage. She will try to hold a man by showing him affection and by treating him lovingly. But by so doing, she acts according to a mistaken projection, since this would be the way to retain her; because only women are held by tenderness and consideration. If she then tried to keep him by sexuality, she is often just as much frustrated, because male sexuality wants variety and she can offer him only homely fare.[1]

Tenderness, consideration, and affection seemed impossible between the sexes. Did men really think that way, act that way? I couldn't believe they were so callous. Were my father's fidelity and devotion as exceptional as my mother made them seem?

In college I had to take a course on Christian marriage taught by a Jesuit. One book I read during that semester explicitly warned wives not to expect to achieve orgasm every time they had intercourse: ". . . for her, there probably will be no definite and complete ending to intercourse at times. Nor need she achieve an orgasm for her physical or emotional satisfaction. If she seeks to fulfill the needs of her husband rather than herself, she will often feel a deep sense of accomplishment in her very communion with him."[2] This "making him feel good will make you feel good" philosophy left me with a headache. I had real doubts about whether "a deep sense of accomplishment" was a worthy substitute for sexual satisfaction. Another book claimed that marriage was woman's earthly destiny and that she was created to comfort man, then went on to say:

> . . . as Christ has loved His own, man will love his spouse with a limitless love, infinitely understanding, protecting and tender, even capable of sacrifice when it is necessary. And the wife will show toward the husband whom God has given her a tender solicitude, an abiding respect, a joyful submission such as the soul feels towards its Saviour.[3]

Such rhetoric further dulled my childish desire to be a bride. I wanted to be comforted as much as I expected to be a comfort. I didn't like the way woman came out on the wrong end of the metaphor: man was to behave like Christ; woman was to act as if he were her Saviour. "Joyful submission" wasn't my style. I was slowly becoming a feminist. The champagne trimmings didn't seem as important as what it really meant to live together happily ever after.

I'm glad I didn't go straight from the playground to being some man's playmate. Over the years, I became less interested in a husband as status symbol and more concerned about what my status as a wife would be. I turned a deaf ear to St. Paul's admonition to the Colossians (3:18): "Wives, give way to your husbands, as you should in the Lord." But I also refused to believe that men didn't grow in their ability to love as much as women. I didn't want men to have a low opinion of me ("homely fare"!), and I didn't want to have one of them. I finally decided that I didn't want a husband as much as I wanted a lifelong friend—someone who would be both comfortable and exciting, someone to make love with and confide in, someone who could look at me at sixty-one and still see the girl of twenty-one.

But wanting a super-friend is very different from wanting a husband. *Vive la différence* has ceased to make much sense as the organizing principle behind a man-woman relationship. Having the same opportunities and responsibilities is much more important than espousing the mere *attitude* of equality typical of those who advocate separate spheres of influence for men and women. Psychological bisexuality can and should take the place of complementarity as the motivating force in female-male relations.

It's still somewhat unusual to think of wife and husband as friends. For centuries women have been expected to defer to the authority of their husbands. To this day, a wife is expected to live where the husband decides (or he can charge her with desertion), to give up her family name for his, to subordinate her career plans to his, to assume primary responsibility for domestic chores and child rearing.[4] All of which perpetuates the notion of wife as chattel, not partner. Marriage became so institutionalized it precluded the camaraderie that is part of friendship. Not only was (and still is in many countries) it customary for wife and husband to pair off because their parents sought the match, but the good wife was expected to fulfill her wifely role without reference to her husband as uniquely hers:

> In a household of the ethical kind, a woman's relationships are not based on a reference to this particular husband, this particular child, but to *a* husband, to children *in general*—not to feeling, but to the universal. The distinction between her ethical life . . . and that of her husband consists just in this, that it has always a directly universal significance for her, and is quite alien to the impulsive condition of mere particular desire.[5]

When someone as important to Western thought as Hegel proclaims that particularity should be a matter of indifference to the wife—"The wife is without the moment of knowing herself as *this* particular self in and through an other"[6]—I understand why I got the impression as a child that who my husband would be mattered less than that *someone* was indeed waiting in the wings. But I didn't just want to relate to *a* husband. I wanted to get to know myself through intimacy with my own, very special *Other*.

Just mentioning the word *Other* presents all sorts of problems to someone pulled between conventional love of a man and feminist love of self. Traditionally, "the *Other*" conjures up images of a basic polarity between the sexes. In fact, the maxim "Opposites attract" has been glorified as the energizing force between women and men. Because there are anatomical differences, female and male are each presumed to lack qualities which the other has. Ideally, the opposites are supposed to come together and complement each other, to form a complete, harmonious, loving whole. Women and men have repeatedly been told they fit together like a lock and key; together they can open the secrets of life. While the fitting together of vagina and penis can be compared to a lock and key, the comparison becomes absurd and brutal if the conclusion drawn is that the sex with the penis holds the key to life's experience, leaving the one with the vagina closed to the same experiences or locked until a man opens her up. Alas, the absurd and the brutal have been foisted on women under the guise of complementarity.

Since complementarity, as applied to female-male relationships, means the coming together of two individuals who each supply what is lacking in the other, the stress has been on differences between the sexes. Such an emphasis on fundamental differences has automatically deprived woman of the chance to express any needs, feelings, and appetites similar to those usurped by man. He is presumed to be the *I*, while she is the *Other*. The reasoning has been, if there are only opposites, and *I* the man am *white*, then you the woman, the *Other*, must be *black*. Therefore if I like adventure, you cherish tranquility, if I am whole, then you are flawed. By definition, the Other then is made weak where the *I* hopes to be strong. The *Other* is assumed to find what the *I* disowns as boring. The *Other* gives what the *I* wants to take, accepts what the *I* wants to give.[7] The *Other*'s role is to offer devotion, comfort, constancy, and admiration so that the *I* can *be*, can grow in self-assurance.

But a woman isn't just her lover's *Other*, she is the universal *Other*—man's shadow, his mirror.[8] She has been expected by

traditionalists to be capable of "a terrible patience, a vast tolerance, forgivingness, forbearance, an almost divine willingness to
forget private wants in the needs of her family."[9] Obviously such
expectations can only tear her apart. Not only is she the *second*
sex, valued primarily as a foil for the first, but also her lot requires
an abnegation of self simultaneously inhuman and superhuman.
But the tortures of always being the good wife not only kill the
woman's humanity, they take their toll on the man too. Feigning
docility so the man can strut and preen turns him into a peacock,
not a virile lover. And the resentments that result from the belief
that life is seldom fair and "woman's chief honor is to know that
and be able to surmount it"[10] eventually boil over. If you spend
considerable energy rising above your situation, you'll soon "surmount" your own husband and scorn him the way the jester does
behind the master's back.

The complementarity concept was presumed to prevent one of
the partners getting the upper hand, because each would have a
sphere of influence with clear-cut boundaries. Instead, it exacer-
bated the battle between the sexes because man wanted to relegate woman to the unimportant or extra difficult tasks, while
woman was always hitting man over the head with her supposed
moral superiority. Contrary to expectation, life is *not* easier when
women are given total responsibility for home life in exchange for
economic support. Competition and rivalry are not eradicated if
women are sealed off from the business world. If you ban overt
aggression, it turns into passive aggression when you are not
looking. It is patently idiotic to attempt to reduce conflict by
emphasizing the differences between two individuals rather than
exploring the aggressive and loving feelings they have in common.
Harmony between two individuals is never a given; it must be
worked for continually. To think a head/heart formula for relationships between the sexes will minimize conflict is to believe in
fairy tales.

Eugene O'Neill's play *The Iceman Cometh* has always impressed me as an example of how complementarity carried to its

obvious conclusion destroys both the woman and the man. Hickey begins his final monologue explaining how he alternated between being homesick and sick of home during his entire married life. The way he contrasts never-complaining Evelyn with his sottish debauchery shows how his love for her has turned into hate, how her love for him has taken on the effect of hate. Finally he cries out, "God, can you picture all I made her suffer, and all the guilt she made me feel, and how I hated myself! If she only hadn't been so damned good—*if she'd been the same kind of wife I was a husband* . . . I even caught myself hating her for making me hate myself so much."[11] (Emphasis added.) It's not just that her martyrdom has made him her executioner or that his lies shut her off from knowing the underlying truth about their relationship, but Hickey now senses that a marriage based on polarity kept them poles apart until they no longer cared to be in touch with each other. "If she'd been the same kind of wife I was a husband"— his impassioned plea, full of conviction now that he spies his waiting grave, sums up, I think, what every husband really wants and certainly what the married feminist wants.

Brian Tate, the central male figure in Alison Lurie's *The War Between the Tates,* is described by his wife as someone who subscribes to George Kennan's doctrine of separate spheres of influence—"If he lost his job . . . it was his fault. If the children became uncontrollable, it was hers"[12]—yet he also comes to a similar conclusion: "He has come to realize belatedly that in love, as in war, whatever is the greatest difference between the principals becomes the central issue. When they are alike except that one is male, the other female, the relationship takes its ideal form."[13] But what does it mean to be alike? Is it possible to be both *I* and *Other?* All I know is that I've tried to combine the two . . .

When I think of my relationships with the opposite sex, I'm tempted to start off: "In the beginning was I . . ." What comes next is the memory of being kissed on the cheek during recess by a fellow first-grader. This young stud had set out like Georgie Porgie to see if he could kiss the girls and make them cry. I had tears in my eyes because the kiss was so unpleasant, his drippy nose compounding the assault on my cheek. . . . My next kiss came five years later when I played spin-the-bottle in the living quarters of a classmate whose parents owned a funeral parlor. For all of us, it was our first girl-boy party, with adults staying in the background. The thrill was in being chosen, not the noisy smooch. In my reveries, rose petals rained down as you kissed your beloved, but the reality was nostrils filled with the stale odor of flowers that had recently accompanied someone else's beloved to the grave. . . . I used to love mistletoe at Christmas time. It provided a splendid excuse for kissing. I tried to get all the experience I could. I was like one of those taste testers on TV commercials, hoping one peck would trigger bells and flashing lights. Since none did, I decided that I had a Styrofoam libido. But in my dreams I was chased by disembodied breasts, genitals the size of Michelangelo's David, and lush nude figures that made me feel whorish. Would the real me please stand up?

I was scared of sex and since males meant sex, I was scared of them. At pajama parties, stories were whispered about couples having intercourse and not being able to get unstuck, about a man sucking a woman's breasts and biting off her nipple. I was titillated—and ready for the convent. . . . There was a drugstore two blocks from my home where you could order a cherry Coke and get an hour's worth of conversation for your money. One of the soda jerks was a few months my junior and handsome, an old acquaintance. I was very fond of him and we had many talks about all sorts of things. I remember him once asking me when I was in tenth grade how often I dated. I think he wanted to get some idea of what was normal, *since ours was an eternal quest for normality. Though I hated all the pressure to have dates every weekend, I said something about "once or twice a week, some weeks not quite so often." I've never since felt so much self-contempt. I'd never even had a one-to-one date. Did he believe me? Was he going to ask me out himself before I made up that lie? Now he probably thought I was either too popular or too much of a liar to bother with. As they say, I had seen the enemy and it was me.*

I was so busy sealing myself off from possible male affronts that it's a wonder I had any boyfriends or friends who were boys. There were times when I bemoaned the fact that I went to an all-girl high school, but it did save me from being self-conscious during school hours. I invited a very kind, shy boy with the most beautiful gray-blue eyes to my junior prom. He accepted and I was ecstatic. He didn't show up at a holiday party I gave because he got the date confused (or so he said), and I was convinced this was his way of telling me that he had had second thoughts about going to the prom. So I quickly rescinded my invitation. I hurt him, but I'm the one left with the scars. I was so unsure of my attractiveness that I couldn't see past my own armor to talk over the misunderstanding. . . . In college, I became very involved in dramatics and developed through that club many friendships with men. I particularly remember corresponding with one alumnus of the "Mask and Bauble" through his first year of graduate school. I liked writing letters and getting mail from him, especially since the two of us had never even dated each other. It pleased me to think that I had solid friends of both sexes. As soon as he became engaged, he informed me that we would, of course, have to stop writing each other. The logic escaped me. Sure, I understood that writing another woman once you were engaged might not please your fiancée. Still it seemed like such a lousy reason for a friendship to die.

I always found it difficult to separate marriage as a personal choice from marriage as a career objective. I remember going to my fifth high school reunion and being one of the few unmarried members of a class something like 120 strong. I was barely into my twenties and already feeling like a has-been when they awarded a prize for who had the most children. (Two, as I recall, already had four.) My being in graduate school was considered something of an admission of defeat, and I found myself hinting that I was seriously involved with an imaginary someone just so no one would feel sorry for me, then hating myself for being sucked into the mad charade. . . . I knew a woman who had lived through three different engagements and had broken them all before she got even close to the altar. She kept all three engagement rings and displayed them like trophies. I wondered if she didn't have the best of all possible worlds: proof positive she was attractive, and her freedom. Her case was not so unusual. There was a woman across the street who had been engaged to the same man for fifty years. Months before his death, he was still bringing her flowers and "calling" on Miss Mamie. My uncle who lived with us was engaged for about twenty-five years. Until he died, he traded in his fiancée's ring every few years for a larger stone. I wondered if a woman wasn't better off being courted rather than married.

When I dated someone I was fond of, I was like a chameleon. I subtly altered my coloring to suit his personality. If he liked football, I tried to learn its rules. If he believed in a particular political candidate, I tried to see his virtues. If he liked John Wayne movies, I pretended to be interested in them too. Books on how to get along with men suggested that you sometimes ask your escort to order for you in a restaurant so he would feel you relied on his judgment. I did it once, but it seemed like such a sham. I never did it again. . . . I've never had much patience and probably never will. I once lived in a dormitory that had a buzzer with a hole which turned white if you'd had a call while you were out. No Greek hero ever suffered the anxiety I did with my Cyclops, my one-eyed overseer. Still, I frequently took destiny into my own hands. I managed to "bump into" favorites after a careful study of their daily routines, and get escorted to plays I wanted to see by just happening to receive two tickets from pretend grateful patients. . . . Somehow, I survived the mating game. I managed to get to know enough different types of men to conclude that a man is not a man is not a man. I survived my stints as wallflower and the graspy hands of men who thought paying for my dinner entitled them to after-dinner cordials of the nonalcoholic sort. Most of all, I managed to survive my own fantasies.

From the time I first heard the music of South Pacific *I wanted* a suave Galahad to come to me across a crowded room and earnestly say, "Where have you been all my life?" He had to be six foot or over to qualify as the enchanted stranger. When I was twenty-two, a man ten years my senior actually did that. He was tall enough for me to wear three-inch spikes and still feel dainty. He had soulful laugh lines and the good looks of a model. We had fun dates peppered with Noel Coward one-liners. He kissed me goodnight with a flourish. "You steamed up my glasses," he said, and I responded, "But I wasn't even trying." There was much to the relationship that made me feel I was the love interest in a Broadway musical, but sometimes I got panicky about the silence that might fall if the patter plodded to a halt. Eventually the show was over, or to be more accurate, I became the audience. The enchantment dissolved as my leading man began to tell me of his worries, longings, and the furies that pursued him, and I realized he needed leading. I became the ear and nodding head that I had been so often in the past. We went our separate ways, but I'm still grateful to him for asking "Where have you been all my life?" and teaching me, in a roundabout way, that you don't have to be six feet tall to be princely.

My husband-to-be was waiting in the wings all the time I was playing "Some Enchanted Evening." Once I fully understood that six feet didn't make a prince, I realized five feet eight inches just might. We knew of each other in college, but only met when we were both graduate students. Bill was so much my friend that when he first came to my home, met my grandmother, and she said in Polish, "Does he go to school with you? Is he Catholic, too? Well, then, he'll make you a fine husband," I even translated her words so we could both chuckle over her futile matchmaking. If I had thought of him as husband material at the time, I would have been too self-conscious to let him know she was sizing him up, too afraid he would think I had my eye on him and run away. Why did I think he wasn't husband material? Because he was so much like me. He enjoyed an outrageous pun and appreciated when you got the better of him. He was ambitious, yet scared of how depersonalizing *ambition can be. I looked at him and could see my own vulnerabilities: he was worried about whether the other sex found him attractive, concerned about whether he made a good impression, eager to please yet pigheaded, someone who thought a caress should mean something and not just be part of the dating ritual. Most of all, he asked me more about myself than any man ever had. I liked our verbal sparring, but had absorbed so many of the he-man images to be dubious about going to bed with a debating partner. If he encouraged me to talk about myself, wasn't he too much like a girl—eager to please? Could I feel passion for someone who thought it was only fair for a man to do the dishes if the woman cooked the meal? How virile was a man who unwound with Gilbert and Sullivan instead of beer and baseball, and was very good about writing "thank you" notes?*

In ways that are now clear to me, it stands to reason that a man with heart would have plenty of libido too. I was worried that we were too alike to be lovers, but I had confused being similar with sameness. Sameness is boring; similarities are always exciting because just finding out they exist implies a sense of discovery. Bill and I are similar, but we're definitely not the same. He likes an ordered house, but doesn't have the hangups I do about doing spring cleaning just because it's spring. I keep track of political developments, but don't feel compelled to comb the newspaper (or two or three) every day. I couldn't kill a mouse if I had to; he could, he has. He loves trains; I'd rather go by plane. I have difficulty reading maps; he thinks I speak gibberish when I talk about research studies and statistics. We had different childhoods. We grew up in very different communities. We belong to different sexes. We have different perspectives, but we're heading down the same road.

Getting married means, of course, having a regular sex life. As someone torn between the traditional and the feminist, I have mixed feelings about virginity. All my girlish preoccupation with staying a virgin so I could wear bridal white with a clear conscience had the net effect of focusing my attention on wondering what intercourse would be like, when I should have been giving serious thought to the advantages and disadvantages of traditional marriage. Wondering what it feels like to have a man thrusting and spurting inside of you leaves little or no time for figuring out budgets or rehearsing what you'll say to your mother-in-law when she announces that you'll obviously feed the whole clan on Thanksgiving. Rather than have my daughters make an unhappy marriage just because they felt the need for a license to sleep with a man, I wouldn't hesitate to advise them to have an affair instead. On the other hand, I'm very pleased that Bill and I were equally inexperienced when we married. Ours was a cooperative venture—learning how to give pleasure to each other and feel it without shame. Sex and mortal sin were so intertwined in my mind that it took time before I ceased to feel guilty every time I felt lusty abandon. The memories we have of our trials and errors give us a shared past that we can tap whenever we're feeling tired or cross. "Do you remember when we first . . . ?" has served as an aphrodisiac on more than one occasion.

What's a self-proclaimed feminist like me doing being married in the first place? The obvious answer is that I didn't even style myself a feminist back in 1965 and was too conventional to think of not marrying if I found the right man. Marriage, in fact, transformed me into a feminist both because of its stifling patriarchal trappings and because I married someone who was more liberated than I was. Once the novelty of being addressed as "Mrs." wore off, I began to be irked by being addressed as "Mrs. William" on Christmas card envelopes. It was as if Angela Barron had become a missing person overnight. I'd go to have a prescription filled at the drugstore and be asked—for their records—who was the head of the household. If "the record" saw Bill as my superior, wasn't I fooling myself when I claimed I was his equal? The sweet talk —"It's only a technicality"—only served to convince me that technically speaking he was expected to lord it over me. On the other hand, Bill never expected me to become a Hausfrau. His own mother worked as a high school English teacher until he, her only child, was born, when she was close to forty. Though she had been a Phi Beta Kappa when few girls even went to college, motherhood ended her professional life, and my husband was not eager for me to become the sort of person who stops living for herself and lives through her child. He didn't want me forever regretting what I gave up because he thought such a mind set aged a person prematurely. Bill always asked me, "What do you want to do next?" The interesting thing is that if someone asks you that you usually have an answer—an answer you might not have known was in you.

Marriage as an institution has all sorts of problems. Like all institutions it is concerned with what is economical, and that so often is assumed to mean strict role division for the sake of "efficiency." The two who constitute the institution can, if they're not on continual guard, stop acting like lovers and start relating to each other as members of a firm, the wife the junior *partner. In traditional marriage a woman is regularly reminded in subtle, and sometimes not so subtle, ways that* famulus *originally meant domestic slave, and* familia, *the aggregate number of slaves belonging to one man.* ¹⁴ *Yet I'm not so angry at the institution that I would want to do away with it; I simply want it to be equitable. There is something very important about pledging your commitment to each other out loud so everyone can hear; it makes you take your relationship more seriously. If you could dissolve your marriage by just saying "I divorce you," then you might run away from conflict instead of trying to work things out. Working out differences in a loving, long-term relationship helps a person grow. I certainly need someone to applaud my triumphs, wipe away my tears, be silly with. And I know the only way I'll keep such a person is to do the same for him. On the other hand, I have several friends who put their husbands through school, cleaned their houses, raised their children, got divorced when their husbands wanted to marry younger women, and heard in the divorce court: "Don't expect me to be generous now, you got a free ride for twenty years!" Maybe a good marriage rests on spelling out the divorce settlement ahead of time. Certainly if you always bear in mind that you may*

*someday have to go it alone, you'll resist all role division that limits
your chances of surviving outside the family circle. I'm ready for
divorce, though I hope it never comes. I've kept up my job skills
and hoarded a little money for my private rainy day. That show of
independence has, so far, served to increase my charms in Bill's
eyes. . . . Sometimes I treat my husband as if he were the enemy.
I overhear a man on the bus snickering about "these libbers who
want to wear the pants in the family" or listen while another asks
my husband, "Aren't you scared of your wife being more successful
than you?" and I find myself feeling hostile to men in general.
Picking on my husband is a cowardly thing to do, but sometimes
I stick pins into him as if he were a voodoo doll, a stand-in for some
enemy not at hand. . . . You try so hard to be equal, but there are
always choices to make: Can you both find jobs in the same
community? Who will stay home when the children are sick?
We've tried to be fair, but my husband has far fewer job opportunities than I do—not every community needs a philosopher, but
psychiatric nurses can work in all sorts of settings—so I was reduced in our last move to having veto power over his options rather
than being able to take the initiative and look for the "perfect" job
for myself. My needs were taken into consideration, but I still
resented being squeezed by his job market. I doubt if such resentments will ever cease to exist so long as couples want to stay
together, but they hurt when you're living through them. What
helped me was knowing my husband felt badly about limiting my
possibilities. Not that I wanted him to pay me off with guilt, but
it was still comforting to know he was the one feeling guilty this
time.*

*Once my husband had a new teaching job, I decided to go to
the "Welcome Newcomers" luncheon sponsored by the University
Women's Club, only to hear the provost say, "You are the most
important group at this university; you put him in shape so he has
energy and enthusiasm for the job." Suddenly I was aware of how
dangerous such women's groups are. The faculty can always be
he if there's an auxiliary group to take care of she. So many men*

think they can take care of the "little woman" by complimenting her, throwing her crumbs. I came to the luncheon to take the edge off my loneliness, but it turned out to be "a word from our sponsor." . . . Just when I think I'm beyond stereotyped thinking, I get annoyed at something I think my husband should have done because he's the "man of the house" (mow the lawn, fix a leak, put on the snow tires), and I'm reminded just how easy it is to push something you don't want to do onto someone else in the name of what is "proper."

I meet an old friend and ask, "What are you doing these days?" and she answers, "Joe and I got married last year." I ask again, "But what are you doing these days?" and she replies, "Joe's gone back to school." Our conversation ends and I still don't know what she is doing, but she looks annoyed. . . . I went to a party in honor of a visiting professor. While one husband was hanging up his wife's coat, the host approached her and said, "What department are you in?" "History," she replied as her husband came back. "Oh," said the host, turning to the man, "I didn't know you were in the history department," and they began to talk while the wife stood there looking off into space. I was appalled by the genteel horror I had just witnessed, once it sank in that she was not in the history department. . . . Is it true that Pat Nixon sent the wives of the members of her husband's first cabinet a memo detailing how to give their men looks of adoring attention when they give boring speeches, or is that just deliciously apocryphal?

I have tended less and less to tell my husband "I love you," because the sentence now has the ceremonial ring of a letter's complementary closing. I prefer instead to say "I like you an awful lot," because still caring after more than a decade together strikes me as quixotically passionate. . . . I wonder if there will be less lesbianism/homosexuality when the sexes learn to be friends with each other. When there's so much fear, distance, and distrust between them, it's easy to understand loving "your own."

My husband makes little distinction between what a woman should do around the house and what a man should do, but I still sputter and fume because so many other people do. When friends remind me that I should be "grateful" for having such a "generous" husband, I find my genuine appreciation of him dissolving to be replaced by a monstrous fury that gratitude is expected from me and not from him. I wind up getting mad at my husband because he even understands why I get so steamed up when he gets canonized for doing his fair share. His understanding sometimes stokes my rage instead of squelching it because he still comes off looking he-man, cool and collected, while I sound like your "average" hysterical female. All those compliments bolster his ego. Mine is riddled with guilt: Would his book have been written sooner if he didn't do most of the grocery shopping?

It scares me to think that I might have married someone with very exact expectations for how I should behave as a forty-year-old or a sixty-year-old. Bill and I never thought to write out a premarital agreement detailing an equitable division of responsibilities and privileges. We exchanged the time-honored vow to love and cherish for better or worse till death do us part, but privately decided to avoid ties that strangle rather than join. Deep down we sympathized with Chekhov's letter to Olga Knipper: "Very well, I'll marry if you wish it. But here are my conditions: Everything must remain the same as before . . ."[15] Not that we really wanted things to remain the same. It's just that we didn't want to lose our hard-earned sovereignty in the name of a happy alliance. . . . Many experiences later, we've changed. His sense of adventure has made mine blossom; his curiosity has rubbed off on me. My insistence on getting feelings out in the open has made him more expressive. He still disapproves of my anger that comes like the thunder and lightning of a summer storm and goes away just as fast. I still don't quite know how to deal with his brooding anger that surfaces in snipes at slow sales clerks. Yet even these differences in style are evening out. He laughs at my superstitions; I make fun of his rationalizations—and we're both more aware of our foibles. In the beginning we confirmed each other's sexual desirability, but that evolved over time to become a mutual celebration of our expanding humanity.

I began the preceding personal reflection by questioning whether one person can be both *I* and *Other*. There is, of course, something contrived about the question, since all human beings obviously think of themselves as *I*, as subject, as the person around whom everyone else revolves. Everyone also has the reverse experience of being defined by one's relation to someone else—a woman is a mother only if she has a child, a man is an employer only if he has an employee. The problem arises for a woman when a man uses her to define himself with little or no reciprocity. To the married feminist, the *I/Other* split is a major issue because marriage has traditionally demanded self-abnegation of the wife, while being a feminist presupposes self-expression.

Taken together, some of the writings of Simone de Beauvoir and Jean-Paul Sartre, intimate friends and trained philosophers, shed light on the apparent *I/Other* contradictions. They have by their own admission influenced each other's thinking, and her *The Second Sex* and his *Being and Nothingness* can be considered together for an accurate understanding of this issue. Sartre's book analyzes, among other things, individual consciousness in terms of the existence of others: "The Other holds a secret—the secret of what I am. He* [she] makes me be . . ."[16] In Beauvoir's book, on the other hand, woman is viewed as the universal *Other:*

> Now, what peculiarly signalizes the situation of woman is that she —a free and autonomous being like all human creatures—nevertheless finds herself living in a world where men compel her to assume the status of the Other. They propose to stabilize her as object and to doom her to immanence since her transcendence is

---

*"He makes me be . . ." The English translation of Sartre's ideas is troubled time and time again by pronoun problems. When Sartre is talking generally about the *Other*, the translator refers to "he," but means by it a sexually unspecified person, for though the pronoun used by Sartre in the original French *(autrui)* is masculine it may stand for either man or woman. Because of this difficulty, Sartre's ideas are distorted since the *Other* is given a specified sex which the original work studiously avoided. Moreover, the pronoun used by the translator is "he" until Sartre starts talking about desiring and caressing the *Other*, when the pronoun becomes "she." This going back and forth simply underscores how much "he" is the norm and "she" the exception.

to be overshadowed and forever transcended by another ego *(conscience)* which is essential and sovereign.[17]

Thus Sartre speaks of the *Other* of private relationships and Beauvoir of the Otherness society imposes on women. This distinction between the personal and the universal *Other* is important; the former is to be desired, the latter repudiated.

A woman doesn't want to stop being the *Other* to the man in her life, just as he is the *Other* for her, but she must resist being the universal *Other* doomed to develop only those qualities men discard as unsuitable for themselves. When Sartre contemplates the pursuit of being, the problem of nothingness, being-for-itself and being-for-others, everything he says about the Self's needs should be applied to a woman as much as to a man. When he points out that the Self and the *Other* are engaged in reciprocal and moving relations, that lovers both resist being made objects yet serve that function for each other, that unity involves assimilation of the *Other*'s Otherness as one's own possibility, he is describing what happens when two people confront each other without assigning subject/object categories by sex. The subtleties of relationship Sartre scrutinizes are exactly what women and men should be devoting their attention to. Beauvoir put it so well: "To emancipate woman is to refuse to confine her to the relations she bears to man, not to deny them to her; let her have her independent existence and she will continue none the less to exist for him *also:* mutually recognizing each other as subject, each will yet remain for the other an *other.*"[18]

In 1929, long before egalitarian marriage was generally discussed, Bertrand Russell championed equality:

There must be a feeling of complete equality on both sides; there must be no interference with mutual freedom; there must be the most complete physical and mental intimacy; and there must be a certain similarity in regard to standards of values. (It is fatal, for example, if one values only money while the other values only good example, if one values only money while the other values only good work.) Given all these conditions, I believe marriage to be the best and most important relation that can exist between two human beings. If it has not often been realized hitherto, that is chiefly because husband and wife have regarded themselves as each other's policeman. If marriage is to achieve its possibilities, husbands and wives must learn to understand that whatever the law may say, in their private lives they must be free.[19]

That such sentiments seem to make increasing sense to both sexes is evidenced by the number of couples rewriting the traditional marriage ceremony to include Kahlil Gibran's words from his book *The Prophet:* "But let there be spaces in your togetherness . . . Fill each other's cup but drink not from one cup."[20] Two are no longer presumed to become one, but to remain two in a special loving way. The mark of long-term love is not a mystical union that suppresses personality, but one that can be expressed this way: the only person to whom I would wish to surrender my autonomy would be the one who would not let me do it.

There are those who fear that to expect one's mate to be also a friend is simply putting another burden on the already beleaguered marital bond. I don't agree. Friendship between the sexes definitely relieves some of the pressures. The classic lovers are always talking to each other about their love; they sit face to face, absorbed in each other, and their conversation consists of variations on the theme "How much do you love me?" But the self-absorption and constant need for affirmation characteristic of lovers is not the stuff of which durable liaisons are made. Shared "I love you's" cloak the couple in a sense of their own importance, but they need to gaze outward if the glow of being valued is ever to be forged into mutually beneficial accomplishments. Friends, on the other hand, sit side by side, absorbed in similar interests, and ask each other, "Do you see what I see and want what I want?" Such good will and common goals are essential to sustaining long-lasting endeavors. The two modes of relating are not mutually exclusive, but go together very well. The lover-as-friend ideal is reflected in the adolescent Simone de Beauvoir's description of married love: "I wanted husband and wife to have everything in common; each was to fulfill for the other the role of exact observer which I had formerly attributed to God."[21]

Any electricity between lovers is not the result of a meeting of positive and negative, but the shock—the very real shock—of finding another person like *yourself.* The beloved obviously need not look like you or act like you (though that happens), but her or his manner may reflect what you would have wanted to be if you had been born the opposite sex; the interests are the same even if they're developed in one and embryonic in the other. It's not a case of passive meeting active or aggressive joining docile, but of one person carrying within her/himself the elements of the *Other.*

Is that the same thing as saying women and men are psychologically interchangeable? Certainly not. But they are each psychologically bisexual. I think women and men have the same appetites, emotions, interests, concerns, and intellectual abilities, but the expression of these qualities is bound to be somewhat different because their bodies are different. This is far from saying "Anatomy is destiny." I'm simply saying biology does shape psychology. Men are not strong and women weak, but each is strong and weak in her or his own way. Women aren't by definition more patient or affectionate or understanding than men, but the expression of these qualities in a woman and in a man may vary. There is *no* quality that you can attribute to one sex that is not to be found in the other. *None.* But each sex grows up acutely aware of what it means to be one sex rather than the other one.

Probably the first label we put on ourselves is "I am a girl, not a boy" or "I am a boy, not a girl," and traditional notions of girlness and boyness start coloring self-esteem. Girls soon realize they can grow up to bear children and that intercourse means *being* penetrated; boys learn that men tend to be physically stronger than women and that their sexual role is *to* penetrate.

They then learn the values that are traditionally associated with these differences. But as the traditional norms are absorbed, both sexes start evaluating what they are told, attempting to figure out how these expectations affect their own personal development. They imagine what it will be like to be a mature adult, which usually translates as "What will I look like when I am a grown-up and am all the things I want to be?" Once the girl and boy are thinking on this level, they're forced to see how their own personalities have been unevenly developed because of their concern with becoming a "woman" or a "man," and the remainder of life becomes an attempt to be truly whole.

But saying that girls and boys go through a stage of learning traditional values is not the same as saying traditional values have to stay the same so that girls and boys can learn them. The current emphasis on giving boys dolls, taking the sexism out of textbooks, and putting girls on Little League teams is important because adults have more of a chance of becoming whole the more they find that what they learned about their own sex as a child corresponds with their later notions of what it means to be mature. But even if society becomes as non-sexist as possible, children will still learn at an early age that previous generations regarded certain qualities as essential to womanhood or manhood. Confronting the history of one's sex will continue to be important to a person's earliest self-identity.

One problem would seem to be that our earliest notions of what it means to be female or male stay with us long after we've processed new information that contradicts the first impression. In a fascinating study in which subjects looked at out-of-focus slide pictures that gradually got clearer, it was found that "the hypotheses the subject forms during the early stage of inaccurate guessing constrain and retard the development of more veridical perceptions of the stimulus."[22] Perhaps this is the key to why we hold on so tenaciously to sexual stereotype.

Margaret Mead points out that some of the present-day concern about father losing his virility is due to a confusion between being masculine and being a man. Masculinity means stress on not being like a woman, but manhood is that part of a male's behavior which makes him a responsible human being. As she says, "If taking care of children is seen as playing a woman's part, being a sucker, being dominated by women, it will be looked at one way. If it is seen as an extension of manhood, as an exercise of strength, imagination and tenderness, it will be looked at another way."[23] Similarly, there are big differences between being feminine and being a woman. Being unlike a man isn't a very positive principle for development, but extending your behavioral repertoire so you can reach *full* womanhood and be a responsible human being is.

A partner of the opposite sex is usually seen as an important step to becoming complete, and the beloved is selected in part because the woman's under-the-skin "maleness" finds expression in a particular man and the man's "femaleness" selects a specific woman as a kindred soul. Philip Wylie had some of these ideas in mind when he wrote:

As men grow older, they tend to become more like women, and vice versa. Even physically, their characteristics swap; men's voices rise, their breasts grow, and their chins recede; women develop bass voices and mustaches. This is another complementarity, or opposite, turn of nature. It is meant to reconcile sexuality and provide a fountainhead of wisdom uncompromised by it, in the persons of those individuals who are hardy enough and lucky enough to survive to old age in a natural environment.[24]

Though his description conjures up some unpleasant images of old age (for we all can see more merit in an androgynous personality than an androgynous form), the blending of female and male in each person is an ancient conceptualization of human wisdom. The fullness of humanity is never pictured as either female or male, but some melding of both which goes beyond mere sexuality. But this fusion ideally starts long before old age.

In her controversial autobiography of her life with the theologian Paul Tillich, Hannah Tillich relates a parable that speaks to many of the issues discussed in this chapter, including the fact that a woman's early desire to be *everything* may sometimes be "submerged in femaleness" after the first heterosexual encounter, but is bound to emerge again with renewed vigor after union with maleness:

> "Why do you always remain on the borderline?" asked the old woman. "Why can't you decide between Yin and Yang, between the mountain and the deep blue sea? I made my decision long ago. I belong to the deep blue sea."
>
> "Why should I decide?" retorted the old man nastily. "I don't know where I belong. Besides, indecision allows for freedom."
>
> "Up to your old tricks," she said. "Freedom, my eye! When I was seventeen, I wanted to be everything, male and female, a self-sufficient hermaphrodite. But you know something? You severed my Yin and Yang. I became submerged in femaleness."
>
> "I don't want to be submerged in either," he said.
>
> "Why don't you want to be the mountain? Why won't you be the man for the woman in me?"
>
> "Poppycock," said the old man. "You are not all woman either. You like to climb mountains too, don't you? You are your own male and female, too."
>
> "We shall meet on the borderline," she cried. "You will come to me from wherever-that-is. I shall rise out of the deep blue sea and join you."
>
> "I shall embrace you," declared the old man. "I shall balance on the rope with you and we'll be two eternal ropedancers."
>
> "We'll do a jig on the rope," promised the old woman.
>
> "We'll rise into the air," they pledged together. "We'll fly over the deep blue sea and the steep mountain in an Ariel embrace."[25]

All of us need to go beyond complaining that the *Other* is not "man enough for my woman" or "woman enough for my man," for we can love each other best if we meet on the "borderline."

I find the picture of these two eternal ropedancers locked in an Ariel embrace most romantic and very liberating.

Egalitarian marriage often gets shrugged off as unromantic. How could so many Frenchmen crooning *Vive la différence* be wrong? But I wonder if the real problem isn't that, to the contrary, equality is such a dazzlingly romantic concept that we shy away from the prospect of developing the complex psychological attributes necessary for such marriage: "the full integration of rational and sexual behavior, the willingness to expose intimate feelings to one another, the ability to cope with the exposure of another's anxieties and hostilities, and the courage to resist fleeing from the dynamic equilibrium of total personal intercourse to a less stressful domination or submission."[26] It's easier to extol the beauty of an hourglass figure or violet eyes or long flaxen hair. But none of the sonnets on these subjects can compare with the intense admiration that John Stuart Mill, author of the classic essay "The Subjection of Women," displayed for his wife, Harriet Taylor:

> While she was the light, life and grace of every society in which she took part, the foundation of her character was a deep seriousness, resulting from the combination of the strongest and most sensitive feelings with the highest principles. All that excites admiration when found separately in others, seemed brought together in her: a conscience at once healthy and tender; a generosity, bounded only by a sense of justice which often forgot its own claims, but never those of others; a heart so large and loving, that whoever was capable of making the smallest return of sympathy, always received tenfold; and in the intellectual department, a vigour and truth of imagination, a delicacy of perception, an accuracy and nicety of observation, only equalled by her profundity of speculative thought, and by a practical judgment and discernment next to infallible. So elevated was the general level of her faculties, that the highest poetry, philosophy, oratory, or art, seemed trivial by the side of her, and equal only to expressing some small part of her mind.[27]

Sure beats being compared to a flower, as Reik does: "Both the beauty of flowers and of women lasts but a day, and fades forever."[28] The love of John Stuart Mill, that married feminist, should inspire us all. He didn't fall in love just with Harriet Taylor's dimples or the nape of her neck, but *all* of her.

Psychological bisexuality should govern a couple's relationship inside and outside the bedroom. Theologian Herbert W. Richardson summed up the issue so well in his book *Nun, Witch, Playmate:*

> As sexual love becomes tender and intimate, the man learns the woman's feelings and response and the woman learns the man's. As they both talk with each other about how they act, react, and interact, each can begin to incorporate, by empathic imagination, the feelings of the other within his own range of possibilities. The man can begin to feel more "feminine," the woman more "masculine." As the motivation in sexual union ceases to be aggression and becomes the loving desire for communion, the sexual differences of the partners are softened and they become "psychologically bisexual" . . . If a person understands his identity only in terms of various social roles, he cannot manage intimacy. If he does not experience himself except in terms of others' expectations, he cannot be a true friend. . . . The human being who is not fully a person must play roles, must be "Male" or "Female" in bed.[29]

The choice is ours to make: mere sexuality, or sexuality expanded into full personhood. The central paradox of a loving marriage of equals is that it calls for the highest degree of awareness of oneself as a person *and* the highest degree of absorption in someone else. But it is this very absorption in what it is to be a woman and what it means to love a man that is the strength of the married feminist; it is this very blending of Self and *Other* that holds out the tremendous promise of *both* becoming complete human beings.

A woman (or a man) doesn't have to marry to become a complete human being. Still, most people continue to think that a long-term union with a member of the opposite sex affords them the best opportunity for discovering the uncharted parts of their personality. But a union between two (wo)men might also provide similar possibilities for self-knowledge. What marriage between a woman and a man does which a homosexual union cannot, however, is provide a needed bridge of understanding between the sexes which, one hopes, will be extended to all other heterosexual contacts. By loving the special (wo)man, you can have more sympathy for other (wo)men and cease to categorize them automatically as the enemy.

If mutual concern and respect can flourish between two individuals, we can begin to envision what society would be like if transformed by mutuality. Virginia Held spoke to this:

> Man and woman each embody within themselves a vast network of group characteristics along with whatever individual characteristics they may have. They bring to their relation their affiliation with two groups possessing an extraordinary disparity of power in the society, and having an armory of conflicting group interests. To transform these antagonisms into a relation of mutual concern and respect is far more significant than is the achievement of such a relation between members of the same sex.[30]

In contractual agreements between lovers, too often the legal arrangements merely become another element of the power that routinely overpowers women; nevertheless, the experience of exploring a relation of mutuality in which both sides renounce the use of power can lead to large-scale social transformation.

On the ninth anniversary of our deciding to get married, my husband wrote me a letter spelling out how he felt about our past and our future. In it, he captured so many of the feelings a married feminist has:

> Sometimes, we go on for hours together after the fashion of two business partners; there are so many arrangements to make. Some-

times, we speak unsentimentally, as if we were afraid that sentimental talk would be either inauthentic or undignified or both, or
that it would all go away if we spoke in that way. And recently we
have had very few times of being together, by ourselves, away from
household surroundings. (We'll have to improve on that score!)
But basically neither one of us sees this day-to-day business routine, at which we are both quite good, as defining our real relationship. We have our secret places, open to no one else, and in those
places we are truly at home.

And in those secret places, sexual differences do count and at the
same time, they don't count.

4

THE CHILDREN

No decision tears a woman apart, if she feels pulled between traditional values and feminist concerns, as much as whether she will or will not bear a child. No other relationship elicits so many conflicting expectations and emotions. On the one hand, she hears voices across the centuries commanding "Be fruitful and multiply," then her attention is captured by those who challenge "Be fruitful, don't multiply."[1] Dr. Richard Rabkin counsels, "Women don't need to be mothers any more than they need spaghetti" (since it's an acquired taste),[2] while the famous Dr. Karl Menninger argues the opposite:

Since the bearing and rearing of children is woman's greatest achievement and the climax of her erotic expression, one would expect it to be not only her greatest joy but the source of her greatest power. By means of it she acquires an inner determined sense of security and is thus in a position to counteract not only her own aggressive impulses but the occasional eruptions of aggression and self-destructiveness on the part of her husband. Hence to be thwarted in this objective, whether by the restrictions of economic reality or by lack of socially approved opportunity or by conflicting wishes engendered within her by her early childhood experiences, makes for a deep inner resentment. To put it another way, it deprives her of her primary safeguard against her own aggressive impulses.[3]

He believes having a baby will defuse a woman's aggressive impulses (her husband's too); Dr. Joseph Rheingold violently disagrees: "If men performed the caretaking duties of the mothering person, it is doubtful that they would exert comparable harmful influence because very few men have the destructive drive toward children common to mothers."[4] Dr. Menninger promises "the climax of her erotic expression," but others rebut in no uncertain terms: "Often when the stork flies in, sexuality flies out . . . It's not only that motherhood may destroy her physical attractiveness, but its madonna concept may destroy her *feelings* of sexuality."[5] Reading the "experts," a woman feels pummeled by all sides.

Erich Fromm sounds as though he's writing verses for Mother's Day cards when he poetically proclaims, "Mother is the home we come from, she is nature, soil, the ocean . . . mother *is* the euphoric state of satisfaction."[6] But Philip Wylie ungallantly labels "Mom" a human calamity who "will exploit the little 'sacredness' we have given motherhood as a cheap-holy compensation for our degradation of woman."[7] Dr. Spock thinks women become mothers "because they love children and want some of their own."[8] But Vivian Gornick suggests complicated unconscious influences: "Woman-the-mother is the golden ideal, the convenient repository for man's most unexamined, sentimentalized, suffocating, ahuman notions about his own composite being."[9]

When the much-read queen of domestic humor, Erma Bombeck, titles her third book *I Lost Everything in the Post-Natal Depression,*[10] you take it seriously because her saucy vignettes are always founded on some basic truth about family life; it's what makes her so popular. And when Helene Deutsch divides her monumental *The Psychology of Women*[11] into two volumes, the first entitled *Girlhood* and the second *Motherhood,* you wonder if the adult female can only be described in terms of motherhood or its absence. Is motherhood at the center of woman's whole psychology, as she suggests? When Dr. Nathan Ackerman emphasizes in his classic work *The Psychodynamics of Family Life* that what is good for the infant is good for the mother, you're ready to embrace maternity without any reservations:

> Through a good quality of psychological union with the infant, the mother fosters homeostasis and effective development of autonomy in both persons; in so doing, she promotes health both in the infant and in herself. The mother makes no sacrifice, therefore, for the welfare of her child.[12]

But if you read Doris Lessing's novel *The Summer Before the Dark* and listen to the heroine's version of motherhood reeking with thwarted autonomy, you begin to wonder:

> Looking back she could see herself only as a sort of fatted white goose. Nothing in the homage her grandfather paid womanhood, or in the way her mother had treated her, had prepared her for what she was going to have to learn, and soon. With three small children, and then four, she had had to fight for qualities that had not been even in her vocabulary. Patience. Self-discipline. Self-control. Self-abnegation . . . Sometimes she had felt like a wounded bird, being pecked to death by the healthy birds. Or like an animal teased by cruel children. And of course she felt she deserved it, because she disliked herself so much . . . Feeling guilty seems almost a definition of motherhood in this enlightened time.[13]

Which is the truer picture?

How much is "maternal instinct" the product of economic and political manipulation, as in the 1974 ban on contraceptive pills in Argentina, which was part of a concerted effort to double the population by the end of the century? *Las Bases,* the magazine most closely identified with the Peronist movement, instituted a propaganda campaign using the same language as many American psychiatrists to implement this plan for national growth: "We must start from the basis that the principal work of a woman is to have children."[14] (At the turn of the century, the German Kaiser was named godfather to seventh, eighth, and ninth sons in order to encourage the large families necessary to any war effort; Nazi Germany also praised loyal motherhood, and American presidents have been known to write letters of congratulations to mothers of large broods.) How much is maternal instinct fashioned by TV commercials? Bing Crosby's smiling family drinks orange juice together, and you wish you had children to smile over their juice glasses at you. Mothers are shown sharing Geritol secrets with daughters, and every woman begins to dream of a daughter saying, "Mom, you're incredible!"

Is motherhood the price you ordinarily have to pay for a sex life, or will it, when it becomes universally a matter of choice, be lifted to a new level of human values? Is contraception a blessing because it lets you control your fertility, or were women less fettered by guilt when they could blame the fates (and their men) for being pregnant, rather than themselves? Are childless women to be pitied or envied? Is the pregnant woman to be admired for her Mona Lisa smile or chided "Is that all she can do?" Is there some sense in which you are not *married* if you don't have a child? Is motherhood stamped by generosity, or is it essentially selfish because there are too many people in this world already? Is nursing a voluptuous experience, if you're confident in your womanhood,* or is it likely to make you feel like a cow? Should every

---

*The popular and professional literature is full of allusions to how much easier menstruation, pregnancy, labor, breastfeeding, and menopause will be for the woman who is happy being a woman than for one full of sexual conflict. While the linkage between self-image and bodily experience has considerable explanatory value, it has also had the adverse effect of making every hormonal dysfunction or anatomical anomaly seem the woman's fault: "If you weren't so uptight about being a woman, so maladjusted, you wouldn't have these problems." It's so easy to go from "The giving woman finds pleasure in breastfeeding"

self-respecting woman avoid what Ellen Peck calls the "baby trap,"[15] or are you bound to be tortured with self-recrimination if you reach menopause without giving birth to a child? These are just a sampling of the questions bedeviling a married feminist as she straddles a position somewhere between seeing motherhood as woman's ultimate fulfillment and regarding it as a sign of carelessness or lack of ambition.

Few women grow up not expecting someday to be a mother. Boys traditionally play at being a fireman or truck driver; girls push carriages and scold their dolls in anticipation of becoming as all-powerful as they imagine the adults of their own sex to be. One of my first school memories is of listening to a Mother's Day story about another second-grade girl who was unruly and didn't appreciate her mother until she got sick and died, and then it was too late. I remember tears dripping down my cheeks as the nun embroidered the moral. By the end, I was actually bawling. Though I was crying because I couldn't bear the thought of my mother leaving me for heaven, I was equally upset because I felt straitjacketed by the unspoken message; I didn't know if I could stop being naughty and thus ensure my mother's health. But my own soggy emotion convinced me most of all that it would be splendid to be a mother in my own right and have a child who would love me as fiercely as I loved mine. Nothing else could ever beat being so admired. The seed was sown.

"First comes love, then comes marriage, then comes Mama with a baby carriage": that playground chant succinctly states what most women have taken to be their destiny. Few, however, imagine this to mean drab seclusion, no matter how unhappy or sad their own mothers' lives may have been. Images of domestic bliss are still so much a part of everyday mythology that it is customary to dismiss discontent as someone's personal problem— "She doesn't know how to handle those kids. She's always yelling

---

to "If you don't enjoy breastfeeding, you must not be a giving woman," but it is bad logic and devastating psychology.

at them. I would never be so callous with *my* children"—rather than question the basic assumptions about blessed motherhood. Since it is woman's traditional status function, there has been widespread reluctance to scrutinize too closely the one role which promises power and honor.

Not long after Gerald Ford became Vice President, *Good Housekeeping* magazine gave its seal of approval in a story that read as if the Fords were the most recent incarnation of our domestic fantasy. In it, *Father* is portrayed as a football hero, successful, affable, hard-working, a self-made man; *Mother*, who is lovely, "gracefully bowed out of the rewarding life she'd made for herself when her husband's career and her growing family claimed all her time." She builds character, molds love, absorbs pressures and tensions, and makes every effort never to short-change her children. Pieces like this one have an insidious effect on our thinking. They inevitably sanitize the family under consideration so that all the normal strains and ambivalence are covered up by a blanket of generalities. Those generalizations, in turn, revitalize archetypal patterns which picture, as this article does, a *male hero* surrounded by *stalwart* sons and a *pretty, bubbly* daughter—all of them held in place by the *all-giving* mother who is rewarded for her untiring efforts by the *profound admiration* of her brood.[16]

The essential dilemma of the married feminist should now be obvious. Such a woman wants to be a mother because she grew up with good feelings about the role and has a variety of expectations about how it will enhance her as a person. On the other hand, so many of the assumptions society makes about what a mother is and can do for her children are preposterous, and are likely to obliterate her as a person rather than fulfill her. There is a big discrepancy between what the woman wants from the child and what the child is said to need from a mother.

I know I wanted to have a baby so my life would be "fuller," my personal world would be "richer," and I would experience a general sense of well-being. I wanted to be happy, and to see if being pregnant would make me look prettier. I didn't want to be accused by my friends of being "too selfish" to have children. I regarded having a baby as a rite of passage; others would see me as fully mature if I could show them my credentials, my children. I wanted to have a baby because my friends all seemed to be starting families and I didn't want to feel "left behind." I wanted some of the sympathy, admiration, and respect society reserves for mothers. I wanted to prove to my mother that, because of my "modern" insights, I could be better at mothering than she ever dreamed of being. I wanted my parents to feel grateful to me for making them grandparents. I wondered if breastfeeding would make me feel sexy; if my husband would look at me with new eyes, loving the Earth Mother–Madonna combination. I saw having a baby as a good way to distance myself from job pressures, a surreptitious vacation. I wanted a baby so I could have a stake in the next generation. I wanted the solicitous attention a pregnant woman gets. I wanted to have someone to take to the zoo. I wanted to feel more "feminine," to immerse myself in the tactile pleasures of cuddling and rocking. I wanted to get presents on Mother's Day. A baby would be my masterpiece, my creation, my work of art. A child would be living proof of the love my husband and I had for each other.[17] It would be a wonderful adventure to combine my genes with his and see what would result. I was also curious to see if what Mary Jane Sherfey wrote in the *Journal of the American Psychoanalytic Association* was true:

> In all women, so long as obstetrical damage does not intervene, pregnancies will increase the volume capacity of the pelvic venous bed, increase the volume of the sexual edema, enhance the capacity for sexual tension, and improve orgasmic intensity, frequency, and pleasure. I suggest that natural selection has taken advantage of every random opportunity to make enhanced sexual pleasure the insurance that motherhood will continue unabated.[18]

All of these feelings left me unprepared for the reality of the role. Society still has a "You made your bed, now lie in it" attitude toward mothers which quickly shocked me out of my romantic reverie. As M. Esther Harding put it, the "bad" mother is blamed for the child's difficulties, while the "good" mother is told she has bound the child to her in an "inescapable fixation."[19] Thackeray's words "Mother is the name for God in the lips and hearts of little children"[20] sting rather than comfort once you fully appreciate that you've signed up for "Mission Impossible": shaping a child who is healthy, adventuresome, happy, sensitive, intelligent, attractive, creative, sociable, kind, generous, ecology-minded, brave, polite, spontaneous, and good—all at the same time.[21] But how can you do this endless job well? Mothers seem to be held responsible for everything that goes wrong, but taken for granted when things go right. It's no wonder Shirley Radl brooded in her book *Mother's Day Is Over* about the enormity of the contradiction she felt: "How was it possible for me to genuinely love my children and yet not like—often to the point of resentment—nearly everything associated with the role of motherhood?"[22] It's very possible . . .

I never gave serious thought to not having children. In my family, you recommended a fertility doctor to childless couples. Once I dated someone who scowled as several screaming children interrupted our walk along the beach; he said he would never want any children of his own because they were so noisy. At the time, I thought he was playing Scrooge just to tease me. I didn't believe anyone but an ogre, which he wasn't, could think that way. . . . I can't say that I always loved children. It would be more accurate to say that I was in love with the idea of loving them. I could see myself picking wild flowers with them, or building sand castles, or blowing multicolored soap bubbles that splattered after a frenzied dance. My daughters have done such things—and more often than not, I've spent the time shooing away attacking mosquitoes.

I grew up assuming that having a child meant quitting work until the school system took over my daytime responsibilities. I looked forward to this enforced retirement because I imagined that it would give me even more time to socialize with my colleagues. By

listening to their troubles with the sympathy that's possible when
you are detached from work, I thought that I would be able to keep
in touch with what was going on at the school of nursing where
I had taught. But people don't keep you up on things if you're not
a part of their day-to-day routine—or, at least, not enough to fill
the void made by becoming an outsider overnight. Long-time
friends began to assume that I was so much into motherhood that
I wouldn't be interested in tales of administrative hassles. Besides,
new people had joined the faculty and their names wouldn't mean
anything to me. . . . I wanted to be a stay-at-home mother because
that's what I thought I "owed" my child. But there was no way I
could be to my children what my mother was to me. When I was
born, she and my father lived on the third floor of the house that
was also home to my grandmother, two uncles, two aunts, and a
cousin. When our first child was born, Bill and I lived in a small
apartment miles away from relatives. We had only a nodding
relationship, if that, with our neighbors, most of whom were from
another state like ourselves. Two summer months of togetherness
and I was going stir-crazy. Bill was very helpful during this time,
but his office was his escape. The days seemed endless, punctuated
only by the sound of burps.

My old boss asked me just before the school year started whether
I would consider doing a little part-time work since they needed
someone with my skills. I almost kissed her feet. What she wanted
me to do involved being at the office a day and a half a week, and
even some of that work could be done at home. Bill and I worked
out a detailed schedule so he would be home with the baby when
I was away. We were still at the "no babysitter can replace us"
stage. But as the school year advanced, we each found ourselves
lobbying for more time away from the baby. It began to be too
much of an adversary relationship for our liking. Sometimes we
fantasized that we'd need an outside team of negotiators to come
in and arbitrate our differences. A friend told me of a grandmoth-
erly person who liked taking care of babies. We hired her twelve
hours a week for the spring semester. But I wasn't very happy when

she seemed to get more strained sweet potatoes on the kitchen floor than into our daughter's mouth.

Because we needed the money and I liked my job, I returned to ever-changing portions of part-time work in the ensuing years until I was back to a full-time commitment. Taking our daughters (now two) to another mother who was home with her own small children kept our kitchen floor clean and gave our daughters the sense of going to their office while we went to ours. This last arrangement, which involved five different families in as many years, had the added advantage of going to play with friends rather than being stuck at home with a sitter. All but one family lived in the same block of graduate-student housing, so there was considerable continuity to their surroundings and playmates. The mothers were glad to earn money without leaving home, and we were pleased that all the fathers substituted for the mothers on a number of occasions. Our girls learned some important lessons: our older daughter had the experience of having an older "sister," our younger daughter had a younger "sister," each learned firsthand what it was like to have a "brother," and, most of all, they observed that their parents weren't the only ones who got angry and had bad moods. Bill and I learned not to expect the surrogate parent to be all-loving, all-patient, etc. It took time for us to realize that we were only modestly accomplished in these virtues, and time again to apply this hard-earned lesson to others.

Since our needs and those of our children remain in a state of flux, our experimentation is not over. We were involved for two years in a cooperative nursery school that required us to help the one hired teacher at least five times each semester. During the summer months we've participated in a play group in which parents alternated hosting the group so you could be free when it wasn't your turn, and hired teenage girls and boys to amuse our children while Bill and I wrote on the second floor (if you want five-day-a-week coverage, different faces on different days makes it less boring for both the children and the sitters). This coming year, our younger daughter is enrolled in a day-care facility that offers a regular *kindergarten program in the morning and play activities in the afternoon. . . . Mine was not a pure feminist desire to be a working mother. I quit work completely and then went back in portions I could tolerate as my guilt about not being the always available mother eased with experience. It took me a solid five years before I became impervious to hints about "If she works, she must not love her children." But my children never knew me not to have some job, so they've grown up thinking that's normal. My older daughter even came home once from playing at a friend's house and said, "Her mother yells so much. I think she should get a job or do something to get out of the house more. She's a nervous wreck."*

Those who watched Bill and me share child care often shrugged off our efforts as possible only if the man had the flexible hours of a college professor. Yet I'm constantly amazed at how many other jobs offer flexibility, and either the father doesn't volunteer his services or the mother refuses to share her turf. I'm also surprised by how many women have jobs and don't see themselves as working mothers. Some of the women who cared for our children didn't see themselves as having a job. Neither did friends who were substitute teachers or gave piano lessons at home or worked evenings at the local library or did bookkeeping at a relative's store. What low self-esteem. . . . It took time not to begrudge ourselves babysitters when we were working, but even more time not to begrudge ourselves them when we just wanted to get away from the children. No one can appreciate how delicious silence and privacy are until they've had children. I'll never forget how sinful we felt on the one occasion we went to a weekday matinee, but we regarded it as therapy—expenses for mental health. . . . How I envied my mother, who had her mother as a live-in sitter. I felt straitjacketed by the constant need to make arrangements; our whole social life hinged on whether neighborhood teenagers needed extra spending money.

All those books that talk about the babysitter as a mother substitute grate on my nerves like squeaky chalk on a blackboard. If the caretaker is a substitute for mother, then mother really does bear ultimate responsibility for the fate of her child rather than sharing that responsibility with father. It's too much for one person's shoulders. Similarly, I've become hypersensitive about the way enlightened professionals talk of mother needing "encouragement to get away from home occasionally." [23] *By using the word "occasionally," hasn't the working mother who gets away regularly been inadvertently censured?*

I've caught myself monitoring how often Bill has changed diapers or taken the children on an outing, because a mother and father should have equal responsibility for their children. Yet I still want to be MOTHER, the favorite parent. I have claimed privilege when it suited me and reminded Bill of his responsibilities when that suited me. I know I can't have it both ways, but I continue to want it both ways. Bill doesn't mind his fair share of child care, but he does mind my vacillation. . . . In the beginning, Bill took his cues from me. After all, I was the mother and should know what to do when the baby cries. I acted as if I was the expert, until I learned enough to admit that I didn't know much more than he did. I'd never really liked babysitting, so I had limited experience with children. Bill became much more involved with the baby once he realized that I wasn't likely to make fun of his awkwardness, if he didn't make fun of mine.

I'm proud of my older daughter's reading ability, but when I see her curled up with a book I'm tempted to give her a sermon on the virtues of regular exercise. I enjoy my younger daughter's dance improvisations, but when she says "I'm going to be a dancer when I grow up," I remind her that it takes years of practice to get anywhere in that profession. It's as if I'm two people: mother enjoys the present moment; MOTHER is constantly reminding, admonishing, worrying, forecasting. One is a person, the other an institution. . . . The dilemma posed by the mountains of art work children bring home from nursery school and kindergarten says something about all the others a mother faces. Part of you resists throwing out even one precious fingerpainting, but the other half knows you'll be buried alive if you're not selective. Similarly, you don't want to concede that you can't do for your children everything the good mother is supposed to do—changing the mobile over baby's crib weekly so there's varied sensory stimulation, reading to your child each night, designing an original Halloween costume, seeing that your child gets enough swimming-dancing-piano-art lessons to avoid later insecurities, fortnightly visits to the library. But it's still hard to admit to strangers that you sometimes substitute a damp dusting for the hallowed daily bath.

I sometimes catch myself playing MOTHER to the hilt as if some emcee were about to open an envelope and say, "Now for the best performance in the role of mother, the winner is . . ." At the dentist's office, they have a film about getting rid of plaque. A cheery male voice extols the advantages of dental floss and says, "Until the child is in his teens, the mother will no doubt have to dental-floss for her child." That too! Another thing to feel guilty about. . . . I love my children with a passion, but I hate being on twenty-four-hour call, feeling that every germ they pick up is my fault, worrying about whether their ears are clean, being cajoled into buying more tickets to the school carnival than I want, being ashamed when their clothes look gray, fretting about whether they're properly socialized, giving birthday parties in ninety-degree weather, finding bubble gum ground into the rug, seeing toys scattered all over, and hearing "I'm bored; I never have any fun."

When the child whines, "I'm bored; I never have any fun," the mother is tempted to say, "Me too." There's tremendous disappointment if the woman feels the role that was supposed to award status has committed her instead to a long sentence in solitary (or suburban) confinement. But the rebellious feelings that surface are a function of the role itself, not just a matter of personal pique. The same woman who defined her femininity in terms of motherhood finds that the role doesn't permit her to develop other vital aspects of her personality, specifically her need for independent achievement. Not only is bearing a child no longer regarded in our society as much of an accomplishment, but the woman is all too aware that it's practically impossible to achieve the psychological astuteness that one is supposed to have in order to rear the child well. What is more, the traditional role prevents the woman from meeting her need for independent achievement outside the family circle. No wonder mothers talk about feeling frustrated.

Psychologist Judith Bardwick describes the dilemma this way: "When a woman is finally in a position to achieve feelings of self-esteem that come from successful femininity she is simultaneously losing esteem because neither she nor the general culture really value the role! Yet the traditional role is conceived as essential to normality."[24] Just when you have done the *expected* —become a mother—and are now ready to go beyond the merely traditional, you find yourself at a dead end. One way out of this morass, I think, is to redefine motherhood so that you don't have to forfeit your self-esteem if you choose to define your womanhood in terms of bearing a child. To do this you have to get very clear about what motherhood is and what it is not.

Let's look once again at the traditional claims that motherhood is woman's destiny, her ultimate personal fulfillment, a noble calling, and proof of successful femininity. As Midge Decter reminds us in her book *The New Chastity,* "Birth control has transposed motherhood from a descriptive category to a normative one . . . unlike her sisters of yesteryear, to whom children happened or did not happen as circumstance decreed, she is a mother by aspiration."[25] So motherhood need not be a woman's "destiny." Venturing into motherhood has, however, become "an act of staking one's life—one's fortune and one's sacred honor— on one's capacity to be adequate to the task at hand."[26] It seems, therefore, that our second category, ultimate personal fulfillment, will not be easy to come by. The new possibility of choice increases the notion of personal liability, which certainly is not conducive to contented-cow feelings. Is motherhood a noble calling? Mothers hollering at their children in supermarkets dispel any pretense of nobility. Is it a career? "Career" implies achievement and aggression, and their expression in nurturing seems dangerous because children are neither prizes to win nor products to package. The last category, proof of successful femininity, contains a glimmer of truth. Delivering a child is proof that you have a fully functioning female body, but patience and all the other approved womanly attributes are far from automatically enhanced by the birth experience and the process of raising a child.

So if the old clichés don't fit anymore, then motherhood must clearly be something else. But what? There are all sorts of ideas that come to mind when I think of what motherhood means to me. It means wanting new experiences, but being unwilling to give up past interests and gratifications. It means deciding to become a mother only when your husband feels ready to be a father. It means reminding everyone that children of working mothers don't have any more problems than children of those who don't; in fact, maybe they're better off.[27] It means wanting a mother's eventual reentry problems to be a consideration in deciding just how much she will commit herself to around-the-clock care. It means wishing everyone realized that women have aggressive, ambitious, and egocentric impulses that demand expression in ways not harmful to those dependent on them for support. It means realizing that even the most wanted child will not be wanted all the time, dispelling the dangerous notion that mothers can love their children without reservation. Acting out that particular lie is such a poor preparation for life (no one loves without putting some riders on her/his affections; that's why only God is supposed to be Love).

Motherhood also means looking at your children asleep and cherishing their beauty and vulnerability . . . the excitement of seeing your child's baby teeth loosen . . . going through "the first kiss" one generation removed . . . dressing up as a witch to accompany your daughter witches on their trick-or-treat rounds . . . reliving how devastating it is to have a "best" friend say, "I don't think I like you anymore" . . . wanting once again to grow up to be a ballerina-dentist-writer . . . playing tag and Scrabble and charades after a fifteen-year lull . . . rejoicing in the forgotten delights of "let's pretend" . . . wondering why leaves turn yellow and how birds fly all over again . . . watching the corn seeds your child planted sprout.

While it goes without saying that motherhood is, on one level, whatever thoughts, feelings, and expectations you've wrapped it in, motherhood is primarily an opportunity to parent. "Parenting" implies a couple's joint investment in the next generation. It doesn't conjure up romantic images of absolute contentment or grand self-sacrifice, but it does imply kindliness, protectiveness, continuity of care, and respect for the dignity of children. Sex-linked role division stultifies, whereas parenting implies an *expansion* of ego satisfactions in order to avoid individual stagnation. (Chapter Eight in my book *The Growth and Development of Mothers*[28] sketches out parenting beyond the motherhood mystique and the importance of dissociating the magic of conception and birth from magical thinking about motherhood.) It is an opportunity to shape the attitudes and values of those to come and a chance to resolve some of the unfinished business of your own childhood experiences. A child's emotions, which are raw, spontaneous, and free of social artifice, reawaken past feelings and conflicts; guiding the child through the inevitable developmental crises leads to a new perspective on your own development. Being a parent is a growth experience: it brings new emotions, new responsibilities, new values, not a "giving up" but a "taking on."

For me "growth experience" doesn't imply the circus-barker enthusiasm of those theorists who huckster phrases like "woman's greatest achievement" or "climax of her erotic expression." It means instead moving from a position such as this expressed by Letty Cottin Pogrebin, "And I truly believed that ripeness, solidity, and wisdom would gestate within me along with the fetus, and that I would give birth to my own adult persona at the same time as I delivered my first child," to appreciating that being a mother won't make you even a little bit divine, although it can humanize: "Though I cannot claim an undifferentiated appreciation of all kids, the existence of my own children gives me a personalized empathy with the children of others."[29] It means learning as Alice Abarbanel did: "I want Amanda [her daughter] to be free, and the only way that's possible is for me to taste my own freedom, so I will not demand respect and love. So I do not, out of desperation and lack of any other meaningful work to do, try to possess and live through her soul."[30] Ideally, it means answering your child's question, "Did you ever wish you never had us in the first place?" by saying, "Sometimes my life is a little too full because I have you children, but, for me, it would be much too empty if I didn't."[31]

As Margaret Mead said with regard to her own family, "I grasp the meaning of puckered eyebrows, a tensed hand, or a light flick of the tongue. The known and loved particular child makes it possible for one to understand better and care more about all children."[32] All adults can profit from what parenting can teach:

> The uniformity of an infant's needs in its earliest days affects the attendant mother with some uniformity. One learns (or learns to use) patience, intuitive insight and imagination, to enjoy the immediate moment in anticipation of change when it comes and the miracle of potentiality that it points at. One learns a good deal about time—that it passes and yet remains solid as experience. One learns that life changes even if one sits still, when it's wise to sit still, and when it isn't. Most of all, one learns other people and one's own limits in terms of relationships with them. All this is important learning, but let us once again refrain from supposing that it is learned only by women and valuable only to them. It is the kind of knowledge that is learned on the way to maturity no matter how the path winds.[33]

Yet child rearing will never be a growth experience if women continue to be isolated, unsupported, and disparaged in that role.

It used to be thought that children provided a woman with an identity; without them she was nothing. Now it's become obvious that a solid sense of self is not conferred but is developed over time, after many experiences. No woman feels enriched by children if their existence has deprived her of all the activities and accomplishments she enjoyed before they came. All those books about what mother should do for the housebound child on a rainy day have to be amended to include what the needs of the cooped-up mother are. Dr. Robert Seidenberg reminds us that you can only become a worthwhile model for a child if you feel you are worthwhile: "A mother before she is anything else must be a person with self-respect, assured of her own worth, and, more importantly, must feel that she has not paid an inordinate price for motherhood in terms of her personal striving and aspirations."[34]

A physician who developed severe toxemia of pregnancy and delivered a premature son told me of the struggles she went through deciding which came first, motherhood or personhood:

> I've had more than my share of busybodies reproaching me for working during pregnancy. When my son and I were both in the intensive care unit, my mother's "I told you so" attitude did more harm to my blood pressure than all my anxieties combined. And now that I am returning to work, I find myself faced with, "After you almost lost him, how could you leave him with someone else?" Of course, the most frightening aspect of these attitudes is how strongly I feel them within me as well. But I am getting the courage to reply, "After I almost lost me, I'm certainly not going to stop being a person now!"

Few women have the authority behind them of being a doctor, so the average woman might resist rating the chicken before the egg, but the notion that a happy mother makes for a happy child is an old truth that deserves renewed emphasis.

Freud believed that a woman of thirty is incapable of much further development but that a man of the same age is at the beginning of his best period of achievement.[35] Though he ignored the cultural pressures (which his own theories in fact reinforced) contributing to woman's quiescence, his observation certainly supports the impression that the period of childbearing has traditionally been more of an end for women than an important beginning. The very word "fulfillment" (so often used to describe motherhood) implies carrying out the expected and bringing to an end, rather than being on the threshold of new experiences.[36] But there's no doubt motherhood can be an important beginning if it is viewed as a growth experience rather than as a time for "settling down" or the beginning of your gradual decline.

We are finally learning, and none too soon, how to strike a balance between mother's needs and children's needs. Children need a long list of things: "adequate nourishment; a speaking social partner to provide language skills and promote interaction; an atmosphere providing reasonable consistency and repetition, but also variety and contrast; toys and playthings; supportive and safe opportunities to move about, play and use skills; appropriate limits and prohibitions as well as support for self-regulation and cooperative behavior."[37] Now that we are able to focus attention on the care itself, we are realizing that it is to the child's advantage to receive such attention from *more than one* loving, interested person.[38] In fact, one person would find it impossible to meet all those needs all the time. Child care is changing, and both mother and child stand to gain.

The rebirth of feminism in the sixties led to a renewed interest in children's rights in the early seventies. Many do worry, however, that the children's rights movement as it is shaping up is actually a movement toward adult irresponsibility.[39] Once the myth that women are instinctively altruistic was rightfully exploded, the needs of children became a matter of concern for everyone, but not everyone has been willing to shoulder this responsibility. In hip-communal settings, for example, children are not usually seen as a class unto themselves, but their status is that of "person," a development which can be understood as part of an egalitarian ethos, yet young children continue to be cared for almost exclusively by their mothers. As they grow out of the primitive physical dependence upon the mother, they are seen as

having their own problems that they must work out for themselves. But isn't this simply a convenient philosophy designed to
gloss over how little some men are willing to do for children?
Communal ideologies tend to be elaborated by men, and there is
growing concern that their inclination to be free from parental
responsibilities is *"a freedom that is itself legitimated in part by the
view of children as autonomous. "*[40] When women say to the men,
"We need your help; we can't do it by ourselves," it's a form of
buck-passing for the men to respond, "You don't need our help;
children don't need that much attention in the first place. Let
them be their own persons."

This chapter has been written from the perspective of a married feminist who decided to become a mother, so that the conflicts of that role could be fully described. A married feminist
could just as well choose not to have a baby. I think it's important,
however, that the decision not to have a child be based, in part,
on the *positive* choosing of another means of expanding ego
interests (for example, commitment to community projects or a
job), not just on avoidance of unpleasantness. Becoming fully
mature implies moving away from being completely self-centered
to being interested in the common good. Raising a child is a
highly personal way of showing concern for others, but there are
many other ways of investing in the development of fellowship
and sisterhood.

In summarizing how this married feminist feels about motherhood, I'm reminded of a weekend when my older daughter's
godfather was visiting us. He was being unmercifully tickled and
punched by his daughter and his godchild, and he said it was time
for a truce. This led to a duly-signed treaty declaring no more
teasing until after brunch and a lengthy discussion of how countries settle their differences, what grievances were named in the
Declaration of Independence, and how the Bill of Rights came
into existence. The two girls decided it was time for them to list
their rights and what those of parents should be; they were out
to convince us that later bedtimes were part of their inalienable

rights. But under mother's rights, my daughter listed: "jobes, going out, loving pepole, working," and she ended by saying, "I am for mothers." I too believe in the rights my daughter gave me —going out, loving people, and working; I am delighted that she saw them as my basic rights. Since she is for mothers, I am even more for children.

5

THE HOME

*The house is a woman; and the
woman is a house, or palace.*

Norman O. Brown
Love's Body (1966)

The quote above bluntly states the potent, almost symbiotic connection made between woman and home which pleases the traditionalist and offends the feminist. Many an old-fashioned woman gets misty-eyed when she thinks of herself as a homemaker; it's pleasant to think of a gracious, warm, inviting home as an extension of your own personality. On the other hand, the fact that "woman" and "house" are so inextricably linked has occasioned many a feminist war cry. It's demeaning to use the word "housewife" to define a woman; she's not wed to a house. After her relationship to her own body and those she has with other people as daughter, wife, and mother, no other relationship has so much emotional hold on a married feminist or generates so much ambivalence as the one she has to her home.

Home. What does the word conjure up in your mind? Shelter from storms and the cold, cruel world? Permanence? Digging in? Refuge? Coziness? Rest? Tranquility? Continuity? A meeting of minds? Understanding? Home may refer to a specific place, but it also suggests a pleasant feeling, a being *at home* with yourself. Home is a place for cherishing, something to be protected at all costs. Home is where you start from and go back to. Home is the opposite of alienation. It is the sum total of domestic affections. You can get angry with parents, your spouse, children, or friends, and your negative feelings may modify your ability to cherish them wholeheartedly, but home is a concept that represents the epitome of all we hold dear. As such, it is not likely to be diminished by the vicissitudes that affect human relationships. Home, of course, presupposes some sense of family, but this can eventually cease to mean specific loved ones and simply mean that which is *familiar.* As Margaret Mead points out, "The need to define who you are by the place in which you live remains intact, even when that place is defined by a single object, like the small blue vase that used to mean home to one of my friends, the daughter of a widowed trained nurse who continually moved from one place to another."[1]

To appreciate how loaded with expectations the word "home" is, just think about all the emphasis on making a house a home, or "home is where the heart is," or "there's no place like home." Consider all that has happened in the name of "a man's home is his castle" or the powerful lure of home as the place where they have to take you in when you want to go there.[2] Finally, ponder the appeal these words of Rudyard Kipling have to women: "Daughter am I in my mother's house, but mistress in my own."[3]

Being mistress of a manor or "the lady of the house" suggests importance, authority, being in command, even its own brand of romance. I've always been impressed with the appeal gothic novels have for women. They inevitably revolve around a smart-pretty woman becoming the wife of a secretive-attractive man; the story line almost always centers on her discovering that the mysterious, brooding man will not harm her (no doubt a basic female fear) and her delight in exploring his many-roomed estate. Love of man and love of house are classically intertwined. The woman loves the man more because he has given her complete power over his manse as a symbol, in part, of her power over him (it's also *de rigueur* in gothic novels to have one scene of conflict between the new mistress and the old housekeeper).

For men, love of woman and the notion of her being his home

are more perniciously intertwined. Woman as welcoming receptacle and house as welcoming receptacle have been seen to have much in common by those inclined to view everything *entered* as "feminine." Then, too, the qualities of home and the virtues of woman have become synonymous because both are essential in conferring upon man the domestic blessings he yearns for. The French philosopher Emmanuel Levinas put it this way: "And the other whose presence is discreetly an absence, with which is accomplished the primary hospitable welcome which describes the field of intimacy, is the Woman. The woman is the condition for recollection, the interiority of the Home and inhabitation."[4] A couple of pages later he expands this notion of woman as the incarnation of hospitable welcome to say that every home presupposes a woman:

> The home that founds possession is not a possession in the same sense as the movable goods it can collect and keep. It is possessed because it already and henceforth is hospitable for its proprietor. This refers us to its essential interiority, and to the inhabitant that inhabits it before every inhabitant, the welcoming one par excellence, welcome in itself—the feminine being. Need one add that there is no question here of defying ridicule by maintaining the empirical truth or countertruth that every home *in fact* presupposes a woman? The feminine has been encountered in this analysis as one of the cardinal points of the horizon in which the inner life takes place—and the empirical absence of the human being of "feminine sex" in a dwelling nowise affects the dimension of femininity which remains open there, as the very welcome of the dwelling.[5]

While the prose is extremely opaque, the message is clear: woman as "welcoming one par excellence" ensures that home is a place of welcome. But even if she's not physically present, a home bespeaks the female presence. Levinas' reference to a woman's "interiority" is echoed in Erik Erikson's belief that women are attuned to "inner space."

In what has become a classic study, Erikson saw 150 boys and 150 girls three times and asked them to construct out of toys and blocks "an exciting scene from an imaginary moving picture." Girls typically built simple, low enclosures with elaborate doorways to house people and animals, who, in a number of cases, were attacked by other animals or dangerous men. Boys favored high walls and towers, placed people and animals either outside the enclosure or moving along the streets, and staged a number of automobile accidents. From this, Erikson reaffirms what he considers to be an already promulgated truth:

> . . . here sexual differences in the organization of a play space seem to parallel the morphology of genital differentiation itself: in the male, an *external* organ, *erectible* and *intrusive* in character, serving the channelization of *mobile* sperm cells; *internal* organs in the female, with vestibular *access*, leading to *statically expectant* ova.[6]

The biology is inaccurate—ova do not stay in one place, and the rest of his conclusions seem too pat. It was a girl he labeled "tomboyish" who arranged the one sports field on the play table. He is quick to talk in terms of girls' "goodness" indoors and "peaceful" interiors as *descriptions* when they are, in fact, his judgments. He gives short shrift to the fact that these ten-, eleven-, and twelve-year-olds have already been conditioned to think in terms of girls indoors and boys outdoors, that he may be seeing the result of social learning, not differences "in the experience of the groundplan of the body." But Erikson can be criticized most, I think, for concluding that his study of preadolescents can be applied directly to women's experience throughout the life cycle: "The data was [*sic*] 'awaited,' above all, as nonclinical and nonverbal support of pervasive clinical and developmental impressions concerning the importance of the 'inner space' throughout the feminine life cycle."[7] Sounds like he got what *he* wanted!

Whether Erikson's study "proved" that women are attuned to

"inner space" or not, there is a long psychiatric tradition that has seen the home as an inorganic womb—a nesting place—and interior decorating as an unconscious extension of a woman's love for her own body. Menstruation is supposed to endow her with a special feeling for personal cleanliness. This impulse she then generalizes to all her surroundings:

> . . . the care and maintainance [*sic*] of beauty and charm is entrusted to them [women]. I do not mean only the beauty of their own bodies which we all admire, but the creation of beauty in the home, which is an unconscious extension of their bodies. In this aspect we are indebted to women for the comfort we enjoy. The cradle into which the baby is put signifies a recapturing of a situation similar to the one which the embryo found in the womb; the home you live in is merely an extension. The secretions of the female body have the effect that the girl acquires a special feeling for cleanliness not only for herself, but also for her surroundings . . .[8]

The ideas are couched in language that makes them seem part of the order of nature, as if all women felt a primal urge to scrub, decorate, and do maintenance work. Being responsible for "the creation of beauty in the home" sounds so much more inviting than being told you're responsible for fighting the endless battle against dust, dirt, and decay, but they amount to the same thing. The word "entrusted" has the ring of a holy mission, but housework is housework and you can euphemize it only so far. What an insidious ploy it is to deem it *natural* for women to feel like cleaning. Any woman who objects is called unfeminine! Home and woman, object and person: Where does the one leave off and the other begin?

Since woman as the "welcoming one par excellence" transforms the home into a place of welcome, she is imprisoned by the very sentiment that at first sounds so complimentary. If the notion of a home suggests the female presence, husband and children demand that she be there when they *come home* so she can welcome them, listen to what they have done during the day, and affirm—by her approval—their endeavors. How many times have you read articles saying a wife can do whatever she wants to do as long as she is back when her husband and children *come home?* That conceptualization has always disturbed me because it further suggests that the woman herself can never *come home* quite the way the others can; if she's been out she returns to an empty building, while her family can come home to her.

When object and person are described as incarnating the same domestic virtues, the dangers to the person are several: the house can start seeming like an old friend; the woman herself may be seen as just another piece of furniture; if she devotes herself to the house, the house *will become* an extension of her. The traditional notion of a fine house is a very attractive one, but it presupposed the presence of a servant class. (At the turn of the century, there was an estimated average of two servants for every middle- or upper-class family of five.)[9] What happens when there is no more servant class *per se* to handle the maintenance work? If sole responsibility for the house is left in the hands of women, if household chores are considered "woman's work," then the answer is obvious: the female sex has become the last servant class, unpaid and unsung.

Thorstein Veblen noted in *The Theory of the Leisure Class* that "according to the ideal scheme of the pecuniary culture, the lady of the house is the chief menial of the household."[10] And economist John Kenneth Galbraith writes frankly about the conversion of women into a crypto-servant class: "Menially employed servants were available only to a minority of the preindustrial population; the servant-wife is available, democratically, to almost the entire present male population."[11] He argues that the development of woman's crypto-servant status was prodded by an economic order based on indefinitely expanding consumption. The prime tenet of modern economic theory is that happiness is a function of the volume of goods and services consumed. Since family happiness is the woman's business, intelligent shopping for goods, their preparation and use, and the care and maintenance of the dwelling are among her prime directives. Our consumer-oriented society has further encouraged isolated, single-family housing units rather than apartments, as in European communities, because more furniture and appliances get sold that way. The larger the space, the more things you need to fill it; and the upkeep grows proportionately. And the more housekeeping devolves on women, the more they need gadgets and mechanical devices to help them forget that it is they who are stuck with the day-to-day maintenance work.

But it isn't just the work itself or even the derogatory title "chief menial" that gets a woman down. Total responsibility for housework affects the woman's time perspective, with damaging results to her own personality development. In the traditional family, the husband is able to be much more future-oriented than his wife. He regularly goes beyond family interests to shape his own future, get one more step up the ladder of success. And through his job he presumably helps shape the collective future —i.e., add to the gross national product, improve health care, fight injustice, increase the value of his company's stock, etc. The past—preserved in the form of furniture, heirloom silver, and antique glassware—and the present, with its emphasis on endless repetition—the daily rhythm of the clean becoming soiled and the soiled becoming clean—are his wife's domain.

The successful life requires both maintenance and progression: "To go forward, each existence must be maintained, for it to expand toward the future it must integrate the past, and while intercommunicating with others it should find self-confirmation."[12] But traditional marriage provides only the man with a happy synthesis of the two. While the woman is limited to past and present, he confronts the future. He goes out into society and comes home each evening, where he is refreshed by the familiar in its place. Though he might not notice, it probably took many hours of work, especially for the young mother, to get everything back in place for his return.

The woman, on the other hand, responsible for maintaining the status quo, doesn't have much energy left over to go beyond her own situation, to do new things. Over the years her life may even come to be totally shaped by a negative philosophy—"the good is attained through the abolition of evil and not by positive action"[13]—which is bound to kill her spirit, her curiosity and creativity. The sun is shut out so the rug won't fade, chairs are covered with plastic so they won't get stained, silver wedding presents are never used because they tarnish easily. How many of us don't know the woman whose life has become an endless series of warnings: "Don't play with that, you'll break it . . . Stop touching that, you're smudging the glass . . . Can't you keep your dirty fingers off that counter?" It's tragic, but just keeping the house up may mean that the woman doesn't have time to keep up with anything else—friends, political events, reading, hobbies, job skills, etc.

The commitment to "home" as object, if not geographical location, is accelerating as we become more and more a nation of transients. Possessions have come to represent the only continuity in many people's lives, for the friends of one year may not be living near you the next, one in every three marriages ends in divorce, and children grow up and strike out on their own early. Fifty years ago, you bought a house and didn't feel compelled to redo it immediately because you knew the house would still be there next year when you had more money and energy. Now you are more likely to feel that all the painting and wallpapering should be done right away because if you spruce up one room per year, you know you may be gone before you've had a chance to see what your dream living room would have looked like.

But no sooner do I list the pitfalls of "home" as a traditional ideal than I'm reminded once again of the pleasures of clean sheets, a cozy fire, flowers on the table, and polished wood. Home is a powerful need for all human beings. We all want warmth and comfort. A home of one's own is part of the American dream, but can it be realized without women having to be a slave to that dream? . . .

I grew up listening to my grandmother tell of emigrating from Poland because she honestly believed the streets of America were paved with gold. Instead of wealth, a job as a charwoman awaited her, but she and my parents and my entire family continued to regard a home of your own as the goal to work toward, something Americans could have that was not easily available in the "old country." I have been heavily influenced by their dreams and by the fact that our family of four lived in just two rooms during my early years. There is something about growing up without a room of your own and studying at a desk jammed into the bathroom that makes you want gracious living as pictured in Better Homes and Gardens.

The television commercial drones: "What I want to know is how can any one woman hold so much love?" asks the touched husband. "It shows everywhere. In your needlepoint, and in your cooking," continues the admiring man. "Mm-hmm," murmurs the wife with an it's-all-been-worth-it-to-be-noticed-by-the-master smile. They then launch into a commentary on her brilliant choice in fabric softeners. The scene ends with the man sniffing the baby's diaper and patting his behind. "She even finds a fabric softener that whitens, too. Tommy, you got terrific taste in mommies." [14] I stare at the set wondering myself how any woman can hold so much love. The ad for Royal Doulton says, "Your taste has probably changed since you first said 'I do' to your china and crystal." (Sometimes I think I married a house instead of a man, but to have it confirmed in The New York Times Magazine *of all places!) The ad goes on to say that seeing the new line of Royal Doulton English china and crystal will "make you want to say 'I do' all over again. And this time, it will really be forever." [15] Now, I understand: marriage to the man was a fling, but exchanging vows with china and crystal has a permanence beyond the merely mortal. "I do, I do, I do" my heart cries out, enjoying the thought of infidelity with the china right under my husband's nose. . . . Lake Havasu City, Arizona (where the London Bridge went), is selling the American Dream. Astroturf lawns are featured there instead of* grass. *"Why, gents, you can send your wife out to vacuum the front lawn,"* suggests one of the salesmen. [16] *If it's grass and mowing, it's masculine work, but if it's Astroturf and vacuuming, it's feminine work. Now let me get that straight: lawn mower = male, vacuum = female, inside things = female, outside things = male.*

There are days when I see the dust particles dancing in a beam of light and the sunshine fades before the fact that my newly polished table is being bombarded by film every second of every minute of every hour of every day of every . . . When it's freezing outside and I'm home several days in a row, the icicles seem to be nailing my door shut and me into my casket. . . . The catalogs stream in daily; I feel like a potentate. I only have to affix a magic Master Charge number to a sheet of paper for the riches of Araby to pour through my door. But ordering through the mail is so lonely; at least going shopping in the center of a city is a chance for human contact. I remember a passage in Arthur Miller's The Price: ". . . the main thing today is—shopping. Years ago a person, he was unhappy, and didn't know what to do with himself—he'd go to church, start a revolution—something. Today you're unhappy? Can't figure it out? What is the salvation? Go shopping." [17] When I'm unhappy, it's so much easier to bandage my hurt with a bauble than face what's bothering me. But it's a short-lived placebo.

If you don't have the measurements of a nymphet, you'd better be a good Hausfrau; at least you can be admired in that role. All those beautiful women advertising products don't have to get the wash "really clean," but they're reminding me I'd better do so. [18] If he doesn't like my figure, at least he might be proud of my neatness. From ring around the finger to ring around the collar! . . . Some fine day, one machine too many will break down and so will I. . . . Most men seem so oblivious to the boredom and burden of housework. But an inordinate number of women friends who have visited our new house commented, "How will you ever manage with all those windows to wash?" Men see a house; women see a series of windows to wash, rugs to vacuum, tile to rid of mold, *wood to polish, sinks to clean, books to dust, plants to turn so they won't slant in the direction of the sun.*

At various Christmases I have gotten a freezer, a serving tray, sheets, a quilt, tablecloths, a salad bowl, knives, and all sorts of other things "for the house." But I am not the house. Five Christmases ago I decided to give my husband glasses, towels, and potholders "for the house." Ever since, I've gotten perfume, stockings, and lingerie. . . . I see things around the house no one else sees—cobwebs on the ceiling lights, dust balls in a closet, mold in the vegetable bin, fingerprints on the woodwork, stains on the back of the seatcovers, grease spatters around the stove, chipped paint on the window sills, the place under the counter where the wallpaper ran out, papers that have fallen behind the bookcase, parched plants, clogged filters, and water spots on the stainless steel. Am I destined to go through life seeing the sticky underside no one else cares about?

Our local paper ran a special feature on June brides. It asked, "What's the one strong link between contemporary Ms. and her home-bound predecessors?" "Housework" was the answer. [19] Is housework what binds women together? Will housework always be woman's ball and chain? My God, I hope not. . . . My husband calls from his office and asks what I did this morning. How do you explain to him or anyone else that it took an hour to get air bubbles out of the radiators and refill the pans of water sitting on top of them so the warm air won't be bone dry? "Milking" the radiators sounds like a domestic obscenity. . . . After being in the house for several days in a row, I find myself a little scared to go out. It's as if I were Rip Van Winkle and didn't think I could handle all the changes that had taken place while I was asleep. . . . A lady on one of the talk shows points out that if you clean the filter on your dryer and collect the fuzz, eventually you will have stuffing enough for a pillow or doll. "Nothing need ever be wasted around the house if you have imagination," she solemnly declares. I used to clean the filter without thinking; now it's a moral decision. To how many dolls have I denied existence? Pretty soon the "Right to Life" people will be after me. The guilt pricks my wasteful heart.

I hate Tupperware parties. Selling your body strikes me as more honorable than selling your friends plastic under the guise of being at a party. . . . Sometimes I read Heloise's newspaper hints just to revel in all the things I'm not doing. I don't collect bits of string, empty egg cartons, bird feathers, fallen-off sequins, baby food jars, toilet paper rolls. I've never made a pencil holder out of an old soup can, a lamp out of a wine bottle, or a vase out of a plastic bleach bottle. I don't press my ground beef into hamburger patties before freezing them or wash all my fruits and vegetables before putting them in the refrigerator. I've never made a Styrofoam Christmas tree out of bits of jewelry and other trifles that happened to be in my attic. In fact, I have a most undistinguished attic—nothing that, "with a little paint, would be a real treasure." . . . I haven't ironed in nine years; my husband has learned to sneeze into a handkerchief without anyone seeing the wrinkles. He hasn't minded his rumpled state enough to take up ironing himself, and we have the only children in our neighborhood who went to nursery school and asked "What's that?" when they saw a toy iron. . . . Now that garbage compactors can compress a week's worth of stinking refuse into one antiseptic package, is garbage woman's work or man's work?

It took a solid eight years for me to stop apologizing to guests "My house is a mess" in that pro forma way so many women unthinkingly do. I want neither someone else's absolution for my sins of omission nor the ritual compliment that usually follows such protestations of guilt. It took another year for me to stop playing the role of chief inspector every time my husband and children did some cleaning. It's still hard for me to see a missed patch of dust without clucking over their incompetence, but I choke down most of my complaints. I don't want them to have good reason to say "If you don't like it, do it yourself." I don't want ever to go back to doing it all myself. . . . I had an aunt who always used to scrub her kitchen floor when she was upset, and I'm quite a bit like her. The day after we returned home from burying my *mother, I silently scoured every surface I could reach. I was a mad Lady Macbeth crying over and over again, "Out, out damned spot." Putting my house in order eventually brought back some order to my feelings. Hard work does ground a person in reality, but you have to be on guard so you're not ground up in the process. . . . There's a famous James Thurber cartoon in which a henpecked husband sees his home and his wife as the same being.* [20] *I don't want to become an object, and I don't want my husband to see me as a monster with windows for eyes and a door for a mouth. I don't want my husband to think our home will swallow him up.*

When a woman considers her relationship to the home, it's easy to feel like this character in a Doris Lessing novel:

> The virtues had turned to vices, to the nagging and bullying of other people. An unafraid creature had been turned, through the long, grinding process of always, always being at other people's beck and call, always having to give out attention to detail, minuscule wants, demands, needs, events, crises, into an obsessed maniac. Obsessed by what was totally unimportant. [21]

Home isn't unimportant, but all the things that have to be done to run a home certainly lack importance in themselves. And an insidious twist has been added by the invention of "labor-saving" devices. Dislike of domestic chores may be mocked as neurotic self-pity when housework isn't realistically appraised but is considered just a matter of pushing a few buttons. Newspapers regularly recount how some man, tired of his wife's complaints, took over the housework for two weeks and found there was nothing to it. After tallying the hours spent on dusting and cleaning, he declared them to be a mere pittance. What was left unsaid was that it was a *temporary* assumption of eternal chores and that none of the miracle machines he used broke down during those particular weeks. He didn't have to hang around the house for a couple of days waiting for a repairman who didn't show. (All services are founded on the principle that there's a lady of the house prepared to be the "welcoming one par excellence" whenever the repairman decides to come.) Probably none of the "you don't have to do them every week, but you have to do them sometime" jobs reared their ugly heads (cleaning the oven, defrosting the refrigerator, then washing it with disinfectant, putting the clothes in mothballs, getting the Christmas decorations out, shopping for school supplies, wiping the dark woodwork that doesn't show the dirt, airing the mattresses, polishing the silver, dusting tops that can only be reached by a ladder, washing the curtains, etc.). And that two-week adventurer didn't shoulder the day-to-day responsibility that saps energy, but enjoyed the excitement of doing something for a lark.

Housework isn't simply a problem that can be solved by the pushing of buttons. Actually the menial role of the woman becomes more arduous the higher the income and the more consumption-oriented the family.[22] As Betty Friedan pointed out:

> The modern American housewife spends far more time washing, drying, and ironing than her mother. If she has an electric freezer or mixer, she spends more time cooking than a woman who does not have these labor-saving appliances. The home freezer, simply by existing, takes up time: beans, raised in the garden, must be prepared for freezing. If you have an electric mixer, you have to use it: those elaborate recipes with the puréed chestnuts, watercress, and almonds take longer than broiling pork chops.[23]

Having automatic washers hasn't meant the end of laundry as a major chore, but it has meant new standards for cleanliness, softness, brightness, and smelling fresh. Drip-dry clothes are still presumed to need a "touch" of ironing, and many wash-and-wear materials have to be extracted from the dryer as soon as they are dry or they will get wrinkles (considerable time must be spent hovering around waiting to get them out before they're overcooked). There has been a heightening of expectation; luxuries have become necessities. Cake mixes have created more demand for "homemade" cakes even when it's not someone's birthday. The availability of canned soups and processed foods has increased the expectation that all cooking should be gourmet, and culinary variety is seen as a basic family right.

Homes may sparkle with chrome and throb to the beat of machines slurping and whirling, but they are also expected to be aesthetically pleasing in ways our foremothers wouldn't have thought possible. You don't buy just any toilet paper; you coordinate the color with the color of the walls, the facial tissues, the soap, and the shower curtain for the "ensemble" look. There's more pressure to entertain, chauffeur, garden, and comparison-shop than ever before. Housewifery has expanded into a full-time career in order to keep the welcoming one busy when she isn't welcoming everybody home, but also because new standards for such work enhance market expansion and stimulate the total economy.

Some household improvements are of indisputable value—fitted bottom sheets, for example—some have increased the feeling of being lady or lord of the manor, but others have led to a reactionary espousal of those time-consuming activities that technical ingenuity was supposed to liberate us from in the first place. All that plastic has made us sick and tired of plastic. In the last few years there's been repeated emphasis on what feminist Susan Sands calls the "new organic housewifery." The packaged ice cream which was supposed to save us from all that cranking is full of chemical additives, and ice cream makers are now being advertised as fine gifts for those discriminating enough to appreciate "natural" things, who want to start from scratch. Spaghetti *aficionados* have found canned Parmesan cheese to be tasteless, so it's back to finger-scraping grating.

The "progress" from homemade to factory-made and back again was prompted in part by renewed appreciation for old-fashioned female virtuosity—"restoring the element of skill and creativeness to cooking, decorating, sewing and gardening"[24]— but all the emphasis on making your own yogurt, candles, soup, preserves, and bread once again threatens to chain women to the hearth and make them feel guilty if they are tasteless enough to buy ready-made.

The concept of "home" may conjure up all sorts of sacred and reverent feelings in the traditional corners of a married feminist's head. But homemaking in reality is a vicious circle—and that is not a perception unique to proclaimed feminists. There is a tradition too of looking at homemaking with a dash of malevolent humor. The most orthodox women have seen something sadly funny in the juggling act of running a home. Jean Kerr described having to write in the family car in order to be alone while she recorded her misadventures with four sons and a big house; the result was one of the fifties' bestsellers. Yet when she admitted to writing so that she could have money for household help, she wasn't labeled a troublemaker; millions of women read *Please Don't Eat the Daisies* and identified with her ambitions and perceptions. When she pictured domestic bliss as freedom from household chores for herself and her husband, there was universal understanding of what she meant: ". . . my husband and I often sit together in the deepening twilight and listen to the sweet gentle slosh-click, slosh-click of the dishwasher. He smiles and I smile. Oh, it's a golden moment."[25] Her triumphal attitude was not seen as revolutionary, but her bemused comments on how frustrating homemaking can be and her desire for household help, privacy, and a job of her own could easily be translated into NOW (National Organization for Women) rhetoric. Jean Kerr's whimsy and obvious commitment to family life simply sweetened the message.

Feminists have repeatedly been upbraided for lacking a sense of humor. It could be they seem dour because their deadly seriousness is in such contrast to the cheerful, always smiling wife men have come to need and expect. Psychologist Naomi Weisstein wrote an interesting analysis of this subject entitled "Why We

Aren't Laughing . . . Any More." She denied the existence of a woman's survival humor comparable to the "self-deprecating but fighting back" humor of other oppressed groups: "I remember no redemptive or fighting humor about my [female] condition."[26] Though I found much to agree with in her article, I cannot agree with her on that point. There is a strong American tradition of women fighting the oppression of housework, ridiculing it, but retaining their dignity despite daily adversity.

The widely syndicated Erma Bombeck is but the latest manifestation of that tradition. This point needs emphasis because any rapprochement between the traditional and the feminist attitudes can be greatly enhanced by seeing the sugar-coated barbs of Erma Bombeck as really another form of feminist protest. Her millions of admirers and those of Betty Friedan have much in common; the difference is in what they do with their respective insights. Bombeck admirers are content with feeling better after reading an ironic but affectionate description of their situation; it's good just to know someone else understands what you are going through. Bombeck's wit amidst chaos and hardship helps one achieve a bemused dignity too. A card-carrying feminist may possess the same understanding as Bombeck, but focuses on political ways of fighting an oppressive situation instead of grinning and bearing it. This person may feel the issues are so serious that it behooves her to be serious so she'll be taken seriously.

There are many gradations of feminism. Bombeck admirers and feminists may share many insights, but differ on the ways to cope with the problems they both identify. It may be true that Bombeck and her readers fear that too brazen an attack on the drudgery and inequities of housework may ultimately mean having to take a stand against family life and the entire concept of home. As believers in many of the traditional values, they may be unwilling to go that far, whereas a number of feminists do not shy away from criticism of the nuclear family as part of a sexist social system.

Maybe it's not obvious that Erma Bombeck and Betty Friedan

have all that much in common. But consider this choice bit of Bombeck prose:

> My mother won't admit it, but I've always been a disappointment to her. Deep down inside, she will never forgive herself for giving birth to a daughter who refuses to launder aluminum foil and use it over again. She was definitely not amused when I held my annual "Breakfast With Mommy" at Christmas time and passed out candy canes to my children and told them to be good until Mommy saw them at breakfast next year. Mother has dedicated her remaining years to bleaching my dish towels and getting me ready for a deathbed conversion to domesticity. During a recent visit she pulled out a piece from the rack and a small envelope dropped to the floor. She picked it up and gasped, "Oh my soul. Do you have any idea the expiration date on this packet of yeast?" Without waiting for an answer she read, "It expired July 28, 1957. What happened?" "I don't like to be pressured by a deadline," I said.[27]

This passage is brimming over with protest. She's critical of mothers forcing an oppressive domesticity on their daughters and of the pettiness of housework. Her desire to distance herself from her children is a bittersweet refutation of the myth of the always available mother, and her disregard of deadlines is a strike against never-ending pressures.

When Erma Bombeck describes filling out a form at the Bureau of Motor Vehicles and having the man behind the counter ask if she wants her driver's license to read "housewife" as her occupation, both traditionalists and feminists understand the edge in her response, "Would you believe, Love Goddess?"[28] When she asks, "How can we serve a husband, kids, an automatic washer, the Board of Health, and a cat who sits on top of the TV set and looks mad at you because you had her fixed and still have something left over for yourself?"[29] she's posing the basic problem of a married feminist: How do you meet the needs of others without short-changing yourself?

What could be more explicit than "... my life is like a treadmill with stops at tedium, boredom, monotony, and the laundry room"?[30] When Bombeck declares, "Since age thirty-five, I haven't had an original thought, done anything significant and while others were making giant steps for mankind, I was making giant steps with the garbage,"[31] she is admitting to having what Friedan calls "the problem that has no name"[32] or what others call "housewife fatigue" or what Dr. Robert Seidenberg describes as "the trauma of eventlessness."[33] And when she comments that "men don't really know boredom as women do. If we had offices with secretaries with appointment books you could do our week with one original and six carbons,"[34] I see connections between what she is saying and Dr. Mabel Blake Cohen's words, "Indeed, constructive use of the long hours alone, which are part of the experience of the housewife, requires a considerable degree of inner richness if retrogression and inertia are not to set in."[35]

Housewives know from their own experience what it's like to feel you haven't done anything significant, so they avidly drink in Bombeck's words. But they also know she's not quite to be trusted. After all, she's a celebrity. They have read her columns and books and have seen her interviewed by Barbara Walters; what she's saying about housework isn't really true for her. That's probably the most dangerous aspect of such domestic humor. The writer who accurately describes the housewives' plight attracts a large readership, but she herself by becoming famous and financially independent isn't *just like* her readers. Those who don't want to treat the boredom and monotony as serious complaints are likely to say she exaggerates, and the overall effect of her writing does have a bubbly flavor. You can sustain that bubbly quality if you are a successful writer, but how many full-time housewives can?

Erma Bombeck would probably not agree with my conclusion that she and avowed feminists have much in common. At the end of her book *I Lost Everything in the Post-Natal Depression,* she proclaims her love for Edith Bunker (of "All in the Family" fame) and says she doesn't know many women with her tolerance, generosity, and optimism. "The people I know . . . are bored, miserable, depressed, and unfulfilled because in 1965 Betty Friedan told them they were. (Would Betty lie?)"[36] That put-down is troubling. Friedan didn't *make* women feel bored, miserable, depressed, and unfulfilled. She simply reported their feelings, allowing women to see it was "safe" to admit their own unhappiness. If you're feeling good and someone says you're miserable, you don't suddenly become miserable, you tell them they're all wet. Tolerance toward your friends' peccadilloes is generally desirable, but tolerance of out-and-out oppression is foolhardy, for it encourages dictators—both on the home front and on a national scale. The Erma Bombecks and the Betty Friedans need each other to shape a more equitable and truly fulfilling world, peopled by women who are neither dupes nor harridans.

If there is substantial agreement that women should be freed from their "crypto-servant" status, how do we go about accomplishing that? The most important change necessary is to see maintenance work as everyone's responsibility. No one should grow up with the attitude that she or he is entitled to a maid (for men, read "wife") who will do the dirty work and take over the thankless routine tasks. I am very sympathetic to the position T. E. Frazier takes when one of the visitors to Walden Two (in B. F. Skinner's 1948 classic of that name) asks: "Why should everyone engage in menial work? Isn't that really a misuse of manpower if a man has special talents or abilities?" Frazier responds:

> There's no misuse. Some of us would be smart enough to get along without doing physical work, but we're also smart enough to know that in the long run it would mean trouble. . . . The really intelligent man doesn't want to feel that his work is being done by anyone else. He's sensitive enough to be disturbed by slight resentments which, multiplied a millionfold, mean his downfall. Perhaps he remembers his own reactions when others have imposed on him. . . . That's the virtue of Walden Two which pleases me most.

I was never happy in being waited on. . . . Here a man can hold up his head and say, "I've done my share!"[37]

Such an attitude means the end of "loving service," that is, proving love by subjecting oneself to others. It also puts an end to the complacent belief that others enjoy what you don't want to do. While a man may want a "wife" to free him to do "manly" things and a wife may wish she had a "wife"[38] so she could be free of trivia and concentrate on the important, such desires are essentially childish. They're childish because they assume you could be whatever you wanted to be if only others would cooperate and make life easy for you. That is certainly anything but taking responsibility for your own life.

Being responsible for your own maintenance work would not necessarily mean everyone had to do the same thing. But it would avoid the all too common attitude that every time a man does something around the house he's *helping* the woman rather than doing his fair share. The man who shirks responsibility should feel guilty, rather than the wife feeling inadequate because she can't do everything around the house herself. The highly trained individual who took years to develop her or his complicated skills would, of course, continue to perform these skills during most of the working day. But no individual, no matter how famous or important, should be allowed to disown menial tasks completely (even the *planners* of Walden Two were expected to do one credit of straight physical work per day).[39] President Harry Truman used to rinse out his own socks and underwear every night because he felt no one should have to do that for him. My father read that in the newspaper and it really impressed him. That the President of the United States would be that sensitive to want to save someone else an unpleasant job touched him, and my father started to do the same thing—and has continued to do so for almost twenty-five years. One wonders if inflation would gallop on and on if government leaders had to do the weekly shopping (and not just as a publicity stunt). At least newspaper headlines wouldn't be likely to read, "Housewives upset with supermarket prices," as if it were solely their concern.

Not all housework is equally boring or tiring. Women have repeatedly been encouraged to take pride in housework and they have with good reason, but the truly creative aspects of homemaking should be distinguished from monotonous drudgery so that no one member of a household gets saddled with all the unpleasant tasks. In the novel *Small Changes*, Marge Piercy has one of the characters describe her household's division of labor this way:

> There were the shit jobs, the jobs that provided little satisfaction and involved little skill: dishwashing, disposing of garbage and trash, cleaning, laundry, shopping. Then came jobs that required mastering and gave satisfaction: cooking, painting, putting up shelves or doing carpentry, working on the car, sewing. Last there were tasks that required dealing with others: landlord, doctors, insurance agents, the electric company. Each had to do some jobs in every category. That way nobody ended up getting all the jobs that involved creativity, nobody ended up doing all the things that aroused anxiety and required aggression, nobody ended up stuck with the repetitive tasks empty of prestige or reward. They all spent time with the children. There were specific times each was responsible. . . . To run properly it required that every few weeks they sit down and review the categories and tasks ahead.[40]

I like these distinctions because they do not imply all housework is exciting enough to dedicate yourself to it nor so demeaning that only a fool would enjoy it. Some periodic assessment of who is doing what also makes sense because tastes change and the boring jobs will be less boring if you do different ones each month. Alternating who does what also has the added advantage of preparing family members to handle emergencies. The limitations imposed by an accident or disability won't be so disruptive if a man can take over the cooking when the woman develops heart trouble and she can do the banking if he has to spend eight weeks in traction.

While there aren't any easy answers to the servant problem (except that no one should be a servant), let me end this chapter by listing ones that are currently being discussed: Wife and husband could equally share the maintenance work and teach their children that everyone has a responsibility to do daily chores; no job would automatically be designated as female or male. This approach has old-fashioned appeal because it emphasizes family solidarity, yet it is new-sounding because it assumes that children do not enjoy privileged status just because they might get bored by housework. In fact, parents who readily admit housework can be boring but go ahead and do it *together* get much more willing cooperation from their children than those in homes where mother does all the housework and tries to make the children think dusting can be glamorous. Marriage contracts may formalize the notion of wife and husband sharing homemaking functions (though as of now they're legally unenforceable), and family councils may be necessary so that work can be periodically reallocated to avoid any one person cleaning more than her/his fair share of toilets. On the debit side, sharing makes couples sometimes feel like an arbitration team when they would prefer to be just bed partners. For this solution to work, it would help if the spouses had flexible work weeks and if *all* children learned maintenance skills (cooking, sewing, plumbing, carpentry, etc.) in school from an early age.

Hiring a housekeeper is another option, but who wants the job? Getting "good help" is a problem for all but the very rich, but, more important, as sex discrimination disappears, class becomes an even greater issue. Drudgery despised by middle-class women is still drudgery when done by the lower-class cleaning woman (or man). Still, it is better to be a wage-earning housekeeper with paid sick days, vacation, and Social Security benefits than to be a *spent* wife.[41] (There is a movement to unionize houseworkers and to give housewives regular salaries and their own Social Security benefits.) Housework could possibly be incorporated into the "public" economy; each family would buy needed services from agencies organized for that purpose. The bill for window washing or rug cleaning would then be calculated as part of the gross national product,[42] though it would raise family budgets considerably. The trend toward upgrading jobs by professionalizing them could be extended to a broad range of domestic activities, and "women's work" would finally get the unionized, financial remuneration it deserves.

Collectivizing housework in a commune, an apartment complex, or on a neighborhood level could eliminate the high cost of service agencies and bring about more neighborly neighborhoods. Of course, someone still has to do the organizing, and getting someone to take on this responsibility would be no little problem, but having community rooms set aside for doing laundry, mending, and babysitting could bring back the shared pleasures of old-time quilting parties and roof-raisings. Finally, and fantastically, domestic robots, maybe like the ones in Woody Allen's film *Sleeper*, will become the super-appliances of the future. Still, someone would have to take the responsibility for their programming and taking them to the repair shop when necessary.

Home can be a very special place, but only if all family members make an investment in it. The love and welcome and warmth that are supposed to emanate from the home can only truly develop when no one feels put upon. I hope the time is soon approaching when no one will have to be a housewife but everyone will be a homemaker—one, however, who knows that self-realization can only come from being *at home* within oneself.

6

COOKING

*Every morning Matilda Titus Hastings fixes her
husband, Wayne, a panful of biscuits and gravy to
go with his specially fried eggs. Perhaps as a subtle
consequence of this repeated alchemy, in the same
way that dogs come to resemble their masters,
Matilda looks something like a biscuit herself,
wholesomely puffy. "Only one woman in Atkins,
West Virginia," she likes to say, "is bigger than I
am—the lady who runs the tavern."*

Jane Howard
A Different Woman *(1973)*

After spending a chapter on woman's relationship to the home,
it might seem somewhat excessive to devote another whole chapter to cooking. But cooking isn't just a part of housework; it is the
outward manifestation of another role felt to be basic to women
as that of mother—woman as nurturer. Erich Neumann put it
this way in his study of the primordial image of the "great
mother": "The woman is the natural nourishing principle and
hence mistress of everything that implies nourishment. The
finding, composition, and preparation of food, as well as the fruit
and nut gathering of the early cultures, are the concern of the
female group."[1] It is generally accepted that woman was responsible for the invention and development of agriculture.[2] That
woman has traditionally been responsible for finding and gathering the food is not without tremendous political significance.
Quite literally, the preindustrial woman was the family breadwinner, and this gave her considerable status. In parts of Africa and

Southeast Asia, a woman is still expected to support and feed herself, her husband, and children with the food she grows. Such women may bear a large part of the work burden, but they also have some economic independence, considerable freedom of movement, and an important position in the community.[3] Since woman was the original breadwinner, modern-day women who want to be financially independent and earn their own daily bread are not usurping a male prerogative, but reasserting a traditional female one.

Cooking deserves special analysis not only because it is an activity considered fundamental to the feminine principle, but also because it carries associations of erotic gratification, motherliness, and hospitality. It would seem, therefore, that a look at woman as nurturer must be much more than a discussion of the pros and cons of feeding the family three nourishing meals a day. Cooking is not only the one homemaking skill most often described as an art and a science, but the one laden with the most symbolism. From the moment the bride cuts a piece of wedding cake and has her husband eating out of her hands, connections between food/cooking and woman/sex are constantly reinforced. A married feminist needs to understand the nexus of meaning contained in the simple acts of preparing and serving food.

Feeding has always been seen as feminine. The fertile earth is referred to as "she." Think of Eve and you're immediately reminded of apples. The pregnant woman obviously provides the growing fetus with sustenance. Mother *is* food: her breasts give milk and provide an infant the first sensual satisfaction.[4] If the classic male stance is "I will protect you," the female counterpart is "I will nourish you and make you feel good"—a sentence which suggests oral gratification, sexuality, satiety, sociability, communion, gift-giving, and the civilizing of raw nature. All these elements associated with food reveal the weight of meaning attached to woman's role as nurturer. To be a woman has meant catering to the needs of others, providing bread and comfort.

There is a very strong sexual component to eating. Claude

Lévi-Strauss wrote that the Caingang dialects of southern Brazil have a verb that means both "to eat" and "to copulate." In parts of Africa, cooking is associated with coitus between husband and wife: "To put fuel into the fire and to blow is to cohabit; the hearthstones are the posteriors; the cooking pot is the vagina; the pot ladle is the penis."[5] A number of scholars interpret the "fall" in Eden as a poetic description of intercourse rather than apple-eating. The snake is an obvious phallic symbol, and the fruit is a feminine representation; Adam and Eve's carnal *knowledge* is what angered God. The interesting feature of this interpretation is how easily eating and copulating are transposed. Dr. Karl Menninger noted that "in the light of modern psychoanalytic theory, living and loving are almost synonymous; one may say that eating one's food and kissing one's bride are merely differently directed expressions of the same drive."[6] Many have been quick to add, "Kissing doesn't last; cookery does!"

"The way to a man's heart is through his stomach" has been one of the favorite maxims of those books on dating which purport to tell teenage girls all they need to know about love and marriage. I remember one that was very popular in the late fifties and early sixties entitled *On Becoming a Woman,* which suggested that the girl whose social life was sagging take the initiative and give a party: "One way to make the party memorable (especially to boys) is to serve really good food. . . . Try to dream up something a little different, and you'll be intriguing." But is there always a direct connection between the food and the woman? This same book said the girl is supposed to learn how to handle boys by watching her mother "handle" her father: "He can come home hot, tired and disgruntled, but somehow your mother can turn him back into a big, powerful man, king of all he surveys, just by a few warm words, a smile, a good meal." But does all this handling transform him into a king—or her into a loyal retainer? What happens when the mother is feeling hot, tired, and disgruntled at the end of the day, or isn't she permitted those feelings? According to this book, an engagement means "she learns to cook, he learns to carve"; and "every husband wants a wife who's a combination of Marilyn Monroe, Fanny Farmer (the cookbook one, not the candy one), and Florence Nightingale."[7] This widely circulated advice shaped my consciousness and that of many of my peers. But just think about the images that were glorified. It pictures woman as cunt-cook-consoler, not a partner; it says a man wants a woman to meet his physical needs and that's all. The woman who *services* and the man who is *served* both come across as soulless machines.

Food has a long history as a preliminary to sex or as an expression of affection. A man may view cocktails and dinner at an intimate restaurant as a necessary prelude to the seduction scene, while a woman blandishes her prey with a demonstration of her culinary skills. Freud's wife-to-be sent him a homemade cake to "dissect" several weeks after they were introduced, which he interpreted as proof that the attraction between them was mutual.[8] The common rooms of my college dormitory all had small kitchenettes "for the girls to fix themselves an evening snack." Relatively few snacks were ever prepared, but the ovens hummed each weekend when countless refrigerated rolls of chocolate-chip cookies were baked for the boyfriend hungry for such tokens of affection. I grew up in a period when a "good girl" thought a "French kiss" was daring, but a French pastry of your own making was presented and received as the sexual overture it was. And how many marriage proposals have been proffered after a candlelit dinner? I suspect their number is legion; the Pillsbury jingle, "Nothin' says lovin' like somethin' from the oven," trades on a truth few would dispute.

If it's possible to talk about archetypal pornographic poses, one of the all-time classics is of a woman bending over a stove naked except for black mesh stockings, high heels, and a brief lacy apron.[9] The "sensuous woman," in the book of that name, is encouraged to try oral sex with the "whipped cream wriggle" in a section headed "Nibbling, Nipping, Eating, Licking and Sucking."[10] In Greece and Rome and in the European Middle Ages, mills and bakeries were often connected with brothels.[11] The bread of life and the one who brings forth life have been associated for so long that even today the pregnant woman is described as having "a bun in the oven," or as my obstetrician said to me when I went to her office to have my second pregnancy confirmed, "So you think you're cooking once again!"

Anthropologist Lévi-Strauss noted that in Cambodia, Malaysia, Siam, and various parts of Indonesia, the postpartum women used to be laid on a bed under which there burned a slow fire. Pueblo women gave birth over a heap of hot sand which was supposed to transform the child into a "cooked person," and various California tribes put women who had just given birth into an "oven" hollowed out in the ground. Those who were "cooked" were deeply involved in a physiological process: "The conjunction of a member of the social group with nature must be mediatized through the intervention of cooking fire, whose normal function is to mediatize the conjunction of the raw product and the human consumer, and whose operation thus has the effect of making sure that a natural creature is at one and the same time *cooked and socialized.* "[12] From this viewpoint, the twin female roles of cook and socializing agent have much in common, for both transform the raw into a finished product. That those roles have been ascribed to women probably has much to do with woman being seen as more a part of nature and thus an obvious intermediary between the natural and the civilized.

Recipes have always been treated as aphrodisiacs of sorts. Often, they have been secretly handed down from mother to daughter with the promise that this special cake or that hearty dish will reduce him to eating out of her hands.[13] The man thrusts his penis and offers his sperm, but the female is the cornucopia of plenty, the mana figure.[14] She conjures up toothsome dainties, the cup of Circe, a heady nectar, ambrosia to make you feel like a god. The woman offers a glass of wine and she herself becomes intoxicating. She garnishes and is the garnish; she serves the tart and is the tart. You taste her trifle and trifle with her. The smooth sauce and her sauciness are both savored. She brews an elixir but is herself the restorative. Tempting food transforms her into a temptress. Butterscotch confections and toffee-colored hair both whet the appetite. She with her blueberry eyes, strawberry lips, peaches-and-cream complexion, and breasts like ripe grapefruits is supposed to be good enough to eat; even the hymen is described as a cherry waiting to be plucked.

One of the basics of love poetry is to compare the woman to food, and the words of the bridegroom in the Song of Songs is one of the most ancient examples:

> . . . Feed me with raisin cakes,
> restore me with apples,
> for I am sick with love . . .
> Your cheeks, behind your veil,
> are halves of pomegranate . . .
> Your lips, my promised one,
> distil wild honey.
> Honey and milk
> are under your tongue . . .
> Your navel is a bowl well rounded
> with no lack of wine,
> your belly a heap of wheat . . .
> May your breasts be clusters of grapes,
> your breath sweet-scented as apples,
> your speaking, superlative wine . . .

Woman/sex, woman/food, food/sex—the connections are made again and again. No wonder the bride-turned-matron bakes raisin cakes. What woman can resist the comparisons, even though it means being *consumed* by the man?

Women have used food as a weapon, as tribute, or as gifts of propitiation. An enormous amount of libido has been poured into cooking because women have traditionally feared brutal sex and unwanted pregnancies. Cooking has always been a way of making a man feel good, mellowing him so he would not harm the woman. Sated from a rich meal, he might even fall asleep and forget about sex. Good cooking brought a woman praise and honor—in a wealthy Victorian house the cook was the highest-ranking female servant, and her word was law. Good sex, however, might make her seem a trollop. Too, a woman might fear that her man would find her lacking in bed; if she could cook, she would feel secure knowing that no one could make his stomach feel contented quite the way she could.

Artie Shaughnessy, the main character in John Guare's award-winning play *The House of Blue Leaves*, is having an affair with the woman who lives in the apartment below his, Bunny Flingus. Bunny knows she's not particularly good in bed, so she sleeps with Artie right away but refuses to cook for him until he leaves his wife and marries her. Meanwhile, they both slobber over the scrapbook he's put together featuring pictures of all the dishes she knows how to cook as she plaintively explains:

> . . . if I cooked for you now and said I won't sleep with you till we're married, you'd look forward to sleeping with me so much that by the time we did get to that motel near Hollywood, I'd be such a disappointment, you'd never forgive me. My cooking is the only thing I got to lure you on with and hold you with. Artie, we got to keep some magic for the honeymoon. It's my first honeymoon and I want it to be so good, I'm aiming for two million calories. I want to cook for you so bad I walk by the A&P, I get all hot jabs of chili powder inside my thighs.[15]

"Food equals love" is a familiar equation. The formulation has so much meaning all through life because food literally is the first expression of love we experience, the first gratification all human beings know. Developmental psychologists call the first stage of life the oral stage because babies are all mouth. They need nourishment every few hours if they are going to survive. This taking in and feeling full becomes associated in the mind with being held and fondled. The tension build-up of hunger and the satiation of feeding have much in common with the tension-release pattern of sexual orgasm.

Breastfeeding is touted in much of the child-care literature as an expression of love; the mother is advised to pour out her love at the same time she gives her child milk so the infant will learn to trust the outside world. This sense of experiencing the world as you ingest your food leaves an indelible impression on many a psyche. As children grow, their oral needs are supposed to recede so they can master other developmental tasks, but the primary gratification no doubt colors all subsequent conceptualizations of pleasure.

As if testifying to the crucial importance of eating for the young child, Simone de Beauvoir recalls that "the principal function of Louisa [the maid] and Mama was to feed me."[16] Such an egocentric view of those who love and care for you is typical of small children, but it is obvious how devastating such self-centeredness can be later in a marriage if a husband has failed to progress beyond the childish expectation of woman as mother and nurturer. If he is still basically immature, he may think the principal function of his wife is to feed him, or conversely label his wife's lack of interest in cooking his food as evidence that she does not love him.

For women, too, the equation of love and food presents problems. It's easy to move from the infantile view of food as love to the belief that any cry for comfort can be satisfied by food. The woman who confuses loving and feeding may build her own self-esteem by having a roly-poly child. Or she may become like the mother in Joyce Carol Oates' novel *Them*, who dismissed her daughter's total withdrawal with the comment "She eats everything I make for her, so she's all right."[17] The woman who prescribes chicken soup for every ailment is part of our folklore. It's so easy to dispel tears with a chocolate bar; it may seem better than trying to comfort in other ways, ways which leave you open to being rebuffed, "Yuck—who wants your wet kisses? They don't

make the hurt go away." As Dr. Hilde Bruch reminds us, "To
many mothers, the offering of food represents the only way of
expressing their affection and devotion, and of appeasing their
anxiety and guilt about the child."[18] But food as an expression of
affection or a way of appeasing guilt is fraught with dangers. No
amount of alchemy can change food into love. Yet I keep trying
to put kisses into my cookies . . .

*I love to read French cookbooks. All those recipes with twelve
major steps, each with fifteen sub-steps, make me feel like a scien-
tist cracking the secrets of nature. I'm a pilot sitting in front of my
oven controls, on my way to . . . nowhere. I've seen one good cook
offer another one a portion of fluffy flan, radish roses, slivers of
spiced beef, and a dollop of blancmange as if executing a maneuver
in some grand duel to the death. . . . I'm like all those dentists and
doctors who warn against too many sweets but dole out lollipops
to their small patients. I know food shouldn't be a bribe, yet I find
myself sometimes bellowing, "If you don't clean your room you're
not going to get any dessert tonight, and it's your favorite, strawberry shortcake." Food is sacramental; it is communion. Is that why
I treat every supper as if it were the Last Supper? . . . When I was
a little girl I used to dab vanilla extract behind my ears because
I wanted to smell wholesomely delicious. Now I don't want to
smell like a piece of food, because I don't want to be eaten up.
. . . When my family devours with appreciation food I spent hours
preparing, I smile a happy smile; but haven't they just eaten up my
time?*

*Why aren't there any nifty ethnic recipes that feature raw carrots
and celery sticks? "Soul food" is always fattening. Why? Because
you need something heavy to squelch anxiety or poverty? . . . A
scrumptious four-course meal is the only artistry I know. No one
regards a clean kitchen floor as a masterpiece, but a flaky pastry
elicits appreciative oooh's and aaah's. And I like applause. . . .
Sometimes I'm so busy baking Gold Medal memories, I lose touch
with the present. . . . All women are expected to know how to cook,*

yet they're rarely considered to have what it takes to be a great chef. Another example of women not being accorded full respect even in areas that are supposed to be their specialty.

Why do all the happy moments have to revolve around food? Anniversaries, birthday parties, Christmas, Easter, Thanksgiving —all the holidays rush by and I see them pass as I look over the mounds of dirty dishes. . . . Some women talk so earnestly about the importance of children "coming home for lunch," as if their peanut-butter-and-jelly sandwiches contained a magic that the school lunch program can't bottle. . . . Famous people now publish their memoirs and their cookbooks side by side. There must be some profound meaning in that. . . . Why do I feel I have to keep the home fires burning even though my stove is electric and I should conserve as many watts as I can? . . . I avoid admitting that I don't make everything from scratch. It kills me to confess that the delicious pumpkin bread was baked by the local bakery. Why do I act as if my identity depended on a piece of bread? No one really cares. In fact, most people appreciate knowing the name of a good bakery. Should I tell them and end this senseless competition? No, I'm not going to tell them.

If the energy crisis persists, will waiting long hours in gas-station lines be defined as woman's work because it's her function to nourish and cars need someone to feed them? . . . Commercials keep advertising food that no one over twenty-one can eat every day without gaining weight. Are we afraid to admit we shouldn't eat them because we don't want to acknowledge we're not as young as we used to be? The convenience foods clog the arteries, but all those crunchy crisp vegetables take so much time to wash and prepare. Guilt—I taste it with each mouthful. . . . I deeply resent it when the woman does all the cooking and then sets the dishes before the man so he can distribute the goodies like an old-fashioned patriarch, yet I like other formalities—saying grace, candles, flowers. . . . For years, I cleaned my plate for the "starving Armenians." I felt duped when I realized that they had starved long before

I was born. "Eat, eat, eat, eat, eat"—does the command mean life or death?

My mother always wanted me to watch her cook so I would learn the basics, but I told her that I would learn all I needed, when the time came, in the same way I had learned everything else—from books. She was scandalized when I compared cooking to chemistry and said both were a simple matter of effecting the transmutation of substances. She didn't think a recipe and a formula amounted to the same thing. To her cooking was a gift, creation, magic— nothing like adding two parts of hydrogen to one part of oxygen and getting water. . . . I learned to cook from books and surreptitious glances at what my mother was doing. I used to take great delight when she would come for a visit and tell me that I was a better cook than she ever was: "And you didn't learn it at your mother's knee, that's for sure." It was the triumph of book learning over magic! Yet the recipes I most enjoy making are those she gave me. . . . As my mother's health deteriorated, she wanted me to take over the cooking when we visited her. I found it a very difficult thing to do. Her kitchen was her ship, and a first mate doesn't easily replace the captain. Though my father took over the day-to-day cleaning of the house, my mother continued to be the cook until the day she died. (My father came home from work and found her slumped over on the sofa waiting for him; the table was set for supper—strawberries, rolls, and burnt steaks in the broiler.) It was only simple fare, but serving dinner every evening meant she could still make him feel good at the end of a long day.

Now I want to teach my daughters all I know. But when I chastise them for spilling the sugar I realize that what I'm also yelling at is the competition. Will I ever be as gracious as my mother was when my children have learned all my secrets and have some of their own? . . . I enjoy having company. It's a chance to cook on a grand scale, in a way you can't for a family of only two adults and two children. Sometimes I feel like a double agent when I've gotten some man who I think is a male chauvinist pig to admit *after his stomach is full of my delicacies that women have good reason for complaining about their second-class status.*

My husband and I don't share cooking as equally as we do the other housework. He fixes most breakfasts, but I still do most of the other cooking, and I'm good at it. I complain that I get stuck with the big meals, yet perversely I sabotage his efforts when he does take over by grunting my annoyance when he's slow (beginners are always slow). It's not just his ineptness that bothers me; I'm finally admitting to myself just how much I resent his "taking over" something I excel at. My pride isn't so hurt when he does what I don't know how to do, such as Chinese wok cooking. I'm learning to laugh at myself and to turn over the kitchen to him when he wants to make something. I no longer feel hurt when the children say, "Daddy, you're a good cook!" He is.

Cooking is the most prized of the traditional homemaking skills, but being defined as *the* nurturer is not a role the feminist can embrace without reservations. Being a galley slave means you will often be shut out from stimulating conversations. Or as Peg Bracken put it in her humorous bestseller *The I Hate to Cook Book,* "When the sun is over the yardarm and the party starts to bounce you want to be in there bouncing, too, not stuck by yourself in the kitchen, deep-fat frying small objects or wrapping oysters in bacon strips."[19] The rhythm of the centuries may be captured in the classic image of a serene woman ladling out an aromatic stew, but who wants to be a vestal priestess if that role makes your husband a two-bit god? The planning, marketing, preparing, cooking, serving, and dishwashing that accompany every meal are tremendously time-consuming, and yet there's nothing to show for your efforts when it's all finished except bulging stomachs and leftovers. There's also the very real danger that all that preoccupation with food in the name of developing your "femininity" will lead to a good many more pounds of femininity than your frame can easily carry. Bunny Flingus may aim for the magic of two million calories; that's not magical, it's suicidal.

The stereotype of the woman cheerfully devoted to perfuming the air with baking smells may make her seem fragrantly earthy, but that representation, because it emphasizes the sensual, also indirectly reinforces the notion that she is naturally disinterested in intellectual pursuits. Samuel Johnson said, "A man is in general better pleased when he has a good dinner, than when his wife talks Greek,"[20] but the more a woman devotes herself to good dinners, the more you assume she doesn't have it in her to master Greek. Image makers repeat the cliché every time they portray the woman as preparing a meal, while her husband reads the newspaper.

Cooking can even literally be the death of a woman, as this 1973 *Newsweek* story proves:

> Noël Carriou likes his roast beef just so—not too well done and not too rare. Back in 1956, the Paris night watchman became enraged when his wife cooked the roast too rare—and he kicked her out of bed in the middle of the night. She broke her neck and died, and Carriou was given twelve years at hard labor. A model prisoner, he was released after seven years and promptly took a new wife—Clémence. She, unfortunately, did not measure up to Carriou's culinary standards either, and one day when she pulled a thoroughly overdone roast from the oven, his exasperation knew no bounds. "You cook like a Nazi," he exploded. With that, the irate Frenchman picked up a kitchen knife and stabbed his second wife to death. In Paris, a jury showed some sympathy for Carriou's *crime passionnel* and recommended leniency. But the court gave the 54-year-old Carriou eight more years behind bars, and this week he begins his second term in prison.[21]

While few men murder their wives over a burned roast, the fact that these two murders could still be written off as *crime passionnel* in this day and age is reprehensible. If he had seen his wives as human beings instead of cooks, presumably he would never have murdered them. Lest anyone think such rage is possible only with the French, who have a reputation for feeling passionate about food, a similar incident happened a few miles from my home last Mother's Day. A man admitted to knocking his sixty-one-year-old wife unconscious when she declined to fix him breakfast at 1 A.M. He put her to bed and went to sleep in another room. Her grandson found her body when he looked in at 8 A.M.[22] (On Mother's Day no less!)

No amount of culinary wizardry can make food a worthy substitute for listening to what another person has to say or openly sharing your feelings and dreams. Good times are a combination of many things. Women have to stay out of the kitchen long enough to participate in the conversations, games, storytelling, jokes, music, singing, and dancing that go along with feasting. Men have to be allowed entry into the warmth of the kitchen and, more important, be permitted to develop the nourishing principle in themselves.

Food is necessary and food is good, even delightful. It dominates holiday merrymaking because it is a time-honored way of sharing happiness and prosperity or celebrating a noteworthy event. Mealtimes also provide a forum for the exchange of thoughts and interests. And it's because food serves this function that it's necessary for women and men and children to share the responsibility for its preparation. Sharing is desirable, not because it's cute or even because it's the ideologically correct thing for a married feminist to do, but because it's a way of enhancing the sense of communion that is at the heart of feasting together. When the preparation (chopping, kneading, stirring, etc.) becomes a shared prelude to the meal, all the participants enjoy the finished product with extra gusto. Not every meal can be a joint venture, but I've found that holidays and weekend dinners are much more festive and relaxing if all four of us work on a menu that can use more than one pair of hands. There may be a little extra mess if you include small children in the preparation, but hearing our younger daughter say "I'm a good cook, aren't I, Mommy?" is worth it all. You have to share the applause when the meal is ready, but it's worth it to share the work.

No one should be ignorant of the basics of cooking. The new widower, the hungry teenager, the young bachelor, all need these skills to be self-sufficient. If everyone knows how to cook, some of the mystique goes out of an elegant meal. The woman can't pose as a sorceress if the man knows how to bake a meringue. What you get in the place of awe is genuine appreciation for how ticklish the beating of egg whites can be. Sharing the cooking won't turn every couple into the Romagnolis, but it can lead to new appreciation of each other's tastes and talents. And there's something wonderfully new-old about a man having a woman eating out of his hands.

7

RELIGION

*Bishop Gran of Oslo speaking for the Scandinavian
Bishops' Conference on the question of priestly
celibacy favoured the acceptance of some married
priests. He referred to the marriages of Lutheran
clergy, whose wives play an important part in parish
affairs. He added, "They are good housekeepers,
something not to be overlooked at a time when
servants have become practically extinct and the
number of nuns is diminishing."*

Reported in The Catholic Citizen
(November-December,
1971)

The devout are fond of saying that religion cannot be confined
to just one day a week of formal worship because the purpose of
religion is to influence all our values all the time. Likewise, it may
be foolish for me to try to analyze the conflicts religion elicits in
a married feminist in just one chapter when religion has an effect
so all-pervasive as to touch one's every thought and action. This
chapter, however, isn't the only one to scrutinize religious pronouncements as they affect women; previous chapters have referred to religious practices, if only in a cursory way, in order to
discuss what has been considered "traditional." Religion is in fact
the repository of traditional thinking because it embodies a particular system in which the quest for the ideal life has been codified.
Unfortunately, in this search for the good, the true, the beautiful,
and the everlasting, woman hasn't fared very well.

In the Judaeo-Christian tradition, God is male. (The historical

Christ obviously was male, and the voice Moses heard coming from the burning bush is also believed to have been a baritone.) Eve, that is, woman, has been held responsible for the expulsion from the Garden of Eden. It is assumed that woman's subordination to man was divinely ordained, and her very existence is described as "derivative" by those who take the "Adam's rib" fable seriously. As a result, women have been denied priesthood and positions of authority in church and synagogue affairs, although at long last some protest and a little response is taking place today.

Woman's nature is usually portrayed as either evil (Eve) or pure (Mary), but rarely as human. Orthodox Jewish women are not allowed to say the prayers of mourning, the Kaddish, or to be counted in a *minyan,* the quorum of ten necessary for public prayer, or to say anything during the marriage ceremony—only the groom enacts the one-sided ritual. As Rabbi Judah said to one unhappy wife, "Why are you different from a fish? You have no more right to complain against your husband's treatment than the fish has the right to object to the manner in which it has been cooked."[1] In the Talmud, women are frequently presumed to be troublesome: "A daughter is a vain treasure to her father. From anxiety about her he does not sleep at night; during her early years lest she be seduced, in her adolescence lest she go astray, in her marriageable years lest she does not find a husband, when she is married lest she be childless, and when she is old lest she practice witchcraft."[2]

Reading what some of the Christian patriarchs have said of women is likely to make most feminists call these pillars of religion an unholy name or two. St. Paul wrote, "I am not giving permission for a woman to teach or to tell a man what to do . . . it was not Adam who was led astray but the woman who was led astray and fell into sin" (I Timothy 2:12–15); in another place he says, "A man should certainly not cover his head, since he is the image of God and reflects God's glory; but woman is the reflection of man's glory. For man did not come from woman; no, woman from man; and man was not created for the sake of woman, but woman was created for the sake of man" (I Corinthians 11: 7–10). St. John Chrysostom wasn't showing his more charitable side when he said, "Among all savage beasts none is found so harmful as woman."[3] St. Thomas Aquinas believed that, apart from procreation, a man is always better helped by another man than by a woman.[4] But according to him, woman doesn't even have an equal role in her own specialty, reproduction: "Father and mother are loved as principles of our natural origin. Now the father is principle in a more excellent way than the mother because he is the active principle, while the mother is a passive and material principle. Consequently, strictly speaking, the father is to be loved more."[5] And Tertullian vented his spleen this way: "Woman, you are the devil's doorway. You have led astray one whom the devil would not dare attack directly. It is your fault that the Son of God had to die; you should always go in mourning and in rags."[6] As Arlene Swidler noted sadly in her book *Woman in a Man's Church:* "There's a saying that the only things women can do better than men are bearing children and singing soprano, but Catholics have been pointing out that the Church disputes even this; some of our people still feel that any self-respecting cathedral choir should use little boys rather than female sopranos."[7]

From the Jewish prayer of the man—"Blessed are you, Lord our God, King of eternity, who has not created me a woman"[8] —to Luther's pronouncement—"No dress or garment is less becoming to a woman than a show of intelligence"[9]—women have been portrayed by authors of religious doctrine as inferior to men. This degradation stems from woman being held responsible for the fall from Paradise and the religious emphasis on sexual virtue which has converted woman into mere sexual object. The one other reason usually given for woman's second-class status is, of course, the "Adam's rib" fable, but that account of creation is easily criticized in light of the fact that Genesis (1:27) contains another version of the same story which emphasizes the simultaneous birth of both sexes. (The "Adam's rib" fable seems, if anything, to be a prime example of "womb envy," a basic male yearning first postulated by Karen Horney. It stems from the tremendous patriarchal need to have the whole human race be derived from one *man*. Such a poetic denial of biological realities has much in common with the practice of *couvade* among some present-day primitive peoples, in which the father takes to his bed just before the birth of his child to enact the birth experience.)

What is more important to an analysis of woman and religion isn't which story of creation is accurate, but the fact that theologians have systematically ignored the one which promotes full parity between the sexes. In the same way, there's actually nothing in the "Adam's rib" fable to account for the servitude that has been exacted of woman because she was created after man; "helpmate" doesn't by any stretch of the imagination imply servant or even what's been called "God's chain of command"— God to husband to wife to child.[10] In fact, Genesis very explicitly says man should "join himself to his wife"; this suggests partnership to me.

No scholars believe that Genesis was written during the time the events recorded actually occurred, so it could be that the emphasis on man as the *firstborn* was inserted because the authors of Genesis lived in a period when the firstborn had all the rights. The privileged status of the firstborn preceded the written justification of man as firstborn rather than the reverse. (Similarly, the emphasis given childbirth as a painful ordeal because of Eve's disobedience was probably also after the fact: man observed woman's suffering and decided it must be a punishment for some past misdeed.)

Much of the exegesis on the Fall from Paradise is an attempt to shift blame, and I take this position to be important as an expression of man's need for a scapegoat. One can look at the Fall two ways, as fact or as metaphor, but either view supports the scapegoat theory. If the first woman and man attacked God's sovereignty by flouting His express command, then both deserved punishment. Saying "she coaxed me into doing it" does not erase man's culpability; it simply shows his eagerness to blame someone else for his transgressions. Tertullian fumes, "Woman, you are the devil's doorway. You have led astray one whom the devil would not dare attack directly," but his bitterness cannot alter the fact of Adam's responsibility for his own actions; his words simply underscore a male pride that even a good swift kick out of Eden didn't diminish. (Eva Figes reminds us in her book *Patriarchal Attitudes* that earlier creation myths feature gardens of delight ruled over by women. The Greek goddess Hera inhabited the Garden of the Hesperides guarded by the serpent Ladon; Gilgamesh went to a Sumerian paradise ruled over by Siduri, goddess of wisdom. Both were eventually ousted by male gods. We see in these stories the strong male wish to usurp the power of a commanding female figure.)[11]

St. Augustine is similarly equivocating in his *City of God:*

> . . . he [the serpent], at first, parleyed cunningly with the woman as with the weaker part of that human society, hoping gradually to gain the whole. He assumed that a man is less gullible and can be more easily tricked into following a bad example than into making a mistake himself . . . we must believe that Adam transgressed the law of God, not because he was deceived into believing that the lie was true, but because in obedience to a social compulsion he yielded to Eve, as husband to wife, as the only man in the world to the only woman . . . though not equally deceived by believing the serpent, they equally sinned and were caught and ensnared by the Devil.[12]

Notice how he minimizes man's responsibility for the Fall with a clever choice of words. The serpent was able to entice the "weaker part" of human society; the man was "less gullible." He distinguishes between Adam's being "tricked into following a bad example" and what would have been more serious, "making a mistake himself." Note the clever phrase "obedience to a social compulsion"; the mere mention of man's obedience to a principle makes his disobedience seem far less severe. "He yielded to Eve" sounds so much better than he sinned with Eve. St. Augustine is clearly trying the case of woman's guilt versus man's guilt in the court of world opinion and finding it useful to distinguish between who was deceived and who sinned. But why is it necessary for man to pin the blame for the Fall on Eve?

Basic to religion is the yearning of mortals for immortality. Before the expulsion from Eden, there was no death. We lost immortality through our sinfulness. But the story of the Fall also promises a Saviour who will regain Paradise. It's believed that primitive man came to associate the menstruating/childbearing woman with the cycle of life and death. Without birth, there is no death. So the givers of life, women, were also responsible for the inevitability of death. In the same way, woman could be held responsible for the torments of living, for bringing children into a vale of tears. It doesn't take any mental gymnastics to go from "Why did you give me life? I didn't ask to be born" to protesting, "Why didn't you fix it so I wouldn't have to die?" The belief that Paradise once existed, was lost, but can be regained is a human desire which many find consoling because it gives meaning and direction to existence.

In his book *Bare Ruined Choirs*, Garry Wills suggests another way of analyzing the Fall which has considerable explanatory value:

> Adam fell out of his self-sufficient isolation into human need—into complex possibilities created by the existence of another person. He fell to his "own flesh," the rib that yearned outward and turned back wearing a different face; and he fell because it is not good for man to be alone. The fall was an escape from Aristotelian self-sufficiency into history and mutual need.[13]

Certainly, even to this day man blames woman for impinging on his self-sufficiency and resists acknowledging their mutual need. Many a man believes the Fall was his own *falling* for a woman.

While the woman sensitive to the nuances of collective guilt may want to exculpate her sex from responsibility for the expulsion from Paradise, most women and men are content to treat that story as a mist-shrouded part of ancient history which needn't affect their day-to-day lives. However, the religious emphasis on sexual virtue has played a much more obvious role in woman's degradation over the centuries. Philosopher Bertrand Russell made the point very well:

> The Christian ethics inevitably, through the emphasis laid upon sexual virtue, did a great deal to degrade the position of woman. Since the moralists were men, woman appeared as the temptress; if they had been women, man would have had this rôle. Since woman was the temptress, it was desirable to curtail her opportunities for leading men into temptation; consequently respectable women were more and more hedged about with restrictions, while the women who were not respectable, being regarded as sinful, were treated with the utmost contumely.[14]

Though the early Christians were supposed to be distinguished by their great love and charity, morality became identified with sexual purity almost from the beginning. St. Athanasius even claimed that the appreciation of virginity and chastity was the supreme revelation brought into the world by Jesus.[15] Sexual continence became the indispensable condition of righteousness. Woman = sex, sex = sin, therefore, woman = sin: these were the connections made by the early patriarchs. Christ went out of his way to treat women as persons, so much so that he astonished onlookers. But his Sermon on the Mount urged new, higher standards of sexual morality. "You have learnt how it was said: *You must not commit adultery.* But I say this to you: if a man looks at a woman lustfully, he has already committed adultery with her in his heart" (Matthew 5: 27–28). Many church fathers found the new teaching difficult, and began to hold women responsible for their troubles.

As celibacy became the ideal, conjugal love became but a reluctant concession to human frailty. (To love your wife too ardently constituted adultery to St. Thomas Aquinas.)[16] The sexual act was regarded as an ugly necessity to be justified only in the name of procreation; marriage was a state inferior to celibacy but tolerated because it helped man avoid temptation. Identified as an occasion of sin, therefore, woman could only be denigrated and feared. Perhaps the most misogynistic vision of all belongs to the apostle John, who described the redeemed as "ones who have kept their virginity and not been defiled with women" (Revelation 14:4). It sounds as if women cannot themselves be redeemed. Whether marriage led to redemption or ruin was a much-discussed issue in the first few hundred years of Christianity. And many besides St. Jerome resolved the question by assuming this attitude: "I praise marriage and wedlock, but I do so because they produce virgins for me. I gather roses from thorns, gold from the earth, the pearl from the shell."[17]

The history of Christian views on marriage is long and complex. Even St. Augustine, who thought concupiscence was *the* original sin, could not totally reject marriage, because it had been sanctified by Jesus. Though male superiority continued to be assumed, marriage itself acquired some respectability over time as its status as a sacrament gained widespread acceptance. Romantic love flowered during the Middle Ages, but poetic sentiment toward a woman was impossible unless she was regarded as sexually unattainable, so few marriages were touched by this new respect for women. By 1532, however, Martin Luther was able to dissociate himself from patristic tradition, take a wife, and say, "You can't be without a wife and remain without sin."[18]

Protestant rejection of the cloister brought with it increased regard for the dignity of marriage. Marriage was considered as good as celibacy and virginity, if not better. Women gained from these changes, though the good wife was still one who kept her place. In Catholic circles, the androcentric assumptions of the early church fathers and medieval theologians were preserved.

(Though some Eastern rites have a long history of allowing married priests, the Latin rite—the dominant form of Catholicism in Western Europe and in North and South America—has demanded celibacy of its clergy since the end of the thirteenth century.) Raw fear and dislike of women, however, were replaced with unctuous condescension.

My emphasis in the remainder of this chapter will be on the Catholic Church, since that's the religion I was raised in and know best. Unlike Christianity, Judaism has always seen marriage as a necessary, positive force, and the woman's sexual nature was even recognized in the sixteenth-century code of Jewish law, the *Shulhan Arukh,* to the extent that it stipulated, depending on the man's occupation, the number of times per week a husband had to have intercourse with his wife. "While a laborer was expected to perform twice a week, and a man of leisure every night, the pampered scholar had to meet his sexual obligations only once a week. . . . In fact, woman's sexual nature was recognized to such an extent that it prevented the Madonna syndrome from developing in Judaism."[19]

In his *Introduction to the Devout Life,* St. Francis de Sales (1567–1622), who was a liberal for his age, suggested that married people take a lesson from the elephant's good and modest habits:

> Although a huge beast, the elephant is yet the most decent and most sensible of all that live upon earth. I will give you an instance of his chastity. Although he never changes his mate and has a tender love for her whom he has chosen, he couples with her only at the end of every three years, and then only for the space of five days and so privately that he is never seen in the act. When he makes his appearance again on the sixth day, the first thing he does is to go directly to a river. There he washes his body entirely, for he is unwilling to return to the herd till he is quite purified.[20]

The sense of intercourse as a necessary defilement continues; contact with a female remains shameful even though fidelity is championed. In another passage, St. Francis de Sales finds St. Louis an example of the stalwart husband: "The great St. Louis, equally rigorous to his own flesh and tender in the love of his wife, was almost blamed for the abundance of such caresses. Actually, he rather deserved praise for being able to bring his martial and courageous spirit to stoop to these little duties so requisite for the preservation of conjugal love."[21] One is not sure if St. Louis was seen as "stooping" because he displayed the "female" virtue of tenderness or because he was consorting with an inferior, but both views emphasize how lowly the position of woman still was.

While no one now debates whether a woman has an immortal soul the way they once did, she is acknowledged as man's spiritual equal only to be told she should subordinate herself in the temporal world: "The wife, in her role as helpmate and companion, owes to her husband complete loyalty and obedience."[22] Since Christian theory is supposed to be egalitarian, many writers feel compelled to stress equality—as if mere mention of the word made it so—then, that out of the way, go on to talk about how necessary differences between the sexes are. One counselor, while protesting that husband and wife are of equal value, urges the man to "give way to your wife about all small matters; but take care to get your own way in the important things!"[23] Woman is described as "the less rational of the partners," and she is encouraged to perform her domestic duties with joy: "It should never be the case that a wife feels, sadly, that the button she is now sewing on for her husband is so different from an exactly similar button she sewed when the two were engaged."[24] The diatribe of centuries past has been replaced by double-talk which stresses that "true emancipation" will not involve "false liberty and unnatural equality with the husband."[25]

In recent times the Church's emphasis has shifted from whether intercourse is a defilement to how to do it the proper way —that is, without using contraceptives. That turn, however, is a classic example of the famous line "The more things change, the more they remain the same." Contraception is frowned on because too much intercourse is still thought to dull one's moral sensibilities, and the observance of periodic continence is recommended to drive out selfishness.[26] But if physical union between a woman and a man is the outward manifestation of their sacramental bond, how can there be too much unless you disapprove of such mutual pleasuring in the first place? Pius XI, in his encyclical *On Christian Marriage,* spoke about the evils of contraception in language surprisingly similar to the old rhetoric:

> ... The Catholic Church, to whom God has entrusted the defense of the integrity and purity of morals, standing erect in the midst of the moral ruin which surrounds her, in order that she may preserve the chastity of the nuptial union from being defiled by this foul stain, raises her voice in token of Divine ambassadorship and through Our mouth proclaims anew: any use whatsoever of matrimony exercised in such a way that the act is deliberately frustrated in its natural power to generate life is an offense against the law of God and of nature, and those who indulge in such are branded with the guilt of a grave sin.[27]

Moral ruin, defilement, foul stain—the ancient specters still hover around intercourse. Intercourse still is justified primarily in the name of procreation. As the sex most eager for safe and effective birth control, woman is once again identified with sin.

"Sex is dirty" gave way to "God purposely made vagina and penis to be joined, so sex isn't dirty," which in turn led to "If you marry, you *must* use your vagina and penis to have children." This biological approach to morality had the effect of making the most moral aspect of intercourse between the sexes its most animal side. It's as if male moralists couldn't imagine any other relationship between a woman and a man except what they so quaintly call the right to "perfect copula."

As mother, woman had finally achieved some status. Pius XII proclaimed: "A cradle consecrates the mother of the family; and more cradles sanctify and glorify her before her husband and children, before Church and homeland."[28] But at what a cost! What comes through loud and clear in all the talk about what's "natural" is man's need to justify the very existence of woman in terms of her breeding abilities, as if she were not also a full human being. The woman isn't allowed to dominate nature the way man does; her existence is grounded in making a fetish of nature. Her fertility is honored more than her mind or spirit. Motherhood is the straitjacket Pius XII would have every woman wear: "The creator has disposed to this end the entire being of woman, her organism, and even more her spirit, and above all her exquisite sensibility. So that a true woman cannot see, and fully understand all the problems of human life otherwise than under the family aspect."[29] Woman is chained to family needs. She is a role, not a person. No wonder Teresa of Avila lamented, "The very thought that I am a woman is enough to make my wings droop."[30]

These obsessive views constricting women have led to tremendous unhappiness. The woman who has been advised by a doctor that she may die if she becomes pregnant again is offered this advice by the priest: "Experience shows both that such predictions are frequently false and that these dangers are often overstressed by many doctors."[31] The woman who fears pregnancy because of the real possibility of bearing a defective child is told should that happen "no real injustice is inflicted upon the new life and the infant will at least enjoy an eternal state of natural beatitude."[32] And what of the woman's peace of mind? If her husband uses a condom, the woman is reminded of her obligation to resist his advances:

> If resistance is futile, the most she can do is remain absolutely passive. The venereal pleasure that she may experience is illicit and she may not consent to it. From a moral viewpoint she is in exactly the same circumstances as a woman who is being raped, and she must conduct herself accordingly. If she can avert this act by physical resistance, she is obliged to do so.[33]

It is horrifying to imagine what this kind of thinking has done to couples in the name of morality. The bedroom becomes a battleground with the blessing of the Catholic Church. What kind of perverse morality would equate marital lovemaking with rape? No questions are asked as to the valid reasons the man might have to avoid impregnating his wife. The wife is challenged to battle him if there's the possibility the penis may be prevented from meeting the vagina.

Obviously, the results of such tortured thinking about sex can be troubling. If intimacy always means anxiety, then husband and wife are likely to see each other as tormentor. If a woman frequently refuses her husband, it's reasonable for him to start wondering whether she finds him repulsive and to get angry. Or he might conclude that women are naturally squeamish and dispirited, even if the real reason is fear of pregnancy. Avoidance emerges as the basic female-male posture; sex becomes an exercise in masochism. It's difficult to imagine blessed motherhood flourishing under these conditions.

Many think contraception is a dead issue even for Catholics: Why waste your time on a natural-law theory that is commonly ignored even by many religious people? But natural-law language doesn't flourish only in narrow religious circles. For centuries men have alluded to the designs of nature to back up their own moral and social preferences. Women have been regularly admonished to act in certain ways, to avoid being unladylike, "unnatural." Sometimes "natural" means "You'd better do this or you won't be *normal.*" Most of the time, such allusions have the desired effect of putting the woman on the defensive, committing her to roles she might not otherwise choose: "Being a mother is the most natural thing in the world." "Cooking only organic foods is so natural." "It's natural for a woman to find sex unpleasant."

The negative view of woman encouraged by the "let nature take its course" morality is still thriving, even if the practice of contraception is gaining momentum. (Shaving, vaccination, circumcision, intravenous feeding, insect repellent, air conditioning, and thousands of other commonplace practices are also "against nature." Human beings are urged to tame nature in every facet of life but sex—proof positive, I think, that men continue to want women chained to their anatomy so they won't be able to challenge male supremacy.) Many Catholics who use contraception still feel guilty about it since the Church hasn't liberalized its official position, and that guilt distorts their view of women. When Pope Paul VI permitted women to attend for the first time some sessions of the Ecumenical Council (in 1964), single women, nuns, and widows were invited, but not one married woman with a living husband.[34] Presumably a married woman is to be avoided because she exudes the corrupting odor of sexuality!

The anti-female bias which developed in Christian thought can be partially explained. For example, St. Paul's status-quo ethics can be understood as a temporary concession to the mores of the time prompted by his belief that the end was imminent—the Kingdom of God would soon be at hand and bring a new equivalence between the sexes in Christ.[35] As it competed with other redemptive cults for supremacy, Christianity was influenced by rival teachings, especially by Gnosticism and Manicheanism, which saw the world in terms of dualities: God, good, and man on one side; Satan, evil, and woman on the other. Early Christianity preached spiritual equality between the sexes and a gospel of love which was in strong contrast to the "life is cheap" values of Roman times. As a result, I suspect some of the first Christians were accused of being effeminate. Accused of weakness, of turning the other cheek, and given the lowly status of all but the most privileged Roman matrons, early Christian men might have been driven to prove they were still men, albeit believers in a Christ who allowed himself to be spat upon and crucified without defending himself. Because of Christianity's radical departures from Jewish tradition—Christianity offered baptism to both sexes (Judaism offered welcome only to males, through the circumcision ceremony), confirmation to both sexes (only Jewish males could be bar mitzvahed), and marriage as a *mutual* sacrament—Christian men may have gone out of their way to prove it wasn't a religion for women only.

It's not difficult to see how the misogynistic inclinations of the early Church fathers were perpetuated by a structure glorifying the value of tradition, but that still doesn't explain woman's total second-class status. Two thousand years later many Christian women feel religion not only doesn't meet their needs, but actively inhibits their development and propagandizes against them . . .

I grew up in a very religious family and my great-uncle was pastor of our local parish for over fifty years. I really loved the man, but watching my grandmother kiss his hands every time he visited (they were consecrated and held the sacred Host) irritated me. The gesture reeked of feudalism. It also bothered me when my father told how this uncle avoided kissing female relatives or riding in a car with them (including his mother) until he was well past sixty, so as not to create any scandal. Talking to a priest, I was always painfully conscious of my femaleness and my potential as an occasion of sin. . . . I've never actually checked, but I'm sure the roster of saints canonized is weighted in the direction of men. Women cannot, for one thing, legally introduce a name for canonization or beatification. [36] Probably few married women ever made it onto that celestial honor roll because to the Church they are sexual objects. The only hope a girl had was to be lusted after by a knife-carrying gardener, like Maria Gorreti, who was very much in vogue during my teenage years, and then choose death rather than submit to rape. It scares me when I think of it now, but I once yearned for such martyrdom. No matter what the conscious message was, the Church managed to convince my unconscious that sex, death, martyr, knife, rape, man, and God all belonged together. . . . Humility was drummed into my head from an early age. I remember losing the election for class president in my freshman year of high school by one vote. I didn't vote for myself because I thought that would have been a "sin of pride," but I never stopped wondering which way my opponent had voted. Since that defeat, I've never again been all that humble.

You were either called to be a nun or called to the married state, but so many religious gave the impression that single blessedness was what a girl got by default. . . . The very first feminist statement I remember making was to tell a very good priest-friend, who was hoping I had a vocation to the religious life, that I would welcome being a priest because you could go places (he had just returned from Europe) and do things, whereas being a nun meant restrictions, not possibilities. . . . Priests are called "Father," but nuns usually are called "Sister." How's that for proof of inequality? I always thought the Madames of the Sacred Heart, an order of nuns who cater to the education of rich Catholic girls, were very smart; every "Madame" is addressed as "Mother.". . . Nuns are "brides of Christ." The nun's divine espousal isn't just a metaphorical description of consecration to the religious life; the theme is acted out in some orders, including wearing a bridal gown and veil when you profess your first vows and getting a wedding band when you take your final vows. I know girls who shopped around to see which orders allowed both. Brochures describing a particular order capitalized on such images, and the frontispiece often featured clasped hands—with the left ring finger encircled by a silver band—holding a candle. How many women have become nuns for the sake of that wedding ring?

The concept of the Blessed Trinity has always aroused profane thoughts in my head. I find the all-maleness of these three Persons oppressive. The Holy Spirit is described as "the Third Person Who is the utterance of the love of Father and Son," [37] but in my blessed trinity I prefer the notion of a child who is the utterance of the love of wife and husband. At least my version has space for a female. . . . I wonder if heaven will turn out to be a Mount Athos in the sky with a sign posted "No females allowed"? . . . In spite of the injustices, the indignities visited on women by organized religion, I think it's harder for a woman to disown religion than it is for a man, because the social life of the traditional woman so often revolves around church affairs. The married woman without a job needs some group affiliation, and scriptural reading groups and fund-raising projects provide that. My mother belonged to the Sodality for years because she enjoyed the fashion shows and bus trips the group sponsored. Yet the influence allowed a woman in church affairs is narrow and limited. Even when women are invited to act as lectors or to serve on the parish council, they still remain the only ones expected to join the Altar Society, whose purpose is to keep the altar clean and vestments in good repair. . . . Ethnic affiliation is almost nonexistent when your children are part Irish, German, French, and Polish as ours are, but a common religion gives a couple a common identity which may be clung to even though the old-time religion seems old-fashioned. Christianity, like Judaism, is as much a cultural heritage as a religious one. . . . The laity are spoken of as the Church Militant, language that suggests a male-oriented Church. I don't want to be a soldier for Christ or anyone else. The liturgy is full of allusions to being a "son of God," and I resent being excluded.

The 1967 edition of the New Catholic Encyclopedia *features thirty-five articles on marriage or related subjects and not one is authored by a female; most are written by priests. Sermonizing and legislating are seen as man's work in the Church, yet the real job of making a marriage work is traditionally handed over to women.* [38] *. . . All the Church's emphasis on man's uncontrollable sexual urges has made some men feel inadequate if they have their passions under control. But every time a single woman gets pregnant, it's she who gets blamed for not keeping the relationship on the "proper" level before marriage.*

The Father-Son pair central to Christianity has usurped all the "good" biological functions of femininity: in Christianity woman is born of man, a male god comforts the sick and dying, and in his name the hungry are fed the bread of life. . . . The Holy Family is supposed to represent the ultimate in family relationships, yet it's hard to find the conventional portraits—Joseph, the silent old stepfather; Mary, the all-giving virgin mother; and Jesus, the twelve-year-old who doesn't tell his parents where he's going—very uplifting. . . . How can women help but feel angry and oppressed when they're regularly excluded from all decision-making and prominence by male priests offering prayers to a masculine God? How do you argue with the crazy logic of the priest who makes this kind of distinction: "Woman cannot be a priest because she is equal but beneath man"? [39] *. . . Why does the thought of a female priest make so many women and men uncomfortable? I think it's because "priestess" conjures up buried memories of vestal virgins selling their favors to passing strangers. Some argue that women cannot be priests because Christ was male, but I'm tired of his maleness being accentuated instead of his humanity.*

I was told as a child to make Mary's prayer, "Thy will be done," my way of life. But I prefer Reinhold Niebuhr's prayer (the motto of Alcoholics Anonymous): "Oh God, give us serenity to accept what cannot be changed, courage to change what should be changed, and wisdom to distinguish the one from the other." I desperately want to be the traditional serene woman, but now know that serenity only comes after courage and wisdom have had their day. . . . I value many of the so-called feminine virtues—gentleness, tenderness, compassion, generosity, patience—but resent the fact that they're so often eschewed by men. Patience is the traditional quality I most admire, because it is so associated in my mind with my mother. She had the ability to wait for the right moment to act and could help others reach their full potentialities by a patient letting-be. But indifference, apathy, and inactivity have no place in the patience I seek. Rather, I want the patience that doesn't make a fetish of the status quo but stands instead at the intersection between reality and possibility, the past and the future, holding both together in delicate balance. [40]

The anti-pleasure stance of the Church disturbs me. It is the by-product of a patriarchal-authoritarian system that cares more about restrictions than about peace, tender humaneness, and happiness. [41] *Instead of sulking for another millennium about paradise lost, we have to direct our attentions to the human evolution of which we all are a part. . . . When considering sexuality up until now, Christianity has based almost all its moral code on procreation. Like Teilhard de Chardin, I think the reproductive function was important until earth reached maturity, but now there's emerging a new role for the sexes: "the necessary synthesis of the two principles, male and female, in the building of the human personality."* [42]

I would find it difficult to have an abortion because it involves ending life, but I don't understand the Church's obstinate stand on this matter when it has endorsed killing at other times; for example, in times of war. Some prelates are said to have become interested in the Vietnam atrocities only after the combatants were described as "former fetuses." Surely this is a distorted sense of morality when you're more concerned about the unborn than about those already working out their destiny on this earth. The Church is implacable on the abortion issue, I think, because of the loss of face it has suffered with respect to its position on contraception. It hopes to regain moral credibility by championing a no-killing position which many instinctively agree with. Yet I'm disturbed as a feminist by how easily the Church excuses men's murder in the name of a "just war" and isn't even willing to consider women ending life in the name of some other justice.

I grew up listening to "She curses like a man. It isn't right for a woman to say 'shit' and 'fuck'; it's ten times worse when a woman uses such language." "Damn it" was all I ever thought of as a reply. ... Matthew 15:32–39 recounts how Christ multiplied the fish and loaves of bread to feed four thousand men, "to say nothing of women and children." But I want a New-New Testament where you say something of women and children. . . . Christ preached the golden rule (Matthew 7:12), "So always treat others as you would like them to treat you," and I think it cannot be improved upon as a way of life. It's time for men to treat women as they themselves want to be treated.

The role models offered to women by the Church have in common a total disregard for their sex. Eve is written off as a troublemaker. Woman as "man," an asexual virginal creature, was the ideal served up by early Christianity. After one thousand years of an absence of femaleness in the liturgy, the cult of the Blessed Virgin Mary emerged. The "Our Father" taught by Christ as the perfect prayer was found in the eleventh century to need a companion, the "Hail Mary." Christianity at that time desperately needed large doses of romance, chivalry, and poetry to counteract the debauchery that had become the rule among clergy and laity alike. But so thoroughly had the Church separated positive sentiment toward woman from sexual feelings that the feminine model brought forth to soften a brutal world was that of a virgin-mother, an ideal absolutely unattainable by mortal women. The need for female values coupled with the low regard for flesh-and-blood women produced "Mary the Mystical Rose," "Mary the Mother of us all," "Mary the Mediatrix from whom all blessings flow."

With a swing of the pendulum, Eve, who did us in, gave way to Mary, who will take care of us, her children. Mary met all the requirements men had for the perfect woman: modest, obedient, generous, understanding, deferential, loving, concerned, uncomplaining, comforting. A completely male-oriented society had proven to be so cold and harsh that it became imperative that "God the Stern Judge" and "God the All-Powerful King" be modified by Mary's intercession on our behalf. The emphasis shifted to underscore the instrumental role of Christ and the expressive role of his mother. Madonna images abounded during the Renaissance, and gradually Marian devotion gave women and family life some dignity within the Church. By Victorian times, however, the female had assumed "the function of serving as the male's conscience, and living the life of goodness, he found tedious but felt someone ought to do anyway."[43] To this day, women are usually seen as temptress or mother, rather than as equal human beings. Even liberal Cardinal Suenens of Belgium describes woman this way: "Woman has the awe-ful choice of being Eve or Mary; she is rarely neutral. Either she ennobles and raises man up to her presence, by creating a climate of beauty and human nobility, or she drags him down with her in her own fall."[44] What an *awful* choice!

I reject being the scapegoat like Eve. I reject the Church's notion of blessed maternity, what F. J. Sheed describes as "love and total willingness to serve."[45] Pius X may call Mary "the first steward in the dispensing of graces,"[46] but I reject the notion of Mary meekly doing spiritual housework for her son. Pius XII may regard woman as "the crown of creation and in a certain sense its masterpiece . . . that gentle creature to whose delicate hands God seems to have entrusted the future of the world . . . the expression of all that is best, kindest, most loveable here below,"[47] but to me, these words are reactionary. He's bending over backward to correct the purple prose of his predecessors, and I'm not going to be flattered into taking responsibility for "the future of the world" or the ennobling of men. The world will never become truly humane until everyone takes responsibility for doing her/his own share. Besides, I do not have delicate hands and am selectively gentle.

Pope Paul VI may see woman as "the most docile, malleable creature and therefore gifted for all social and cultural functions, especially those most related to her moral and spiritual sensitivity,"[48] but I'm too sensitive to the pitfalls of docility to swallow his pretentious rhetoric. I even reject the counsel of Rosemary Haughton, who suggested in her article "Beyond Women's Lib" that "the great need now is for women to reassert their insights as proper human priorities, and save not just themselves but all mankind."[49] Women should assert their insights as proper human priorities, but being blamed for all the world's troubles and being hailed as a possible saviour are two sides of the same coin. I reject both sides. After two thousand years of seesawing between these crazy poles, I look forward to some humanity in the millennium ahead.

When all is said and done, the biggest problem religion poses to a woman is not that it has seen her as evil temptress or self-immolating mother, but the fact that religion assumes it has possession of the truth; all that's necessary for salvation is that human beings conform to the tenets posted by Church authorities. That view posits a human nature that is static and unchangeable rather than subject to continual development and refinement. It further assumes that the proper stance of the laity is to soak up the "truth" like a sponge rather than actively evaluate ethical positions as they affect each generation. Though the Catholic Church has gone to the extreme of designating its leader as infallible when he speaks *ex cathedra,* every major religion protects its doctrinal purity and very identity by saying its major prophet(s) was specially enlightened, in a way the ordinary person now can't be, when the original covenant between God and His chosen people (or chosen leader) was made. Therefore, the old ways must prevail intact. Instead of looking at every change as a repudiation of past good, however, I suggest we acknowledge how much religion has been affected by the political structures of various periods and by the projection of psychic needs onto theological pronouncements.

You have only to read the various statements Christians have made about slavery to appreciate how much Church policy has always been affected by political and economic realities. When the early Christians were too poor to have slaves, all men were created equal; when later Christians became affluent, emphasis shifted to taking good care of your slaves; and when civic leaders began to see a political advantage to freeing the slaves, all men were created equal once again. The religious statements on women's proper social position have likewise mirrored what was regarded as proper by those with the most power. I'm not arguing that religion has always taken a back seat to politics and economics, but a specific moral insight only takes root when social factors are ripe for that idea to emerge. For example, pre-industrial society needed slave (or serf) labor so badly that it was unlikely there would be widespread affirmation of the sovereignty and equality of each person when so many hands were needed to cultivate the land, but a mechanized society can afford to think of a world without slaves. Making this point doesn't negate religious insights, but it does make clear how values are constantly changing as social conditions present new problems or erase old ones.

There is an overwhelming tendency on the part of human beings to embroider doctrine with "what I would do if I were God." One of the proofs given for the Assumption of Mary into heaven by angels is "there was the simple feeling that Christ would want His mother with Him in heaven, not her soul only but herself, body and soul. Any son would want that, and this was the one son who could have what He wanted!"[50] The Assumption as "just what every good Jewish boy would do for his mother" is a perfect example of human beings coloring dogma with their own aspirations. It is significant that the Assumption, Mary's supposed reward for being Christ's mother, only became dogma in 1950, at the height of the feminine mystique. (No doubt Pope Pius XII wanted to remind ordinary women that motherhood would be rewarding for them too.) It's important that we start scrutinizing religious pronouncements in terms of our own unconscious needs because the fair person is duty bound, I think, to separate an article of faith from wishful thinking.

Perhaps Mary truly was a virgin-mother, perhaps she wasn't. It's vital that we start looking at such a proposition in terms of whether it is necessary to our system of belief, or whether it is an expression of man's deep-seated need to have a mother untouched by venereal pleasure, saved only for him. Fortunatus (530–609), Bishop of Poitiers, wrote poetry infused with images of Mary as Christ's sexual object: "Freely He penetrates viscera known only to Himself and with greater joy enters paths where none has ever been. These limbs, he feels, are His own: unsoiled and unshared by any man. Tenderly and with affection He kisses the breast . . ."[51] Erotic verse or divine mystery? How much is Mary's virginity fact, and how much does it reflect man's wish that his beloved belong only to him? Religion must cease to be a device for describing one's secret desires as God-ordained. Its energies should be directed instead to describing what the good life should be. Socrates felt the unexamined life was not worth living; I think religion which cannot withstand such examination is not worth believing.

The very future of women in religion depends upon whether we can exorcise male bias from our beliefs and whether we can admit that human nature is constantly being shaped by new insights and new forces. Arguing that religious insights have to change because the relation between human beings and nature is constantly evolving isn't advocating something new as much as it's asking that we acknowledge how things have already changed over time. For example, the notion of capital punishment has evolved tremendously over the centuries:

> For our Teutonic Christian ancestors capital punishment was left to the individual parties involved. Later, in a more organized society, what had been accepted as legitimate private punishment was rejected as a moral crime; today we wonder whether capital punishment, even when inflicted by public authority, is not against the natural law.[52]

Have the external circumstances changed, or have human beings changed? Louis Dupré, for one, argues convincingly that "the circumstances have changed mainly because *man has changed.* The natural law is the dynamic expression of this ethical development."[53] The day is here, I hope, when we see woman's "inferiority" as just as foolish as calling lice the "pearls of God" when anything which made the body clean and inviting was dismissed as suspect.[54]

Religion poses a further problem for woman in that it is itself perceived as being a female institution (for example, Catholics are fond of calling their Church "Our Holy Mother the Church"). A God who favors love and peace is automatically tilted in the direction of femaleness because those values are seen as womanish. Freud described religion as basically feminine; he saw it as "beneath the masculine dignity of reason . . . To be religious . . . is to be passive, complaint, dependent—essentially feminine traits."[55] (But he sees the origins of religion in patriarchal terms; in *Totem and Taboo* he posits the notion that religion began with the murder of the primal father by his sons. He also terms Judaism as a "Father" religion and Christianity as a "Son" religion.) Men resist giving women power within organized religion because the virtues already seem so feminine. There's widespread fear that female preachers and theologians will mean a complete takeover by the feminine perspective. Some think women priests and rabbis will really mean "God is dead"; but God was killed by men long before women started making demands. God died when men designated religion a female preoccupation, equated goodness with passivity and compliance, and started seeing nothing manly, nothing they could identify with, in love and peace.

In George Bernard Shaw's play *Joan of Arc*, one of the characters says: "Joan, we are all trying to save you. His lordship is trying to save you. The Inquisitor could not be more just to you if you were his own daughter. But you are blinded by a terrible pride of self-sufficiency."[56] Today few women are scared into believing that self-sufficiency is terrible. It's necessary to develop a sense of personal worth in order to comprehend the ultimate purposes of existence. As Teilhard de Chardin said in *The Divine Milieu*, "First develop yourself, Christianity says to the Christian."[57] Blind acceptance of your parents' faith is no longer the mark of a religious person; we are coming to appreciate that we have to be self-possessed in order to comprehend how incomplete mere human answers are. The St. Teresas of the future don't want their wings to droop before they've scaled the heights.

My feminist outrage surfaces in the area of religion more than it does anywhere else because I expect so much from people and institutions that claim to be my link between time and eternity. I am angry because I care so deeply about fathoming the ultimate purposes of existence, about social and economic inequities, about whether there's life after death. These are big issues, too important to be buried under a mound of sexist attitudes and outdated canon law. The Church doesn't need "good girls" afraid of brimstone and damnation, but women of integrity unafraid to seize the whirlwind.

8

THE JOB

The double bind is such that whatever a woman chooses she stands to lose: if she follows the legal and cultural mandate and chooses marriage above all else, she will sacrifice her earning potential for her family, and she may suffer upon divorce. On the other hand, if a woman chooses to combine marriage and a career she (and her family) may also suffer because of the great force of legal priorities given to families with a single earning partner and a housewife.

Lenore J. Weitzman
California Law Review (July-September 1974)

The wife of Proverbs (31: 16, 31) was praised for her work outside the home—"She sets her mind on a field, then she buys it; with what her hands have earned she plants a vineyard. . . . Give her a share in what her hands have worked for, and let her work tell her praises at the city gates"—much more than today's woman. The homemaking rhetoric of the fifties and sixties which emphasized that women didn't need impersonal interests or dedication to a task[1] or to prove themselves through accomplishments and achievements[2] has been partially gagged by feminist rebuttal. Despite the number of women in the labor force—a majority of nearly 34 million in March 1973, 58 percent of whom were married[3]—many people still refuse to consider a job a basic component of a woman's life.

Psychiatrist Theodore Lidz writes convincingly about the importance of occupational choice in determining the course of one's personality development, one's status in the community, one's daily associates, and one's emotional and physical well-being, then goes on to say that marriage is most women's career:

> Problems of vocational choice are more significant to men than to women, for whom, by and large, marriage and child rearing take precedence over a career. The future of most women depends to a frightening degree upon whom they marry. Unless she remains single, a woman's status in life and that of her family will almost always depend upon her husband's career even if she works, and her hopes for the future rest more in the lives of her husband and her children than in what she can accomplish vocationally.[4]

Unlike me, Dr. Lidz doesn't seem to be very alarmed by the "frightening degree" to which a woman's future depends on whom she marries. He dismisses her own work by announcing that her vocational accomplishments will "almost always" bring her and her children less "status" than her husband's career, so her "hopes for the future" will necessarily require an investment in her husband and children rather than be the result of self-direction. Implicit in Dr. Lidz's statement is the conviction that the husband's career should always come first, that a wife should automatically defer to the requirements of his job. After saying how important occupational choice is, he effectively leaves the woman with *no choice.*

In an essay entitled "Women and Social Stratification: A Case of Intellectual Sexism,"[5] Joan Acker notes that the professional literature assumes that the social position of the woman is determined by the status of the male head of household, unless she is not attached to a man. Research studies in many disciplines have categorized women as belonging to one socioeconomic group or another strictly on the basis of their husbands' job, earning power, and education rather than their own. Even more ludicrous, I know of a Puerto Rican woman who lost her minority-group status and a job reserved for a Spanish-American when she married and assumed her husband's English family name.

On the one side we hear the "experts" say, "Most women recognize, even if the colleges they attend do not, that being a good wife, and even more, being a good mother requires many refined skills and forms a career in itself."[6] Then the U.S. Department of Labor proclaims, "Homemaking in itself is no longer a full-time job for most people. Goods and services formerly produced in the home are now commercially available; laborsaving devices have lightened or eliminated much work around the home."[7] The woman is told how noble the wife-homemaker-mother is, then picks up the *Dictionary of Occupational Titles*,[8] which defines some 22,000 occupations on a "skill" scale from a high of 0 to a low of 8 in three categories (skills needed with respect to data, people, and things). How do resourceful and seasoned mothers stack up against, for example, hotel clerks, who have a rating of 3–6–8 (3 for compiling data, 6 for speaking–signaling people, and 8 for having no significant relationship to things)? Homemakers,* foster mothers, child-care attendants, and nursery-school teachers all share a listing of 8–7–8, which means they're presumed to have no significant relationship to data or things and a "serving" relationship to people. So much for public acclaim. Freud said the mark of the mature person is the ability to love *and* work. "Making love your life's work" may sound beautiful and uplifting enough to embroider on a sampler for the kitchen wall, but the married feminist knows that it can also leave you a one-sided person, feeling very *low*.

However, it doesn't stop with the woman's feeling low. Woman's work role in modern industrial societies has a number

---

*The "homemaker" entry is cross-referenced "maid, general"—proof positive that John Kenneth Galbraith's remarks about housewives being a crypto-servant class are well founded (see Chapter 5). In the "skills related to ranking people," 0 is the value assigned to mentoring, 1 = negotiating, 2 = instructing, 3 = supervising, 4 = diverting, 5 = persuading, 6 = speaking–signaling, 7 = serving, 8 = no significant relationship. No matter how fancy the language we use to describe the importance of women's domestic work, the fact remains that the U.S. Department of Labor sees "serving" as their significant relationship to other people.

of characteristics which make her more susceptible to functional disorders characterized by anxiety and/or mental disorganization. First, most women are traditionally restricted to the single major social role of housewife, whereas most men have two major sources of gratification—household head and worker. Second, large numbers of women find their primary activities—child rearing and homemaking—frustrating because they involve being "on call" twenty-four hours a day. Not only are they jobs of low prestige, but they are ones in which the woman is confronted with expectations that are unclear and diffuse. Third, the role of housewife is relatively invisible and unstructured. Sociologists Walter Gove and Jeannette Tudor explain it this way:

> It is possible for the housewife to put things off, to let things slide, in sum, to perform poorly. The lack of structure and visibility allows her to brood over her troubles, and her distress may thus feed upon itself. In contrast, the job holder must consistently and satisfactorily meet demands that constantly force him to be involved with his environment. Having to meet these structured demands should draw his attention from his troubles and help prevent him from becoming obsessed with his worries.[9]

Fourth, even when a married woman works, she is typically in a less satisfactory position than her husband. Men definitely have greater access to prestigious jobs and bigger salaries than women, who frequently hold positions that are not commensurate with their educational backgrounds. Others tend to see them (so they frequently see themselves) as only working for pocket money, which makes their career involvement all the more tenuous. (The reality in March 1973 was that about 17 million women worked because of pressing financial need; another 4.7 million had husbands with incomes between $3,000 and $7,000.)[10] The typical sequential work pattern—work, withdrawal from work for child rearing, and eventual return to work—doesn't enable the woman to build up her experience during the crucial years—late twenties and thirties—when the majority of reputations are forged. (Even with a break in employment, the average woman worker has a work-life expectancy of 25 years.[11] However, more married women have paying jobs than the government knows about, because they do babysitting, mending, cleaning, etc., for neighbors but do not file W-2 forms.)

Knowing she can't earn as much as a man, it's difficult for a woman to persist in the face of her husband saying, "Fine, you work, but I'd like to see the day you bring in $15,000 a year the way I do." Yet if the woman decides to do part-time work to supplement the family income, she is penalized by the fact that most part-time workers are not entitled to pension, health insurance, and vacation benefits. Obviously too, opportunities for advancement are limited in part-time jobs. Men also discourage a woman's working by saying, "It doesn't pay for her to work, considering the taxes we'd have to pay." The added expenses, such as the cost of babysitters, new clothes, bus fare, lunches, etc., also bolster his argument. But these "disadvantages" seem no hindrance to the man's pursuing his career. A man's business expenses are treated as givens, but a woman has to justify the fact that her work is of benefit. And being good for her mental health doesn't seem to count for much.

For the many married women in the labor force, the relegation of domestic responsibilities solely to the wife means that she must perform two jobs. (On the average, working women spend from 0.8 to 3.5 hours more per day in homemaking and child-care activities than their husbands.)[12] The standard argument is that women should hold the entire responsibility for keeping house because men are less able to handle these tasks and don't get much satisfaction from them.[13] It seems to me more accurate to say that this has been a very convenient division of labor—convenient, that is, to men. This kind of "it's the only efficient thing to do" thinking further squelches women by suggesting it is selfish of them to take a job and thus force men to share in housework they find difficult (!) and distasteful. Equating career with a man's

self-respect and image of himself leaves women holding the bag
once more. The woman who wants both a job and a family usually
finds she must shoulder all the household arrangements under
pressure of this argument. As one male college senior said, "It is
appropriate for a mother of a preschool child to take a fulltime
job . . . provided, of course, that the home was run smoothly, the
children did not suffer, and the wife's job did not interfere with
her husband's career."[14] No such onus falls on the husband; he
is not responsible for how the children and house will be cared
for during his absence. Hit over the head with all these guilt-
inducing arguments, the lack of good child care, and the paucity
of well-paying part-time work, many women who might want to
work do not.

Legislators and social scientists are still busily debating whether
they should endorse day care. The ever increasing number of
women in the labor force has already answered the question, but
men continue to play deaf and dumb. We need, as the Bill of
Rights put together by the National Organization for Women in
1968 states, child-care facilities to "be established by law on the
same basis as parks, libraries, and public schools, adequate to the
needs of children from the pre-school years through adolescence,
as a community resource to be used by all citizens from all income
levels."[15] Ironically, it's some of the same conservatives who
glorify the British nanny who maintain a child is entitled to a
mother's undivided attention during the first six years of life.

The government does its share to make working outside the
home less profitable to married women. "She is forced to pay a
full social security tax, but the benefits she receives as an independent worker are not added to those she would be entitled to as
a spouse. The family thus pays a double tax when she works, but
she collects for only a single worker."[16] The Social Security laws
penalize married people with separate incomes: the first $15,300
earned by each is taxed, so if two people earn that, they are both
taxed, whereas if one person works and earns $30,600, only
$15,300 of his income is taxed. Income tax policies discriminate

against couples when the wife works. Until 1977, child-care expenses can be deducted only if both wife and husband are "gainfully employed on a substantially full-time basis,"[17] so part-time work, which most married women with small children might prefer, doesn't qualify for any child-care or household-service deductions; this has now been rectified. Still, you cannot take deductions for paying a relative (brother, sister, mother, father, aunt, uncle, sister-in-law, niece, etc.) for taking care of your children while you work.[18] If you want the deduction, you are precluded from hiring the very people your children might be most comfortable being with during your absence. Presumably the government assumes that grandparents and other close relatives would gladly take care of your children *out of love* (like mother is supposed to) and not want any remuneration. Paying a relative for needed services if you do work can in no way be construed as collusion to avoid taxes. Furthermore, if a couple work in different states, as more and more are doing, and visit each other every weekend, their travel expenses—so necessary to keep their marriage alive—are not deductible either, because they're not business-related.

After tallying the disadvantages of having a job outside the home, some women decide to throw themselves into a life of "vicarious achievement" through their husbands' job; Hanna Papanek labeled this special combination of roles the "two-person single career." She sees this "solution" as "a social control mechanism which serves to derail the occupational aspirations of educated women into the noncompetitive 'two-person career' without openly injuring the concept of equality of educational opportunity for both sexes."[19] In this arrangement, the husband has the formal tie to the job, but the wife serves as hostess to his clients and associates, patron of the arts he wants to sponsor, typist for his briefs, researcher for his position papers, sometimes as the tie to his female constituency—as in the "job" of First Lady. Dr. Von Gagern must have had the "two-person single career" in mind when he described marriage as this sort of partnership:

She [the wife] will do well to interest herself in his work, to keep in touch, to ask questions. With her intuitive mode of thought, more closely bound up with life, she can aid him in the avoidance of abstractions remote from reality, thus making his work more fruitful. Without necessarily being herself intellectual, she can be a valuable co-worker. Her criticism fresh from a more intimate contact with reality, supported by her praise, will stimulate his creative impulse; nor should she be sparing with her praise, when justifiable.[20]

How fortunate for the man who can both bask in all that praise, yet argue that she's obviously being irrational when his wife is critical.

All the book dedications to the wife "without whom this book would not have been written" attest to the fact that the "two-person single career" is alive and well. The scope of this kind of bogus partnership is, of course, another reason a woman may not take a "real" job. Though the wife receives no money from the husband's company, she may get involved in conferences like the one the Ford Motor Company held for wives in 1972 at which a company executive summed up the wife's role in six little words: "Watch your figure and don't nag."[21] At least this man's put-down is there for all to see, not hidden under cyanide frosting like Von Gagern's words! The biggest disadvantage of this life style is, as the wife of a banker said, "Sometimes I feel he's living his life to the fullest, and I'm living his life to the fullest."[22]

Another way for the wife to be "ungainfully employed" is to throw herself into volunteer work. While a tremendous amount of important work is done by volunteers and many women use this option as a stepping stone to a paying job, society takes advantage of the woman volunteer by not allowing her tax credits for travel and child-care expenses incurred during business hours and by not according her experience in an unpaid job the same respect it would get on a *curriculum vitae* if it was paid work. Volunteer work disturbs me the most when I hear women disguise their achievement needs and bill themselves as one seventy-three-year-old grandmother did: "I've always been a strictly female's female, and have loved being helpless and letting my husband take care of me."[23] Yet she has more than fifty years of volunteer work behind her, involving forty organizations, at least twenty-five major offices, the management of many people and thousands of dollars. Who's kidding whom?

So far, I've emphasized the conditions that frequently put women into the double bind about which Lenore Weitzman spoke in the quote that began this chapter. But a job (not necessarily a career) offers so many advantages, I wouldn't be without one for long. First of all, it means having some money of your own, which in turn means not having to justify every penny you spend to someone else who has ultimate control of the purse strings. There's an entirely different mentality operating when you feel you have a right to buy a book or a dress or have your hair styled because you earn a portion of the joint income than when you feel such items can only be bought with the approval of the breadwinner. No matter how generous a man is to his wife in terms of a food or clothing allowance, an allowance implies just that; he is *allowing* her to do something at his discretion, and gratitude is all too often the price exacted for such largess. Even traditionalist Phyllis McGinley thinks a woman should have money of her own, because it makes the "difference between resentful dependence and happy self-reliance."[24] Though she doesn't spell out how you get this indispensable "pocket money" while devoting yourself to home and family (presumably you either have rich parents, or lie about the amount you need to run the household so that you can have some left over for yourself, or squeeze in some profitable writing as she does), her emphasis on having money of your own as essential to a good marriage does point up the same basic needs highlighted by feminists.

Many people minimize a woman's ambition for a job or career by pointing out that rearing children well is much more of an accomplishment than being a good secretary or saleswoman or factory worker. It's true you can feel very proud of your children in a way that's different from (and frequently superior to) the way you feel when you bring home your check each week, but the need to have your own identity or the need for a *regular* feeling of accomplishment is not always met by child rearing. In fact, the more you expect your children to meet those needs, the more you are likely to be disappointed, because your relationship will be geared to what you want from them rather than what you can do to help them grow up to be mature human beings.

A job makes you more discerning about how you spend your free time. A job gives a woman a reason for saying no to the thousand-and-one tasks she doesn't want to do but usually is expected to do. When you don't have a job, it is assumed you can rearrange your time to do volunteer work at the children's school or chauffeur the Brownie troop on a field trip or clean out the church basement in preparation for the spring fair. But if you work outside the home, they leave you alone if you remind them you're just not available during the day and too devoted to your family to deprive them of your presence in the evening or on weekends.

A job gives a woman an affiliation of her own, another place besides home where she belongs and where she has contact with people. A job gives structure to a woman's life, gets her out of the house regularly. Most of us dream of a time when we will have a flexible schedule and can sign up for the art class or fencing lessons we always wanted to take, but few people actually prosper without some sort of timetable.

Staying at home and being your own boss sounds good, but the Puritan ethic is still so all-pervasive that you're forever feeling guilty if you're not doing something you think is "constructive." It becomes necessary to prove you're no slouch, so you either assume all sorts of social and community obligations to show you're as busy as everyone else, or you start taking longer and longer to accomplish what used to occupy a small portion of your time. The stay-at-home wife and mother usually becomes more tired too, because a nonstructured existence encourages the impression that your work is never-ending. The accompanying fatigue thereby seems equally all-pervasive. Commitment to a job doesn't have to be explained to anyone, but being home all day forces most women to be on the defensive about how they spend their time. This is because what they do doesn't show (a full refrigerator, an orderly room, clean clothes go unnoticed), but what they don't do does (still in your bathrobe at noon is easily noticed, and a son with strained carrots matted in his hair obviously hasn't gotten recent attention).

(Boyd C. Rollins and Harold Feldman point out in their article "Marital Satisfaction Over the Family Life Cycle" that husbands are most dissatisfied during the time when they are about to retire, and that child rearing is the period when wives report the highest level of negative feelings. One wonders whether it's the child care *per se* that the women found distressing or their premature "retirement" from productive associations with other adults.)[25]

Much has been said about the importance to children of the always available mother. I think that we ought to explore much more fully the benefits to the children of the mother who works. Leaving aside the financial aspect (which for many families is decisive), a job is important so you don't become excessively invested in your children. Though securing good care for your child when you and your husband both work isn't easy, a working mother does encourage independent children. Alice S. Rossi argues persuasively that if we want assertive, independent, responsible adults we should rear our children in a way which prevents undue dependence on the mother:

> They should be cared for by a number of adults in their childhood, and their parents should truly encourage their independence and responsibility during their youthful years, not merely give lip service to these parental goals. The best way to encourage such independence and responsibility in the child is for the mother to

be a living model of these qualities herself. If she had an independent life of her own, she would find her stage of life interesting, and therefore be less likely to live for and through her children. . . . If enough American women developed vital and enduring interests outside the family and remained actively in them throughout the child-bearing years, we might then find a reduction in extreme adolescent rebellion, immature early marriages, maternal domination of children, and interference by mothers and mothers-in-law in the lives of married children.[26]

Wife-and-husband psychologists Sandra L. and Daryl J. Bem point out that daughters of working mothers, when asked to name the woman they most admire, are more likely to name their own mothers than daughters of nonworking mothers.[27]

In the four hundred marriages reported on by Jan E. Dizard, the most satisfactory marriages were those in which the wife worked and the husband was not overly successful occupationally:

In such circumstances, it seems reasonable to imagine, the possibilities for equality between husband and wife are maximized—both cooperate around the house and share interests and neither spouse is totally dependent upon the other for stimulation and recognition. At the same time, neither is so committed to "success" that concerns about competitiveness and getting ahead dominate their relationship.[28]

The cliché has it that husband and wife need separate spheres of influence in order to complement each other's work rather than compete with each other, but there's growing awareness that this has led to all too frequent invidious comparisons between the importance of the husband's job and the housework of the wife. If they both work and both accept responsibility for home and family concerns, it is less likely that this imbalance of respect will occur.[29]

Career mothers constitute only about a fifth of all working mothers, though they're the ones who have a more difficult time integrating work and family roles (the status and salary that go with being a professional sweeten their struggle, however).[30] There is evidence that women who have jobs in offices, hospitals, and restaurants that aren't coveted by men experience less psychological turmoil than career-minded women because they see what they're doing as a logical extension of the mother-wife role. Such women aren't likely to emphasize self-fulfillment as their reason for having a job the way their career sisters do, but see a job as a way to fill the void left when the last child enters school, to ease the strain on the unemployed husband, to provide a child with a college education, to keep creditors from the door, to get their own mothers into a good nursing home, to be less dependent on their husbands, to be better conversationalists, and even to be more glamorous. Sociologist Jessie Bernard wonders if this trend doesn't presage an increasing assimilation of the worker and the mother role in the future, the first becoming, more and more, a component of the second.[31] The two overlapped in pre-industrial society when everyday commodities (candles, soap, cloth, preserves, etc.) were made both for home use and to be bartered. Men, too, have traditionally seen their role as worker as an expansion of the father-husband role.

Since human beings continually strive for cognitive consistency, some integration of the various components of the self, I think women will increasingly see work outside the home as an extension of their inside-the-home personalities, and self-fulfillment as a requirement for meeting the needs of others. They will adopt the attitude that no work is by definition incompatible with the private side of one's life. I know I've tried to make my work life an extension of my personality, my femaleness . . .

The Catholic all-girl high school I went to had a reputation for educational excellence, but Career Day focused more on which school of nursing to go to (with considerable emphasis placed on which had the most attractive cap) rather than what the choices were besides nursing. There weren't many: if you chose the com-

mercial track, you prepared yourself to be a secretary; if you chose the academic track, you were assumed to be heading for nursing, elementary-school teaching, or library work. Practically no one pictured a female going to school after her twenty-first birthday. . . . If you don't know a woman who has combined a career with family life, you're not likely to imagine that combination for yourself. Since my high school teachers were all nuns (with the exception of the gym teacher and one part-time science teacher) and my female instructors in college were mainly nuns, or single women or married women without children, it wasn't until I did graduate work in psychiatric nursing at Yale that I met a number of working mothers who enjoyed what they were doing and talked openly about the pressures and satisfactions that working entailed. It was only then that I began to consider the possibility of that sort of arrangement for myself.

Your feelings about a job are so much a function of economic necessity. When you're unskilled and have to take any sort of job because you desperately need money, the thought of some future time when you never again have to work captures the imagination. The more interesting the job, the more you appreciate work for its own sake. Of course, the interesting job usually has the added advantages of being well-paying and prestigious too. . . . Long before the recent emphasis on retaining your maiden name after marriage, career women were often known at the office by their maiden names and reserved their married names for use in social situations. It never occurred to me to resolve my own identity problems that way because it seemed a practice so connected with an elite social standing that I would have felt pretentious. . . . Probably one of the best things the women's movement has done is to make a job respectable: neither something to be justified only by dire economic straits, nor something you're entitled to only if your talents are "exceptional." . . . It's no news that success enhances a man's sexiness, whereas success is usually thought of as desexing a woman. Yet the women I know in their thirties, forties, fifties, and sixties who look the most alive and attractive are often *the ones who have careers. . . . A man doesn't choose between a job and having a family, he* must *work. But women have been taught that they can't have both. This led many educated women to choose careers in the "helping professions" so they could acquire skills that would be of use when they became parents. I became a nurse in part because relatives said, "You can use all that psychology on your kids." Twenty years later, I can use psychology that way and to reshape my own views of women's roles.*

When I was working on my master's degree at Yale, I often felt like a quick-change artist. On a date with someone working on his Ph.D., I billed myself as a fellow graduate student. With men who had a college degree or less education, I described myself as a nurse. But the feeling that I could be all things to all people was often replaced by the feeling that I was neither fish nor fowl. . . . As a second-year graduate student, I took a course at the Yale Medical School and got an honors, only to find out a couple of years later when I was on the Yale School of Nursing faculty that the professor had written on the official grade sheet: "I gave her an honors because she was from the School of Nursing, but her work, if she had been a med student, would have warranted only a high pass." I was both mortified and angry when I learned this. Why the double standard; why couldn't he tell me directly that I wouldn't have made the grade judged by more rigorous criteria? Maybe he refused to believe a nursing student and a medical student could have equal ability.

I'm tired of the "only a nurse" attitudes at large. Soon after Yale "went co-ed" (Yale had had women in its graduate and professional schools for years, so all the publicity given to Yale's finally admitting women in the late sixties was annoying to many of us who had been there before the headlines), a booklet entitled "She" was put out listing all the resources available to women and the names of all the women on the faculty. Under the heading "School of Nursing," the dean's name was listed and in parentheses it said, "For a complete list of the School of Nursing faculty, apply to the Dean's office." Every other female faculty member employed by the university had been named, but those at the nursing school were left off, supposedly because it would have upped the printing costs to have included so many additional names. When a protest was lodged, the situation was quickly remedied and all those names managed to fit on a one-page addendum. The School of Nursing hadn't been considered part of the "real" Yale before having women became chic. After the enrollment of female undergraduates, nurses continued to be almost invisible because they were members of the most traditional female profession (all nurses are alike?). A number of the residential colleges which were eager to appoint some female "fellows" culled names from that booklet to find appointees. If you weren't on this list, you weren't likely to be appointed. As so often happens, exclusion one place meant exclusion elsewhere.

When I traveled to promote my first book, I was frequently given the ultimate in backhanded compliments: "You're smart enough, you could have been a psychiatrist instead of a psychiatric nurse." When someone implies you're smart for a nurse, *the praise doesn't take away the sting of denigrating your profession. But then a number of social scientists don't even see nursing as a full-fledged profession; they label it a "semi-profession," whatever that means. Why doesn't anyone believe that you might have deliberately chosen to be a psychiatric nurse rather than a psychiatrist because the former gives you a chance to be therapeutic in informal surroundings and not confine your effectiveness to a fifty-minute hour? . . . A year later, I took a statistics course which began with a historical survey. When he got to the nineteenth century, the professor mentioned that there were three important names in statistics for that period and Florence Nightingale, the founder of public health statistics, was one of them. There were giggles of disbelief when he wrote her name on the blackboard; the laughter reverberated long afterward in my head. . . . We remodeled our kitchen two years ago. I couldn't resist the impulse to tell the various workmen that I was a nurse. Men generally like nurses and feel protective toward them. They're seen as salt-of-the-earth, unas-*

suming and sincere. I was trying to cash in on these good feelings and do what I could to convince them I wasn't someone they would want to rip off. I was annoyed with myself afterward for playing on emotions and sympathies I dislike.

How many times have I heard a man say "I don't want my wife to work," and wondered what he thought she did all day at home with the children. I think only a man who is exhausted from shouldering all the responsibility for earning the money can be so callous as to fantasize his wife nibbling bonbons all day while watching soap operas. . . . When we were first married, I thought my husband's salary existed for all the essentials, but mine was so we could afford some luxuries. One day, when I heard myself grandly suggesting that we use my money to pay for a trip we wanted to take, I realized how much I took him for granted. I was acting as if he had to pay for food, clothing, and the rent because that's what men do; my salary was extra, and I could take credit for giving us the fun things. It occurred to me that I couldn't have it both ways: expect him to do half of the child care and housework and still see my job as icing on the cake. If I wanted him to be egalitarian about "woman's" work, I would have to assume equal responsibility for our finances and not parade about as Lady Bountiful when it pleased me. . . . I've found some advantages to both spouses working that people don't usually talk about: you worry less about being let go in the middle of a depression if both of you are working, because you figure at least one of you will be able to hold on to a job; you don't have to invest enormous sums in life insurance if you know the death of your husband wouldn't leave you and the children with no means of earning a living. . . . It would be foolhardy to ignore the fact that a two-job family does mean the husband will sometimes wonder, "Have I gotten smaller, as she's gotten bigger?" but openly talking about that issue seems much better than normally expecting the woman to contract as her husband expands his career interests.

When Maryland governor Marvin Mandel's wife of thirty-two years first refused to give him a divorce and to leave the mansion, many women admired her gumption. For almost half a year after her husband moved out on her, she kept giving speeches, vowing to continue as first lady, and explained herself this way: "I helped him achieve the highest position in the state. All our lives we worked hard for a goal together."[32] *Barbara Mandel had made marriage her career and had achieved the highest state office possible to her, that of first lady. Who can blame her for wanting to hold on to her two-person single career? You would think she'd have tenure after so many years of service. . . . Cher described ex-husband Sonny Bono this way: "He has a great respect for women, but . . . like [he thinks] a woman could be a great doctor, but when she goes home, she cannot bring being a doctor into her house. She must be just a woman, and the moment she becomes a woman, she must do what a man says. Walk three steps behind."*[33] *I don't understand how you can respect someone you go out of your way to keep subordinate. . . . In 1959 Louis Leakey was applauded for finding the "missing link," remnants of the oldest tool-making man to date, yet few of the news dispatches of the day noted that it was actually Mary Leakey and not her husband who had made the find.*[34] *Because wife and husband are one, and that one is the husband? . . . The wives of San Diego firemen were up in arms when the city decided to enlist female firefighters. Because the women would have to use the same dormitories and washrooms, one wife sneered, "With that kind of a set-up, you no longer will find the firemen whiling away the time between fire alarms over a game of checkers." I am disturbed by the notion that women and men who work together will naturally orgy together every opportunity they get, because it suggests the sexes have practically no impulse control and that wives live in daily dread of their husbands leaving them for someone else. One fireman's wife who admits that if you can't trust your husband you're in pretty bad shape comforts herself this way: "I don't think the women who make it through the academy will be all that great to look at."*[35] *Why is it we assume that the career-minded woman will be ugly as sin?*

A nurse-friend's father used to tease her and her mother by regularly saying, "A hard day's work would kill you. I hope you thank God for me every day." My friend bridled at the suggestion that she never did any work equal to that of a man, yet what upset her most was the effect her father's words had on her mother. She could see her mother swallowing the line that she wouldn't be able to handle the pressures of the "real" world should she choose to stop being a full-time housewife. . . . When a woman is reminded she's better off waiting on her own table than being a waitress in a restaurant, the advice seems very persuasive. Yet if you think about it, it's the jobs that are extensions of housework which often look the most unappealing. That shouldn't be too surprising; the waitress and the wife both work for tips. . . . Not too long ago, I eavesdropped in a restaurant on a conversation two middle-aged couples were having about the country club they belonged to. One of the men was arguing that women shouldn't clutter up the golf course on weekends because that's when men are free to use it, while women can play anytime they want during the week. His wife countered by saying she wasn't that free during the week and she was a member, so she should be able to use it anytime; after all, half of the family's dues represented her contribution to the club. The man turned blustery red and took credit for picking up the tab on everything. She protested that by providing him with a support system which enabled him to be the wage earner, she was entitled to count half his salary as her own: "We're partners, aren't we?" "Partners, yes, but I make the money; you don't," he replied. Both she and the other woman sat smoldering for the remainder of their dinner. I had visions of them urging all their friends to play golf only on weekends.

I think it's best for children not to grow up expecting the mother always to be available, because it's such a shock to them when she does go back to work. Children whose mothers have always worked some portion of the time assume that such maternal behavior is natural—even if others don't. . . . A friend's babysitter called her at the office to tell her that her son was in the hospital because he had fallen and broken his leg. She rushed there and was greeted *by an older nurse who suggested that the accident wouldn't have happened if she had been home with her son where she belonged. Imagine how miserable she felt. It was only after all the excitement was over that she was able to remind herself that she wasn't God and, if she had been home, her son could just as easily have fallen while she was taking two minutes to go to the bathroom. Why did the nurse have to hit her over the head with guilt? Because she was jealous of my friend for choosing to combine a job with having a family? . . . A male personnel director advises housewives looking for jobs: "Don't puff up being a housewife into 'household manager.' Don't try to sell me on the fact that, since you've supervised a husband and three kids, or have balanced a checkbook, you can be a manager. Everybody knows what a housewife does—not much."* [36] *Does everyone know what a housewife does? More important, does everyone know how a housewife feels? . . . Traditionally, women are not directly paid for their most indispensable work, rearing children and keeping house, so their work is seen as either valueless or priceless depending upon the good will of their husbands. Even if women become legally entitled to a set portion of the man's salary, as many are advocating, I am unhappy with the fact that dependence on the man's salary will remain the norm. . . . If you quit your job to stay home until the children are in school, chances are you will be scared about returning to work because you'll imagine your skills are too rusty to be reclaimed. In fact, that may be true, given the speed with which things change. Many of my friends quit work to have a baby because they were frustrated with their jobs, but I don't think they realized that if you work only a couple of years you never have the opportunity to get past those inevitably green first years to gain confidence in your abilities. I feel sad because they don't even know what they're missing.*

There was a time, soon after I confronted the fact that being a wife-mother-homemaker needn't mean retirement from the marketplace, when I felt super-ambitious. Once I didn't have to be just a woman, I wanted to be more than a man. Ideas rattled in my head; I talked an awful lot about what I wanted to do. My husband listened to my harangues with a kindly smile. After a while, I lost interest in whether Newsweek *and* Time *would someday mention my death in their columns. In the mellowing, I became content to be* me. *Now I'm not without a need for recognition, but I'm not committed to SUCCESS (in capital letters).*

I've gone from working as a nurse's aide on the maternity floor during my high school years to working as a practical nurse, then as an R.N. and teacher. My interest in people's troubles led me to major in psychiatric nursing, then I became more interested in normal growth crises than in psychotic behavior. That turn prompted me to start working on a Ph.D. in developmental psychology so I could extend my research and study some of the mental health issues which caught my fancy as a nurse. I'm still a nurse, sometimes a writer, and soon to be a psychologist. When I was a little girl, I thought you grew up to be only one thing; you signed your name on the dotted line and everything fell forever into place. Now I know nothing is decided once and for all. You can put new interests on top of old ones, change jobs, go back to school and become what educators call a "mature" student. Shifts don't come easy. It takes time to point yourself in a new direction; money is tight when you decide to go back to school and can't even deduct child-care expenses on your (1974) income tax return. But at thirty-four, I'm not past my prime the way Freud thought a thirty-year-old woman inevitably was. I'm just approaching my prime.

There is a lot to this subject of work in addition to the special dilemma a married feminist may confront. Women are now having to face the decision that has tormented many a male: Should one be committed to having a career or settle for having a job? For the remainder of this chapter, however, I'm going to leave the general advantages and disadvantages of having a job and focus on an aspect that dominated my diary-like reflections, the dilemma of the woman in a so-called woman's profession—specifically the conflicts a nurse feels, because she is the worker most torn between the traditional and the feminist.

Nursing is the oldest, most honorable female profession, and it is saddled with just about all the problems that women see in themselves as their consciousnesses are raised. First of all, nursing, like women in general, has been deprived of its own history. Physicians claim Hippocrates as the founder of medicine and nurses name Florence Nightingale as the mother of nursing, yet more than two thousand years separate the two and nursing was very much alive during those centuries and even before. Even those who underscore the fact that Ms. Nightingale was the founder of *modern* nursing leave the erroneous impression that the profession floundered in the Dark Ages before she lit her lamp. During those centuries women were the traditional healers because they were the ones familiar with dietary prescriptions, herbal preparations, and poultices. But instead of being praised for their healing abilities, many were burned at the stake for being "witches."

The fact that women could heal was considered proof that they were privy to the devil's secrets. Yet the remedies they used included many things we now regard as miracles of modern medicine: ergot to hasten labor, belladonna as an anti-spasmodic, digitalis for heart ailments. Hundreds of years of witch-hunting have been underplayed by historians. That period has usually been dismissed as one of mass hysteria which "rational man" is far beyond, and it has not been taken seriously the way the systematic extermination of a group of men would have been. There remains more of an inclination to describe the women as neurotics or psychotics rather than their inquisitors. Evidence exists that the suppression of women health workers was to make possible a takeover by male professionals. How could a witch be recognized in the Inquisitor's rulebook *Malleus Maleficarium* [*Hammer of Witches*] of 1484? The answer was, by the judgment of doctors. Since no women were allowed in the institutions which educated physicians, "no woman could ever judge another woman, and no claim of proper education from a woman healer could be made."[37] The two other "crimes" witches were accused of included "being organized" and making men feel lust—that is, they were denounced for female sexuality.[38]

Women complain that they are treated as sexual objects, and you only have to glance at your local movie marquee advertising some X-rated film about swinging nurses to appreciate how often nurses are portrayed that way (Linda Lovelace is the most famous example). Few nursing students escape being teased about Florence Nightingale dying of syphilis; it's a rumor which has been around for years.[39] Apparently it's titillating to imagine that lust lurks deep in the purest heart and that syphilis might be an occupational hazard—and not just because you can get the spirochete by treating an infected wound. Nurses in fiction always seem to be more interested in romance than in their profession.[40] Tracy Crandall, heroine of *Nurse on Vacation,* is typical of the genre: "If anything, her training had been the best in the world for her to become the understanding wife of a young doctor."[41] Nurses are seen as either cruder than the average woman or starchy pure (Eve or Mary once again). What other profession has a pledge in which its members promise "to pass my life in purity"?! (That's the opening statement of the Florence Nightingale Pledge, formulated in 1893. Interestingly, doctors take the Hippocratic *Oath,* but nurses only make a *pledge*—because they're considered to be less serious?)

Throughout this section I describe the nurse as she and the doctor as he only to make my points, but both professions need to discard their sexism if health care is to be improved. While 70 percent of all health workers in the United States are women (most are ancillary workers; few are in policy-making positions), about 93 percent of the physicians are men.[42] About 97 percent of all professional nurses are female.[43] Women in medicine are discriminated against, but so also are women in nursing. The median salary for registered nurses is $5,603 for women and $7,013 for men; women make 80 percent of what men make with the same education. Also, a disproportionately high percentage of men (45.7 percent) are in administration.[44]

Physicians have managed to make medicine synonymous with health care, but it's only one aspect of health care; nursing is another (social work, physical therapy, dietetics, pharmacy are others). Men are assigned the instrumental role in a family, and women the expressive role. Such role divisions have become institutionalized in doctor-nurse relationships, which define the physician as the agent of *change* and the nurse as the compassionate keeper of the status quo who comforts and supports. The doctor diagnoses and prescribes; the nurse carries out the treatment. So much of what a professional nurse does is dismissed as housekeeping, yet a coordinated, smoothly running organization entails tremendous skill. The nurse's self-initiated therapeutic efforts are regularly minimized, but there is a full array of comfort measures, dietary changes, and health tips that the nurse employs without having to ask the doctor's permission. They're overlooked because so much of what she does seems like "common sense"; people forget that what looks effortless might have taken years to perfect.

What nurses do is often overlooked because their efforts are seen as instinctive. A nursing historian once said, "Woman is an instinctive nurse, taught by Mother Nature,"[45] and many still believe that's true. The nurse is frequently described in textbooks as a mother-surrogate and is admonished that "this subrole requires unconditional acceptance of the person; just as the mother loves her infant because he is hers, and for no other reason, so the nurse accepts the patient because he is a human person with inherent worth and dignity."[46] The clinker, of course, is that no human being is capable of unconditional acceptance. Whatever value "creative mothering" may have as a description of what nurses actually do gets lost in the emotional, grandiose fantasies that professionals and laymen alike have about motherhood.[47] The nurse-patient relationship isn't based on kinship, and the sentimental reference to mother obfuscates more than it illuminates.

Good nursing like good doctoring has something in common

with good parenting, but professionals shouldn't expect an emotional payoff for their services the way mothers do; their effectiveness is better measured in terms of a remission of symptoms than in a patient's undying gratitude or a big box of chocolates. But as Germaine Greer makes clear in this passage from *The Female Eunuch*, it has been a long-standing practice to convince nurses that an emotional reward is better than a monetary one:

> The public relations experts seek to attract girls to nursing by calling it the most rewarding job in the world, and yet it is the hardest and the worst paid. The satisfaction comes in the sensation of doing good. Not only will nurses feel good because they are relieving pain, but also because they are taking little reward for it; therefore they are permanent emotional creditors. Any patient in a public hospital can tell you what this exploitation of feminine masochism means in real terms. Anybody who has tossed all night in pain rather than ring the overworked and reproachful night nurse can tell you.[48]

Nurses shy away from demanding adequate remuneration because they wonder if it's "fair" to set a price on what's seen as "instinctive," and because so many of them were educated in schools of nursing where the focus was on charity, not unionization.

The public calls an individual a nurse no matter whether that person has had only a six-week nurse's-aide course, one year of practical nursing education, two years in an associate-degree program, three years in a hospital school of nursing, four or five years in a baccalaureate program, two years of postgraduate specialization, or even a Ph.D. There are all different kinds of nurses educated to do different things (including research, administration, education, writing), yet the term has a leveling effect. Women are dismissed as "just a woman," and nurses experience the same thing: "She's just a nurse." Nurses who make a big impact on a particular health-care system are always discounted as "exceptional." And if you get an advanced degree and use it to work in any position but that of a staff nurse giving bedside care, you're immediately accused of not *really* being a nurse, just as the woman who challenges stereotype is described as unfeminine, no longer a *real* woman. Nursing is a complex and demanding profession, yet what nurse has not heard the comment: "I don't know how you do it. I could never be a nurse; I can't stand bedpans." Characterizing nursing that way reduces all those in the profession to the lowest common denominator: emptiers of bedpans. Many men distance themselves from child care by saying, "You'll never get me to change the baby's diapers," and the same thing happens in nursing. The underlying message is that nursing must be shit work, and anyone in it must be a trifle tainted.

Having painted a rather grim portrait of nursing, do I intend to wallow in my unhappiness, bitterly complaining about the injustices, and become a misanthrope? Do I recommend that all females avoid nursing until the situation improves, as many in the women's movement are advising women to put off motherhood? No, I don't. My outlook is surprisingly affirmative. I think the feminist nurse can feel self-satisfied and self-confident and can put nursing back into proper perspective if she publicly acknowledges she intends to follow the example of Florence Nightingale.

Ms. Nightingale's popular image is that of a saint with a lamp in hand, but that serene countenance belies the fierce reformer beneath. Her lobbying, fund raising, writing, organizing, observational skills, and promotional work were unstinting; she devoured the reports of medical commissions; there was hardly a great hospital or a slum in Europe with which she was not acquainted as she prepared herself for her work. She was the superintendent of a charitable nursing home in London before the Crimean War broke out. Once in Scutari, she reorganized the army medical system, started a laundry, took over the kitchen, financed supplies, improved ventilation, and even helped the soldiers save money to send home. She wheedled and threatened, demanded and cajoled. Because of her efforts, the mortality rate fell from 42 percent to

2.2 percent, and she made political capital of these statistics.

No gentle vision of female virtue, Florence Nightingale was a threat to the smug, conservative medical establishment of her day and had her share of government critics. Her *Notes Affecting the Health, Efficiency and Hospital Administration of the British Army* filled eight hundred pages and remained for years the definitive statement on the medical administration of armies. Her 1859 *Notes on Hospitals* revolutionized the theory of hospital construction and hospital management. She founded the first school of nursing in 1860, which put nursing on a professional basis. Ms. Nightingale didn't know "her place"; she made her place wherever she was needed. I find it interesting that Prince Albert met her and was impressed with her modesty, but Queen Victoria exclaimed, "Such a *head!* I wish we had her at the War Office."[49] *This* is the historical Florence Nightingale, not the "lady with the lamp."

When I was a student, one of the books we used for a class on professional nursing asked, "Should controversial political and social issues be discussed by students in nursing schools?"[50] Now all women are realizing that they not only have to participate in important debates, but they have to go beyond talking to doing. One-third of all working women are clustered in only seven jobs: secretary, retail-sales clerk, household worker, elementary-school teacher, bookkeeper, waitress, and nurse. (In fact, 78 percent of all working women, as opposed to 40 percent of the men, are employed as clerical workers, service workers, factory workers, and sales clerks.)[51] Maintenance and child care are essential endeavors in any society, but women can neither be given sole responsibility for them, nor have their truly creative efforts disparaged as glorified housekeeping. Women are demanding entrance to those male-dominated jobs and professions which traditionally effect change, but they are also demanding that those in the predominantly female jobs and professions be likewise recognized as important agents of change. However, decision-making and financial advantage won't be shared by the sexes in work outside the home until they are shared within the home.

9

COLLISION COURSE OR . . .

*The trick is to be independent without being so
all-fired angry and hostile about it. The fact that
you are beholden to no one doesn't license you to
put others down.*

Jessie Bernard
The Future of Marriage
(1972)

Part of me wants to end this book by saying the women's movement is on a collision course with established conventions. And maybe those of us who feel personally torn between the traditional and the feminist are on one too, because the opposing ideologies could easily rip us apart. The rage that so often accompanies a raised consciousness can be destructive, even lethal if allowed to consume all your energies. That's what I think on my bad days—days when I am angry, feel misunderstood, confused, duped and alone. But those days aren't every day, and I'm more and more excited by what the ". . ." portion of this chapter's title might mean. Filling in that blank isn't going to be easy, but resolution never is when conflict is so strong.

Before considering the possibility of solutions to the dilemmas facing a married feminist, let's look more closely at the anger that is an integral aspect of consciousness raising. That emotion has tortuously threaded its way through this book and is a prominent feature of the women's movement. On the whole, I have considerable respect for anger. Anger has important diagnostic value, because it shows you where you're hurting. It's healthier than being depressed, because your feelings aren't crushingly turned inward but are aimed at the external forces responsible for your unhappiness. Underdog groups particularly, such as women, have been told for centuries that the expression of anger was unacceptable; obviously, an angry word has the force of a defiant declaration of independence. Anger feels good because it has a cathartic effect; it washes the system of poisonous rage and can leave you with a pleasant, spent feeling. That is, it can feel good for a while, as long as the anger doesn't backfire and rain down on your head too many reactions that will leave you feeling angrier than before. Anger does make you feel perversely noble, especially when you can label your anger "just." But it's possible, I think, to become an anger "junkie," to become hooked on indignation.

There are days when I find myself listening to people's opinions and reading only with a view to what I can get angry about. I've developed an uncanny ability to spot a putdown one hundred paces away. I find myself going over and over passages such as this one of Theodor Reik's:

> Do women really believe that men woo them because they are intellectually brilliant? I should think that such an attitude on the part of the male would be highly offensive to women, because it would be possible only at the cost of the man's admiration for the woman's loveliness or beauty. Fortunately, no woman believes, deep within her, that a man is much impressed by her brilliant intellect. She attributes no more value to it than as an accessory to a beautiful dress. I refer, of course, to a woman in her right mind; but when is a woman in her right mind?[1]

I keep wanting to rebut him point by point as if I could erase sexism with logic or woman's vulnerability by unmasking his tactics: notice how cleverly he implies intelligence will cost a woman a man's admiration, how he tries to convince her that what a man finds offensive she will too, how he uses the exaggeration "intellectually brilliant" to make a mockery of average intelligence, how he uses the phrase "deep within her" to buttress his argument with an appeal to instincts, how he cloaks his degradation of women in a romantic flurry of compliments. He waves the red flag and I keep charging. I fume and sputter and rant and rave. I am the bull in the china shop wanting to smash his porcelain put-downs to smithereens. Sometimes it's just about impossible to curb the anger; it's all over the place. It's as if one of the barbs was lodged inside me—always pressing, infecting my entire system with its poison, making me mad.

I know I'm sometimes too feisty for my own good. And I even have come secretly to suspect that I relish the combativeness for its own sake and may not want my antagonists to disappear. Why? I think it has something to do with the fact that I still don't quite know what will follow when all the anger is dissipated, and I dread some sort of final emptiness. The anger is indisputably valid, but what I do after all the male chauvinists recant is open to question. The ebb and flow of anger seems more real than the personal decision-making, political platforms, and social restructuring toward which they lead. To the extent that I am addicted to feeling angry, it's also because I just can't get over the fact that the public, and even more so, trained professionals, didn't protest all those millions of bigoted remarks the moment they were uttered. Deep inside, I know I should strive to reach the point where I can just laugh at a man who dismisses female brains as an accessory to a beautiful dress, because my anger gives his position a credence it doesn't deserve whereas titters and guffaws would reduce him to a joke; but I'm not there yet.

I'm still angry at all those sexist scholars because I find it difficult to believe that they could be so wrong and I could be right (part of the "I'm only a woman" syndrome). I, who grew up with such a profound respect for authority, especially the written word, feel as if I've been "had," and that general feeling of having been taken advantage of seeps out of me even when there's no specific grievance. I think that accounts for why this book has been rather heavy on academic references, perhaps more than were needed to make a particular point. I still can't believe that women have been held in so little regard, and I keep having to quote chapter and verse to remind myself that whatever feelings of persecution I have are real, not just in *my* mind. Reik's goad—"When is a woman in her right mind?"—may gall me, but I have been scarred by those sentiments enough to distrust my own perceptions. And that, of course, makes me even angrier.

But the anger isn't constant. No one's life stands still. I heard a wise person once say, "You can blame your parents for all your problems for the first twenty-five years, but after that you're a bore if you don't recognize that you make your own life," and that perspective makes sense to me. I don't dispute the fact that it's hard to shake what you have been conditioned to believe and feel in your formative years, but that view is essentially too pessimistic for my tastes. I prefer to think that if you can start seeing new options in your life, you can seize those options. Many women structure their lives a certain way because "he wouldn't like it if I did that," but they never even test their assumptions to see if they're accurate. If a woman believes in what she wants and acts decisively to get it, many more things are possible than she might have first imagined to be the case. (Of course, self-confidence isn't easy to come by.) Feeling anger at the "authorities," past precedent, or missed opportunities serves a very real purpose in distancing yourself from those points of view that are oppressive, but after a while you realize that your present had better start being directed by your future and not your past. And the anger starts to recede when you can really imagine a future where you are your own person and can choose what you want to retain of the belief system you grew up with and what you want to reject. And that's the richest legacy of feminism—realizing that you do have choices. No one's life falls into a ready-made mold, but not everyone perceives that she or he has alternatives, and it's those people who are slaves to stereotypes that don't conform to real human needs.

Yet even if women can see more options in their lives, isn't the feminist still on a collision course because she wants access to the privileges men have traditionally enjoyed but also wants to retain some of those qualities that have been viewed as typically feminine? Won't the embracing of masculine strengths mean a repudiation of the feminine? Won't a glorification of female talents mean being submerged in femaleness more than ever before? I think the answer to these questions is to separate what happens to individuals from what is now happening to Western culture. In the long run, there's no collision course, because our society is going through a period of productive social change from which will emerge new notions of justice, maturity, cooperation, and personal responsibility. But since we are all trapped in our own piece of time—daughter, mother, and grandmother see events from different perspectives—many of us are feeling confused and threatened as we live through this reformation.

In the remainder of this chapter I'll sketch out what I consider to be the perceptions most likely to shape our lives in the years ahead; they include the move away from thinking in terms of dualities to a dialectical approach to concepts, the need for more role models, and the ascendance of a psychology which emphasizes full maturity rather than sexual identity. This list doesn't have the pragmatic appeal that a specific forty-point program for legal reform would have, but I think the changes I'm about to discuss will lead to alterations in all segments of society.

Moving away from dualities to a dialectical approach to concepts: What does that mouthful mean? Dualism means thinking of everything in terms of the number two, as if all knowledge could be reduced to two opposite principles—good/bad, right/wrong, body/soul, mind/heart, love/hate, light/dark, pain/pleasure, attractive/unattractive, and so forth. A dialectical approach, on the other hand, implies thinking in terms of the number three, as if all knowledge were shaped by a process of thesis-antithesis-synthesis, a coming together of attitudinal opposites as against the fixed polarities of dualism. For example, the duality independent/dependent is conceived of as opposite ends of a continuum having

having a positive (valued) pole and a negative (less valued or unvalued) pole; a dialectical view is more interested in points along the continuum—how independence is mediated by dependence and vice versa—than in the extremes (which rarely exist in pure form in real life). From what I have said so far, it should be obvious that the feminist would be opposed to thought processes that emphasize dualities because women so often find themselves on the unflattering side of any two principles. Thinking in terms of opposites generally means woman will automatically be described as the opposite of man. Dialectics is more appealing be cause it avoids the rigid point/counterpoint analysis and attempts to look at reality in a less fragmentary manner.

It is not surprising that early women and men thought in terms of dualities, because the simplest way of figuring out who you are or what the world is like is to say, "I am this and not that; this thing and that thing are different from each other in this way." Human beings began to understand themselves by noting that they were different from animals, that night and day seemed the opposite of each other, that men had penises and women didn't, that women were subject to cycles of bloody discharge and men weren't. In a hostile world ruled by seemingly uncontrollable forces, there was a tendency for opposites to be seen as either good or evil. It was comforting to think that if you could identify an evil, you could then exercise some control over it.

Needless to say, women didn't fare very well in this sort of world because they lacked the brute strength that was essential to combat the all-pervasive hostile forces. Women also oozed blood regularly, a substance associated with injury and death rather than life. Masculine strength further ensured that man would name the positive qualities in terms of those he himself had; woman was, thereby, stuck with being his opposite.[2] Tradition institutionalized different sexual traits, which in turn became self-fulfilling prophecy because all social systems are based on precedent and resistant to change. From primitive to modern times, there was little substantial variation in sexual roles because uncontrolled fertility was a fact of life, periodically immobilizing the majority of women. It wasn't until the twentieth century that the average person understood menstruation and conception and could think of woman without the labels "cursed" or "under the evil eye."

I'm convinced that historians a thousand years from now will regard the invention of effective contraceptives as a watershed in social mores because they have quite literally made women independent. (Keep in mind that as recently as 1970 only 20 percent of couples reported that they had completely planned the number and timing of their children.)[3] But contraceptives don't mean being only mechanically free; their development would not have been possible if our fundamental thinking about reproduction hadn't changed to the point where it could be thought of as susceptible to rational control. Once reproduction was conceptualized that way, women were freed from the bondage inherent in their being seen as repositories of dark mysteries.

The knowledge explosion of the last century has made dualistic thinking outdated. The more we know, the more it's difficult to think in terms of absolute good and bad, right and wrong. What looks good on the surface may not be deemed beneficial under scrutiny; what seems wrong at first glance may seem valuable once certain prejudices evaporate. More and more, we are realizing that every idea contains the seeds of its own destruction, and that the intelligent person should look at every obvious good in terms of how it can affect something else adversely. This consideration is likely to lead to a conclusion different from both the first positive assessment and the later negative one. For example, the enthusiasm of the fifties for as many gadgets as one could afford has led to a second look in the seventies emphasizing the dangers of wasting energy resources, and we can reasonably expect a more enlightened use of oil and coal reserves in the future. The exodus to the suburbs has brought home the truth that you can't run forever from urban problems, and perhaps this recognition will lead to something more wholesome than an escapist mentality.

The traditional views of woman-man relations are being assaulted by feminist demands and will, I hope, eventually lead to a new blending of both positions which will be better than either one by itself.

After being torn by all the pulls a married feminist feels, my answer is that such a person, who tries to extract the best from traditional values and the best from feminist analysis, isn't a walking contradiction (though she may feel that way at times); but she should be a walking dialectician. Such a view presupposes that history is always moving ahead to a brave new world—even though it can look like it's standing still when viewed from any particular individual's vantage point; it means holding fast to old values such as justice and love, but steadily shaping them so that they meet the demands of new pressures. This dialectical view of history is different from the Greek belief that there's a cyclic pattern to ideas or from the notion of history as some sort of linear progression. The analogy that best illustrates the dialectical process is not the pendulum with its swings from extreme to extreme, but the spiral which moves from side to side in *connected* but always *original* turns. For example, the machismo philosophy was suited to an era in which fertility was of indisputable value to society; that sort of thinking is now being assaulted by those who fear for the planet's ecology and are acutely aware of how dangerous the population explosion is to the very family life traditionalists esteem. Those who count their blessings in terms of offspring are being challenged to stop defining productiveness mathematically and think instead of the quality of life.

Since social currents are in a constant state of flux, large trends are difficult to see when you're actually living through them. The ecologists may appear to be anti-life and the machismo types may appear indifferent to the quality of life, but they are each influencing the other and pushing the overall climate of opinion away from either extreme toward an entirely new perception of what it means to be alive. This view of development doesn't presuppose a specific end point, but a necessary movement involving the coming together of different concepts in a continual struggle for a higher unity in the name of comprehensiveness.[4]

I think the dialectical view has considerable explanatory value. It's a way of explaining how the traditional view of woman as wife and mother together with the feminist view advocating career and independence for women will propel us all, women and men, toward a healthier balance between love and work. It's this needed realignment that is more important than either of the previous positions. The same thing holds true for every other aspect of a woman's life we have considered in this book: those who glorified a woman's cooking are being challenged by those who see how that activity kept women away from sports; as a result, both activities will assume a more equitable position in the lives of generations to come. Those who extolled a woman's beauty and softness need to be challenged by those who applaud her brains and steely hardness, but both positions will someday be seen only as steps along the way to becoming a whole person.

A dialectical view of change also explains something about one's personal history. Ideas are altered by a process of thesis-antithesis-synthesis, and the three generations in a family go through something similar. Your parents reacted against what they saw as their parents' foibles, just as you react against some of the values of your parents which strike you as dated. The reaction against your parents also means you're free to feel more sympathy for your grandparents' convictions than your own parents could. Every new generation is bound to synthesize the values of the previous two in a special new way, yet there's considerable continuity in the way it's done. Thought of this way, the resurgence of feminism in America two generations after the suffragettes accomplished their primary goal should come as no surprise. The intervening generation reacted to the militant posture of their parents' feminism by embracing family life and trusting that the advances in labor-saving appliances* and child-rearing theories would herald a grand era of truly creative home-making. They wanted the vote, yet also wanted to achieve the lady-of-the-manor dreams of their grandmothers. The result, as they say, is history: the children of this generation have reacted against such total immersion in domesticity and wondered why their grandparents didn't go further in their feminist demands. Voting, after all, is only a seasonal way of shaping your destiny.

And so it goes. My own children may think my generation went too far in a particular direction and may not even understand my brand of militancy, especially if many of the stereotypes I railed against have faded from view. They will evolve their own formulas for combining love and work, convinced—as they should be—that they're about to define the good life in a way their ancestors couldn't dream of doing. I am not saddened by the fact that "truth" seems so elusive, but appreciate with more warmth how the generations need each other to move ahead.

This analysis also helps me to understand some of the problem areas in today's feminism. For example, a number of women who have struggled to combine a family with having a well-paying job sometimes act as if they won't be happy until the traditional roles are actually reversed. But if I consider their behavior an expression of the inevitable conflicts a first generation feels when climbing up the ladder (and women *are* the last "minority" group to be assimilated into the economy), their quarrelsomeness, such as it is, doesn't strike me as proof positive that job and family can't be pleasantly combined or that women and men will endlessly keep

---

*Though I believe every action leads to some sort of reaction which in turn leads to yet another, many separate currents are shaping our lives at any one time. For example, the labor-saving appliances were touted as capable of transforming every wife into the fabled Victorian mistress with a galley full of silent servants because women who remembered their own relatives working as maids and scrubwomen found it an enormously appealing idea, but also because an expansionist economy needed to develop new products to create new markets to up the gross national product. A dialectical view of change has considerable explanatory value, but it can't explain everything because it's difficult even to name all the forces shaping a particular generation.

trying to subordinate each other. I can understand it as a phenomenon that will probably happen less frequently in other generations as we learn from experience how to combine work and love more successfully. Much of what is harsh about present-day feminism can be understood as an overreaction against years of being denied access to varied opportunities. Once our children get used to living in a world that welcomes women into every aspect of personal and public life, they will be able to concentrate their efforts on cooperation between the sexes, which my own generation finds difficult because few of us have had much experience in getting along with members of the opposite sex who are not family members. Besides, I suspect our children and grandchildren will be living in an era when "climbing the ladder" will generally be seen as less important than learning to live with limited natural resources.

My focus on the coming together of attitudinal opposites to effect a synthesis may sound like a fancy way of saying everyone should be middle of the road in her or his opinions, but that is definitely not what I am advocating. "Middle of the road" implies compromising merely for the sake of compromise and suggests staleness rather than vigor. When I talk about a dialectical approach, I have in mind working toward a position that actually goes *beyond* what your first opinions or first reactions were, not mediating them simply because moderation is always desirable. Compromise may be of value in political forums, but dynamic synthesis is what's important to personal growth.

I said earlier that the married feminist need not be a walking contradiction, but that is little comfort to someone who feels torn by inner conflict. Contradictions frustrate us because we have been schooled by our tranquilizer-popping society to assume that contradictions can and should be avoided and, moreover, that we can recognize when we are on the right track by feeling conflict-free. We're often so bent on ridding ourselves of conflicts that we forget how exciting they can be. While we may continue to hope for constant serenity and storybook contentment, it's important to realize we're asking for something that's humanly impossible. It's time we stopped associating contradictions with fuzzy thinking or bad logic and appreciate how necessary they are to growth. To be *alive* means to be open to apparent contradictions, to expand our horizon of expectations, not to be closed to experiences. Growth comes about when the person is comfortable saying, "I am this *and* that; I am sentimental *and* intellectual; I am like my mother *and* father; I am body *and* soul."

Psychology up until now has emphasized stability and closure more than discordance because of the traditional preference for focusing on neat developmental stages, but plateaus should be valued only as points on the way to new questions.[5] For example, you look forward to the time your children can go their own way, only to wonder how you and your spouse will handle being just a couple once again. It's quite possible to hold seemingly contradictory positions—for example, to want to be more like a man, yet not to give up being a woman—without their being mutually exclusive. Instead of assuming every contradiction has to be resolved by choosing one side over another, it seems much wiser to try to expand your world view to accommodate the best of both arguments. If you think this way, you don't automatically assume women should go into those professions embodying the traditional female virtues just so they won't feel any conflict between their personal view of self and their career *persona*. In fact, no matter what road you chose, you would be drawn to trying to combine in your own unique way the best of what is considered feminine and the best of what is considered masculine. The notion of combining a number of positive qualities in one person leads us to a consideration of archetype.

I approach a discussion of archetype with considerable ambivalence. I am wary because archetype easily degenerates into stereotype, yet I'm not prepared to abandon archetype completely as an important concept. "Archetype" means prototype or the original model after which a thing is made, and the concept is most often associated with Jungian psychology, where it is defined as an unconscious image or pattern of thought inherited from the ancestors of the race and present in every person's psyche. To Jung, there are inescapable sexual differences which cannot be denied; if they were, they would prevent a person from achieving any identity at all. What's more, Jung argues that the psyche can be described in terms of a series of polarities (conscious/unconscious, active/passive, etc.) which can be identified with the basic polarity of masculine/feminine. Growth is an ongoing struggle to overcome these oppositions; the self is constructed out of a series of successive reconciliations between the feminine and masculine poles. He sees the feminine as an *original* psychic mode of being, which he describes as eros (or psychic relatedness), and postulates that this feminine principle is most clearly seen in contrast to logos (or objective interest), the masculine principle. Jungians maintain that the feminine modality of being is encompassed in these four fundamental archetypes: the Mother, the Hetaira, the Amazon, and the Medium or "wise woman."[6] No person is ever a complete archetype, nor would one want to be.

There is much in Jung that appeals to someone with a taste for both the traditional and the feminist: namely, the notions that the feminine modality of being is not derivative but fundamental, and that personal completeness can only be achieved by a reconciliation of the feminine and the masculine modalities within oneself. Unlike rival psychologies, the Jungian concept of feminine archetypes sees woman in manifold aspects, not just as the gestating, nourishing (or possessive and overprotective) Mother. The outgoing aspect of the feminine is manifested in the Amazon ("mother's daughter"), who is self-contained, independent, and relates to men as an equal; the Medium signifies a woman's wisdom and potential as a seer; and the Hetaira ("father's daughter") is described as awakening the subjective, psychic life in herself and others. These aspects of the feminine have been ignored or undervalued for too long. It's reassuring to know that there are a number of role models a woman can follow; her wholeness requires the fullest possible integration of all four modalities.

(One of the problems Jung's archetypes present to a feminist is their very names. Hetaira originally was the name given to the select group of cultivated women in ancient Greece who played the social role of the modern "woman of the world." They were artistic and intelligent, they controlled their own wealth, and some were known to share the glory of their lovers. Demosthenes said, "We have hetairas for the pleasures of the spirit," but he also added that concubines existed for sensual pleasures and wives to produce sons.[7] By naming a feminine archetype after an elite, unusual group of women who lived in dramatic contrast to the average woman, the type is hopelessly mired in past cultural prejudices and the subliminal message conveyed is that relatively few women are of this type. Similarly, the self-contained Amazon is limited in its meaning by the Greek legend of a race of female warriors who were able to develop their independence only by living apart from men, and Medium conjures up images of B-movie spiritualists who con widows out of fortunes more than it suggests an honored sage. Archetypes may represent some essential element of human experience, but those who presume to talk about "pure" symbols are deluding themselves if they think their choice of what to focus on is free of hackneyed conventions.)

While appreciating much of Jungian analysis, I am uncomfortable with the description of the psyche in terms of sex-matched polarities. There is no *original* position from which all females proceed. We cannot assume that every female's being will automatically be determined by feelings and relationships rather than spirit and ideas. It makes more sense to treat opposites such as conscious/unconscious or passive/active as polarities all individuals have to struggle with, not tagging one side as feminine, the other as masculine. And it is this struggle that is more important than the qualities.

Jungian Ann Belford Ulanov offers women a very positive self-image when she describes the wisdom of the heart that is the highest expression of the feminine modality of being:

Feminine wisdom is bound to the earth, to organic and psychological growth, to living reality. It issues from one's instincts, from
one's unconscious, from one's history and relationships. It is nonspeculative wisdom without illusions, and it is not idealistic in its
approach to reality but prefers what actually is to what should or
might be. Feminine wisdom nourishes, supports, and develops the
strongest possible ties to reality. It is the wisdom of feeling and
compassion, coordinated to the qualitative moment and the specific instance rather than to an unrelated code of law. Feminine
wisdom is personal, never impersonal. It always evolves out of
relationship to an "other," whether it is the other of unconscious
processes, or numinous contents, or another human being. . . .
Such wisdom brings ecstasy and illumination rather than knowledge.[8]

I assume she wouldn't exclude men from having a share of "feminine wisdom" and would say that the man in touch with his
feminine unconscious (his *anima*) would work toward developing
this brand of nonspeculative wisdom too, but there's something
about defining these attitudes and qualities as feminine that reinforces sexist stereotype more than it endows woman with the
powerful energy of feminine archetype. Such a glowing portrait
of feminine wisdom makes me uneasy because it isn't much
appreciated in the social order of today, even while I'm feeling
grateful for the complimentary description. This same author is
bothered enough by the implication that woman is the feeling
type to caution, "Women have no more monopoly of the feeling
function than men have of the thinking function,"[9] but her
emphasis on women striving for ecstasy rather than knowledge is
an anti-intellectual position.

Branding one group of qualities feminine and another masculine—even if you're separating them only to make the point that
they need to be integrated—reinforces the notion that each sex
lacks certain qualities to begin with just because it was born with
one kind of genitals and not the other. I am never sure when I
contemplate such a point of view whether I should rejoice because

it encourages a woman to get in contact with her own unconscious masculine side (her *animus*) and not stay immersed in traditional femaleness, or whether I should be angry because anything that smacks of cold reason or objectivity will still be labeled basically masculine if it appears in a female. I also feel dismay over the fact that the feminine principle is named after Eros, the *male* god of love. So while I welcome the positive feminine archetypes Jungians acknowledge, I feel the system is sadly weakened by the fact that the mythology which it values so highly apparently didn't have a female god to embody the feminine principle. Perhaps the unconscious desire to keep women in chains as sex objects made Jung blind to prudent Athena, Greek goddess of wisdom?

Women understandably rebel against feminine prototypes that epitomize attitudes for which they themselves feel no sympathy (for example, the notion that woman does everything for the love of a man), yet all of us need models after which we can pattern our lives. As a feminist, I may not like archetype; but humans still think in terms of types, and so long as that is true, we need to have as many models as possible. We needn't look to the distant past or assume that Greek and Roman mythology said it all. We're inheriting new images and acquiring venerable ancestors all the time. Elizabeth I, Sojourner Truth, Florence Nightingale, Marie Curie, Helena Rubinstein, Ruth Benedict, Gertrude Stein, Karen Horney, Eleanor Roosevelt, Helen Keller, Barbara Walters, Indira Gandhi, Agatha Christie, Simone de Beauvoir, Shirley Chisholm, Gloria Steinem, Katherine Graham, Roberta Flack, Melina Mercouri, Barbara Jordan, Ella Grasso, Lillian Hellman, Beverly Sills, Maya Angelou, Anita Loos, Billie Jean King, Patsy Mink, and Jane Goodall considered as types offer me more feminine variety than Aphrodite or Circe or Oedipus' mother ever will. They represent so many different types that they defy the description "typical."

Beyond postulating four major archetypes that women should somehow integrate into their person, we need prototypes that represent all sorts of combinations of thinking, feeling, and doing.

Such rich and complex examples are genuine role models, not cardboard figures you wouldn't want to meet, much less emulate. I look forward to a time when a woman can choose a particular occupation or life style and not have it said, "She's not the type." There should be a "type" for every personality and talent combination. And once there's a glut of types, archetype will cease to make much sense and stereotype should disappear, because it's impossible to press everyone into one mold if there's a wide range of approved life styles.

The discussion of archetype has skirted the issue of whether psychology should emphasize full maturity or sexual identity as the primary developmental goal of the person. Since Freud, sexual identity has received much more attention than the definition of maturity. (It should be remembered that Freud emphasized sexual identity, in part, because he was reacting against the fact that it was a taboo subject to his generation.) This emphasis is all too evident when you pick up a psychiatry or psychology text purportedly on the life cycle only to find that 90 percent of the book is spent on the period from birth to puberty. The reason for this concentration on the early years is that the road to maturity has been defined in terms of sexual directives which the individual has substantially absorbed by the end of adolescence. The sexually mature woman is supposedly someone who is comfortable with her body and her femaleness, has developed those traits that are appropriate for her sex, and looks forward to motherhood and being a wife with an open, warm, generous heart; the sexually mature man is supposedly someone who is comfortable with his body and his maleness, has developed those traits that are appropriate for his sex, and intends to pursue a money-making career with enthusiasm and eventually take on the responsibilities of family life. Genital maturity has been confused with psychic maturity.

As further proof of the importance sexual identity has received in academic circles, consider the attention given to the Oedipal period (age three to six), regarded as the most crucial developmental period in a person's life because it is a time of tremendous sexual curiosity characterized by an attraction for the parent of the opposite sex and eventual identification with the parent of the same sex. Freud believed that an individual is determined by how she or he comes out of this period. He held that females were overwhelmed during this time with their lack of a phallus (*de facto* castration), which meant that their superego development would forevermore be faulty because it could never be as impersonal or independent of its emotional origins as a man's: "For women the level of what is ethically normal is different from what it is in men."[10] In other words, only the concept of a healthy, mature man could define a healthy, mature adult. The concept of a healthy, mature woman must take into account her lack of a penis; she is incomplete.

The surging feminist consciousness was naturally enraged at Freud's theory. We are realizing more and more that making an issue of the alleged fact that all women are castrated (therefore automatically inadequate) has the effect of actually castrating their psyches. And it is this mutilation that accounts for low self-esteem, not genital differences. Still, we are stuck with the basic question of how sexual identity relates to maturity. Are all the differences between the sexes culturally determined, or does anatomy shape destiny in certain ways? My own inclination is to say that biology certainly shapes an individual's feelings, thoughts, and actions (I've considered some of the ways in Chapter 3), but it is a mistake to treat full femaleness or full maleness (that is, successful resolution of whether you are comfortable with your sex, can have a satisfying sex life with a partner of the opposite sex, and desire to have a child) as synonymous with full maturity. An individual has to answer certain of life's questions as a member of a specific sex, but sexual differences should not be an issue in nonsexual matters (career selection, religious preference, political persuasion, intellectual choices, etc.).

Even when feeling/thinking, body/mind, head/heart, strong/weak, passive/active, etc., distinctions do exist between the sexes, they're statistical differences, not universal ones. More men than women may be able to pick up a two-hundred-pound weight, but that doesn't mean that a large number of women can't lift it. The time has come for a more sophisticated view of differences. It isn't simply that men are strong and women weak, but that they're strong and weak in different ways. It's faulty logic to assume that noting one difference gives you license to generalize that difference to thousands of other situations. Men are active in an obvious way during intercourse; women are active in an obvious way when breastfeeding an infant. Which deserves the label "active"? Developmental psychologists should take a lesson from philosophers and start thinking of character and personality traits in terms of the question "with respect to what?" Before a person should be allowed to get away with saying women are emotional and men rational, she or he should be forced to specify those situations in which this rule applies and what the exceptions to the rule are. (For many years, the emphasis on sex differences led to the publication of only those research studies that found differences; now sophisticated researchers are becoming increasingly careful to point out when no differences are found.)[11]

As the similarities between the sexes are studied with new rigor, we no doubt will find that far fewer indisputable differences exist than we had previously expected. A case in point is the work on tomboyism of Janet Hyde and Benjamin Rosenberg of Bowling Green State University which was reported in the August 1974 *Psychology Today*. They surveyed college women, junior high school students, and women at a shopping mall and found that the majority in each group reported themselves to have been tomboys in childhood:

> Behavioral scientists, who are subject to the same biases as everyone else, have tended to assume that demure little girls represent the norm in female development. They have often viewed tomboys—little girls who wear jeans, climb trees, and love aggressive sports—as atypical, or even abnormal. At best, our culture has

treated tomboyism as something one eventually grows out of, like an allergy. . . . If self-reports reflect reality, rather than wishful thinking or the current sexual and political views of the respondents, then tomboyism may be much more common than previously supposed. Hyde and Rosenberg speculate that "tomboyism is not so much abnormal as it is *typical* for girls. The stereotype of the little girl sweetly staying indoors and embroidering while sitting at mother's knee, which behavioral scientists have tried so diligently to document, may well have to fall in favor of the empirical data. Motor activity and expressive acting out are characteristic of *children*, whether male or female."[12]

These findings wouldn't have surprised anyone familiar with the reading preferences of girls. Two of the favorite books of adolescent girls are Louisa May Alcott's *Little Women* and Jane Austen's *Pride and Prejudice*. There are a number of different female types in these books, but I have never known a girl who didn't identify with the intelligent and spunky heroines, Jo and Elizabeth, in contrast to their frivolous or saintly sisters. Jo March's words, "I'll try and be what he [father] loves to call me, 'a little woman,' and not be rough and wild; but do my duty here instead of wanting to be somewhere else,"[13] capture the pulls between social expectation and personal preference the majority of females have always felt. The Hyde and Rosenberg conclusion that motor activity and expressive acting out are characteristic of children in general, not determined by sexuality, certainly supports my own position that there exists a whole range of issues important to maturity—handling boredom, surviving failure, channeling aggressive impulses, developing intellectual curiosity, putting off the need for immediate gratification, coming to terms with the inevitability of death, etc.—which are largely unaffected by sexual identity.

Biology shapes behavior in the first two decades of life much more than it does thereafter. The toddler's character is affected by how easily she or he arrives at sphincter control; adolescence is defined in terms of puberty changes. Beyond genital maturity, however, sheer life experience and opportunity determine personality more than physical powers. For one thing, there is far greater variability in the chronological age at which a given developmental crisis (marriage, parenthood, career advancement and decline, retirement, widowhood, illness, etc.) arrives in later life than is true of the mastery issues of youth. Physique-based values give way to wisdom-based values in self-definition. As Robert C. Peck points out:

> If a person takes positive action at this point, redefining men and women as individuals and as companions, with the sexual element decreasingly significant, it would at least be understandable that interpersonal living *could* take on a depth of understanding which the earlier, perhaps inevitably more egocentric, sex-drive would have tended to prevent to some degree.[14]

Instead of the very narrow view expressed by Peter Blos—"puberty represents the demarcation line beyond which bisexual admixtures to gender identity become incompatible with progressive development"[15]—it seems increasingly obvious that the opposite happens. Progressive development becomes impossible if the boundary lines of sexual identity remain rigid in the last five or six decades of life. (Pushing for sexual differentiation is a masculine feature. Women are more observably bisexual than men because the "tomboy stage" in the girl has always been more socially acceptable than girlish behavior in a boy [mainly because dependence is rightfully seen as regressive conduct]. The boy is urged "Don't be like a girl," but his first five or six years have traditionally been spent in the company of women. This puts males in a double bind—they want to be boys *and* be like their role models—which they try to resolve by overreacting to any inclination toward gentleness in themselves and by feeling antagonistic to girls of their age. Part of the fear of women is a fear of psychological bisexuality, which up until now has erroneously been confused with homosexuality. If boys had more contact with male care-givers during their early years, some of these problems would disappear.) I'm inclined to agree with David Bakan: "The proper way of dying is from fatigue after a life of trying to mitigate agency with communion."[16] When communion is defined exclusively as a feminine trait and agency is urged only for men, the results are an unmitigated disaster.

I was asked not long ago to comment on a manuscript a psychiatrist and psychologist were putting together for use as a nursing text. In it, these two men said: "In the mid and late forties the major transition for women is the great change in occupational [*sic!*] role, from mother to mother-in-law." Needless to say, I saw red at the thought of these educated authors seriously believing that a woman's life could be summed up as going from daughter to wife to mother to mother-in-law to grandmother. In no way do I want to denigrate those relationships, but woman— any more than man—does not live by relationships alone. I don't think it's too much to ask that the qualities of the mature woman be synonymous with those of the mature adult, and that the developmental issues across the life cycle be freed of sexist claptrap.

I end this book the way I started it; I am still a woman full of contradictions. But the big difference between where I was and where I am now is that I understand them better. I'm comfortable with saying, "If I'm pulled in two different directions, they are not as contradictory as I once thought," and then trying to work them out over time. I no longer buy arguments that state "If you're not this, you must be that," because I know from personal experience that the choices are far greater than most of us realize. If you're not a liberal, that doesn't make you a conservative; if you're not a traditional man, that doesn't make you feminine. The pluralism in my own personality has, if anything, helped me appreciate all the more the pluralism in society at large.

A better world—that's what both sexes want and are afraid they won't get. Men understandably shy away from equality because it looks like inferiority if you're used to thinking of yourself as belonging to the first sex. Women worry that widespread economic depression might be met by a reactionary return to propagandizing about how "economical" and "stable" the traditional role divisions are. Parents see their daughters wanting new possibilities for themselves, but worry how they're going to manage if everyone else's sons still want to marry old-fashioned girls. But things have improved in so many ways. Men have become less scared of getting close to their children, and more readily admit that their wives are their best friends. Women don't resist getting old as they once did because they now appreciate that pursuing youthful beauty means looking backward; in job situations, it *pays* to be experienced. Couples find themselves busier than ever before—sharing everything from sex to laundry to work hours— and much less bored than they once were with each other.

The married feminist is alive and well, even if (s)he is experiencing some growing pains. As traditional ideals are modified by feminist concerns, more and more people will fit that description. What will they be like? They certainly won't all think the same way, but they will have in common an openness to change of the sort that takes the best of the old and the best of the new and tries to fashion a better world. The married feminist will be someone like my first-grade daughter. For several months she kept bringing notes home that were addressed to "Dear Mother." The papers included a request for cakes for a bake sale, lists of words the child should be encouraged to spell and read in sentences, and other bits of information the teacher wanted to communicate. I reacted to "Dear Mother" by getting angry at such blatant sexism and worrying about what my husband and I should do to correct the situation. We couldn't make up our minds just how to register a protest without being thought of as troublemakers. While we were weighing the pros and cons of writing a note to the teacher or arranging an informal chat, our daughter came home with another note which began "Dear Mother," but penciled in were the words "and Father." I asked her if the teacher had added the reference to father, but she said she had done it, explaining to the teacher that she didn't want her father to feel left out. From that day on, all notes from the teacher were addressed "Dear Parents." I was ready to fight, but my daughter was able to see the more direct and more loving solution.

Like Milton, the dark side looms large
When I try to name where I am.
The good, the happy are shadowed,
And fade into tomorrow's wish.

But things are changing, so am I;
Paradise stands to be regained.
Daughters make us all feminists;
Will our sons be strong and join hands?

Whole together; armed together—
Heaven and hell in each person,
No vice, no dream shoved on one half.
Mere promise? Without it we're lost.

NOTES TO CHAPTERS

INTRODUCTION

1. Alix Shulman, "Organs and Orgasms," in *Woman in Sexist Society*, ed. Vivian Gornick and Barbara K. Moran (New York: New American Library, 1971), p. 302. Ms. Shulman ends this essay with the advice "Think clitoris."

2. Carolyn G. Heilbrun, *Toward a Recognition of Androgyny* (New York: Alfred A. Knopf, 1973), pp. x–xi. Here "androgyny," from *andro* (male) and *gyn* (female), is defined as "a condition under which the characteristics of the sexes, and the human impulses expressed by men and women, are not rigidly assigned . . . Androgyny suggests a spirit of reconciliation between the sexes; it suggests, further, a full range of experience open to individuals who may, as women, be aggressive, as men, tender; it suggests a spectrum upon which human beings choose their places without regard to propriety or custom."

3. Leon Salzman, "Psychology of the Female: A New Look," in *Psychoanalysis and Women,* ed. Jean Baker Miller (New York: Brunner/Mazel Publishers, 1973), pp. 175–76.

4. Naomi Weisstein, "Why We Aren't Laughing . . . Any More," *Ms.,* November 1973, p. 90.

5. Shulamith Firestone, *The Dialectic of Sex* (New York: Bantam Books, 1970). This book established Ms. Firestone as one of the leading theoreticians of radical feminism.

6. Midge Decter, *The New Chastity* (New York: Berkley Medallion Books, 1972). This book established Ms. Decter as the most gifted critic of feminist writing.

7. Eleanor Emmons Maccoby and Carol Nagy Jacklin, *The Psychology of Sex Differences* (Stanford, Calif.: Stanford University Press, 1974). In their landmark analysis of the research on sex differences, Maccoby and Jacklin concluded that there are only four fairly well established differences: (1) that girls excel in verbal ability; (2) that boys excel in visual-spatial ability; (3) that boys excel in mathematical ability; (4) that girls are less aggressive than boys.

8. Erik H. Erikson, *Childhood and Society* (New York: W. W. Norton and Co., 1950), p. 366.

9. Elinor Langer, "Confessing," *Ms.*, December 1974, p. 69. Ms. Langer is critical of the exhibitionistic confessional style that has become a self-congratulatory tradition in the women's movement: "Confession, under the auspices of the Women's Movement, is getting to be a messy business." She doesn't call for an end to self-revelation but urges that it be accompanied by analyzing the political structure in which personal events take place.

CHAPTER 1. THE BODY

1. Elinor Wylie, "Let No Charitable Hope," in *Collected Poems of Elinor Wylie* (New York: Alfred A. Knopf, 1932), p. 65.

2. Arthur Schopenhauer, "On Women," in *Studies in Pessimism*, 4th ed., trans. T. Bailey Saunders (London: Swan Sonnenschein and Co., 1893), pp. 105–23.

3. Sigmund Freud, "The Infantile Genital Organization of the Libido" (1923), in *Collected Papers*, Vol. II, trans. Joan Riviere, (New York: Basic Books, 1959), p. 249.

4. Sigmund Freud, "On the Sexual Theories of Children" (1908), in *Collected Papers*, Vol. II, p. 67.

5. Judith S. Kestenberg, "Menarche," in *Adolescents*, ed. Sandor Lorand and Henry I. Schneer (New York: Paul B. Hoeber, Inc., 1961), p. 37.

6. J. M. Tanner, "Physical Growth," in *Carmichael's Manual of Child Psychology,* Vol. I, ed. Paul H. Mussen (New York: John Wiley, 1970), pp. 77–156.

7. Schopenhauer, *op. cit.,* p. 107.

8. Ruth Herschberger, "Society Writes Biology," in *Adam's Rib* (New York: Har/Row Books, 1948), pp. 71–87.

9. Attributed to Aristotle by Matina S. Horner, "Femininity and Successful Achievement: A Basic Inconsistency," in *Feminine Personality and Conflict,* ed. Edward L. Walker (Belmont, Calif.: Brooks/Cole Publishing Co., 1970), p. 54.

10. Aristotle, "De generatione animalum," in *The Works of Aristotle,* Vol. V., trans. Arthur Platt (Oxford: Oxford University Press, 1912), pp. 729a-b.

11. Thomas Aquinas, *Not in God's Image,* ed. Julia O'Faolain and Lauro Martines (New York: Harper Torchbook, 1973), p. 131.

12. Don E. Hamachek, "Development and Dynamics of the Adolescent Self," in *Understanding Adolescence,* 2nd ed., ed. James F. Adams (Boston: Allyn and Bacon, 1973), pp. 43–44.

13. Quoted by Natalie Shainess, "Images of Woman: Past and Present, Overt and Obscured," in *Psychoanalysis and Women,* ed. Jean Baker Miller (New York: Brunner/Mazel Publishers, 1973), p. 261.

14. Joyce Maynard, *Looking Back* (New York: Avon Books, 1973), p. 74.

15. Joreen, "The Bitch Manifesto," in *Radical Feminism,* ed. Anne Koedt, Ellen Levine, and Anita Rapone (New York: Quadrangle Books, 1973), p. 55.

16. Klaus W. Berblinger, "Obesity and Psychologic Stress," in *Obesity,* ed. Nancy L. Wilson (Philadelphia: F. A. Davis and Co., 1969), p. 155.

17. Kate Blackwell and Karen Ferguson, "Pensions: Are There Holes in Your Security Blanket?" *Ms.,* October 1973, p. 14.

18. Hilde Bruch, *Eating Disorders* (New York: Basic Books, Inc., 1973), p. 21.

19. Phyllis Chesler, *Women and Madness* (Garden City, N.Y.: Doubleday and Co., 1972), p. 41.

20. Bruch, *op. cit.*, p. 20.

21. Joyce Carol Oates, *Them* (New York: Vanguard Press, 1969).

22. Berblinger, *op. cit.*, pp. 157–58.

23. George Gilder, *Sexual Suicide* (New York: Quadrangle Books, 1973), p. 224.

24. Margaret Atwood, *The Edible Woman* (Toronto: McClelland and Stewart Limited, 1969), pp. 267–73.

25. Theodore Isaac Rubin, *Forever Thin* (New York: Gramercy Publishing Co., 1970), p. 66.

26. Marjorie Palmer, "The Effect Weight Loss Has on Your Life Together," *Weight Watchers Magazine*, March 1974, pp. 22–23.

27. Hilde Bruch, *The Importance of Overweight* (New York: W. W. Norton and Co., 1957), pp. 238, 242.

28. Bruch, *Eating Disorders*, p. 97.

29. Robert F. Suczek, "The Personality of Obese Women," *American Journal of Clinical Nutrition*, 5, 2 (March-April 1957), p. 198.

30. Bruch, *Eating Disorders*, pp. 97–98.

31. *Ibid.*, pp. 98, 79.

32. *Ibid.*, pp. 100–101.

33. Joanne Koch and Lew Koch, "The Marriage Savers," *Chicago Guide*, February 1974, p. 96.

34. Rudolf Ekstein, "Puppet Play of a Psychotic Girl in the Psychotherapeutic Process," in *The Psychoanalytic Study of the Child*, Vol. XX, ed. Ruth Eissler *et al.* (New York: International Universities Press, 1965), pp. 465, 445.

35. Simone de Beauvoir, *The Second Sex*, trans. and ed. H. M. Parshley (New York: Vintage Books, 1952), pp. 369–73. Not only does Beauvoir link confidence in one's body with confidence in oneself, but she is very explicit about how a grounding in the art of self-protection leads to self-assurance.

CHAPTER 2. THE PARENTS

1. Simone de Beauvoir, *Memoirs of a Dutiful Daughter*, trans. James Kirkup (Cleveland: World Publishing Co., 1959), p. 45.

2. Lawrence Galton, "Decisions, Decisions, Decisions," *The New York Times Magazine*, June 30, 1974, pp. 26–27. Though the author carefully lists the pros and cons of choosing the child's sex, a bias toward male preferability shapes his entire presentation. Granted he's largely parroting the pro-son stance of the larger society as he sees it (and you can't fault him for the fact that many people see girls as naturally the *second*born), but his notion of why women would themselves favor a male majority is sexist. For example, he thinks women might enjoy an imbalance favoring men because it would eliminate "lonely widowhood or spinsterhood for many older women." That is the only advantage his whole article lists for women, and it is dripping with stereotype. Why drag out the old cliché that life without a man means loneliness or, worse yet, the stigma of being a spinster? Mr. Galton's article suggests a frightening future in which the notion of male domination is extended from politics to numbers, but it also says a good deal about the present low regard for women.

3. Leviticus 12:1–8. All biblical quotes throughout the book are from *The Jerusalem Bible*, ed. Alexander Jones (Garden City, N.Y.: Doubleday and Co., Inc., 1966).

4. Genesis 29:15–35; 30:1–24.

5. Carolyn G. Heilbrun, *Toward a Recognition of Androgyny* (New York: Alfred A. Knopf, 1973), p. 35.

6. Barbara Howar, *Laughing All the Way* (Greenwich, Conn.: Fawcett Publications, 1973), p. 28.

7. Margaret Mead, *Blackberry Winter* (New York: William Morrow and Co., 1972), p. 41.

8. Lois Gould, *Necessary Objects* (New York: Dell Publishing Co., 1972), p. 14.

9. Genesis 6:1.

10. Alfred Lord Tennyson, "The Princess," *The Poems and Plays of Alfred Lord Tennyson* (New York: The Modern Library, 1938), p. 273.

> Man for the field and woman for the hearth;
> Man for the sword, and for the needle she;
> Man with the head, and woman with the heart;
> Man to command, and woman to obey;
> All else confusion.

11. Ruth 4:16. Impressed by Ruth's heroic fidelity toward his kinswoman Naomi (the mother of her dead husband), Boaz marries her. Her women friends tell Naomi that Ruth "is more to you than seven sons," but what a double-edged compliment. Sons are assumed to be valuable regardless of merit.

12. Beauvoir, *Memoirs of a Dutiful Daughter*, pp. 153–54. Similar sentiments are expressed here: "If in the absolute sense a man, who was a member of the privileged species and already had a considerable lead ahead of me, did not count more than I did, I was forced to the conclusion that in a relative sense he counted less; in order to be able to acknowledge him as my equal, he would have to prove himself my superior in every way."

13. Jean Libman Block, "The Betty Ford Nobody Knows," *Good Housekeeping*, May 1974, p. 141.

14. Florence Rush, "Woman in the Middle," in *Radical Feminism*, ed. Anne Koedt, Ellen Levine, and Anita Rapone (New York: Quadrangle Books, 1973), pp. 43–45.

15. "Learning Dependence Early," *Human Behavior*, 2, 5 (May 1973), p. 41.

16. Simone de Beauvoir, *The Second Sex*, trans. and ed. H. M. Parshley (New York: Vintage Books, 1952), pp. 376–77.

17. Matina Horner, "Why Bright Women Fear Success," in *The Female Experience*, ed. Carol Tavris (Del Mar, Calif.: Communications/Research/Machines, Inc., 1973), pp. 55–57.

18. Reported by Dorothy Rogers, *Adolescence: A Psychological Perspective* (Monterey, Calif.: Brooks/Cole, 1972), pp. 118–19.

19. Mary Jane Moffat, *Revelations: Diaries of Women*, ed. Mary Jane Moffat and Charlotte Painter (New York: Random House, 1974), p. 5.

20. Quoted in *ibid.*, p. 14.

21. Phyllis Chesler, "Patient and Patriarch: Women in the Psychotherapeutic Relationship," in *Woman in Sexist Society*, ed. Vivian Gornick and Barbara K. Moran (New York: New American Library, 1971), p. 383. Clinicians see a healthy mature man and a healthy mature adult as one and the same, but are likely to assume a woman is more submissive, less independent, less adventurous, more easily influenced, less aggressive, less competitive, more excitable in minor crises, hurt more easily, more emotional, more conceited about her appearance, less objective, and less interested in science and math.

22. Reported by Thomas J. Cottle and Stephen L. Klineberg, *The Present of Things Future* (New York: The Free Press, 1974), p. 99.

23. *Ibid.*, pp. 116–22.

24. Walter Mischel, "Sex-Typing and Socialization," in *Carmichael's Manual of Child Psychology*, Vol. II, ed. Paul H. Mussen (New York: John Wiley, 1970), pp. 36–39.

25. Judith Bardwick and Elizabeth Douvan, "Ambivalence: The Socialization of Women," in *Woman in Sexist Society*, p. 229.

26. Bernice L. Neugarten, "Adult Personality: Toward a Psychology of the Life Cycle," in *Middle Age and Aging*, ed. Bernice L. Neugarten (Chicago: University of Chicago Press, 1968), p. 140.

27. Erik Erikson, *Identity: Youth and Crisis* (New York: W. W. Norton, 1968), p. 283.

CHAPTER 3. THE HUSBAND

1. Theodor Reik, *The Need to Be Loved* (New York: Bantam Books, 1963), p. 88.

2. James T. Geddis, "The Act of Love," in *Marriage Guide for Engaged Catholics*, ed. William F. McManus (Glen Rock, N.J.: Deus Books, Paulist Press, 1961), p. 63.

3. Daniel-Rops, *Of Human Love* (Notre Dame, Ind.: Fides Publishers, Inc., 1960), pp. 16, 52.

4. Lenore J. Weitzman, "Legal Regulation of Marriage: Tradition and Change," *California Law Review*, 62, 4 (July-September 1974), pp. 1170–1288.

5. G. W. F. Hegel, *The Phenomenology of Mind*, 2nd ed., trans. J. B. Baillie (London: George Allen and Unwin Ltd., 1956), p. 476.

6. *Ibid.*, p. 477.

7. Jerome Kagan, *Understanding Children* (New York: Harcourt Brace Jovanovich Inc., 1971), pp. 25–26. This well-known psychologist takes the attitude that each sex is "gratified by what the other disregards," but he has the woman being gratified by what the man disregards and is upset that what woman is now disregarding will rob man of "the healing power of her love."

8. Virginia Woolf wrote in *A Room of One's Own* (New York: Harcourt Brace, 1929) that women have served all these years as looking-glasses having the delicious power of reflecting the figure of man at twice its natural size.

9. Phyllis McGinley, *The Province of the Heart* (New York: The Viking Press, 1959), p. 17.

10. *Ibid.*, p. 18.

11. Eugene O'Neill, *The Iceman Cometh*, in *The Plays of Eugene O'Neill* (New York: Random House, 1951), pp. 713–14.

12. Alison Lurie, *The War Between the Tates* (New York: Warner Paperback Library, 1974), p. 13.

13. *Ibid.*, p. 280.

14. Friedrich Engels, *The Origins of the Family, Private Property, and the State,* trans. Ernest Untermann (Chicago: Charles H. Kerr and Co., 1902), p. 70.

15. Quoted by translator Randall Jarrell in Anton Chekhov's *The Three Sisters* (London: Collier-Macmillan Ltd., 1969), p. 104.

16. Jean-Paul Sartre, *Being and Nothingness,* trans. Hazel E. Barnes (New York: Washington Square Press, Inc., 1953), pp. 477, 445.

17. Simone de Beauvoir, *The Second Sex,* trans. and ed. H. M. Parshley (New York: Vintage Books, 1952), pp. xxxiii-xxxiv.

18. *Ibid.,* p. 813.

19. Bertrand Russell, *Marriage and Morals* (New York: Bantam Books, 1929), p. 97.

20. Kahlil Gibran, *The Prophet* (New York: Alfred A. Knopf, 1964), p. 15.

21. Simone de Beauvoir, *Memoirs of a Dutiful Daughter,* trans. James Kirkup (Cleveland: World Publishing Co., 1959), p. 153.

22. Walter Mischel, "Sex-Typing and Socialization," in *Carmichael's Manual of Child Psychology,* Vol. II, ed. Paul H. Mussen (New York: John Wiley, 1970), p. 10.

23. Margaret Mead, "The Job of the Children's Mother's Husband," in *The Contemporary American Family,* ed. William J. Goode (Chicago: Quadrangle Books, 1971), p. 135.

24. Philip Wylie, *Generation of Vipers,* 2nd ed. (New York: Rinehart and Co., 1955), p. 209.

25. Hannah Tillich, *From Time to Time* (New York: Stein and Day Publishers, 1973), pp. 15–16.

26. Herbert W. Richardson, *Nun, Witch, Playmate* (New York: Harper & Row, 1971), p. 86.

27. John Stuart Mill, *Essays on Sex Equality,* ed. Alice S. Rossi (Chicago: University of Chicago Press, 1970), pp. 91–92.

28. Reik, *op. cit.*, p. 87.

29. Richardson, *op. cit.*, pp. 89, 113.

30. Virginia Held, "Marx, Sex, and the Transformation of Society," *The Philosophical Forum*, 5, 1–2 (Fall-Winter 1973), p. 153.

CHAPTER 4. THE CHILDREN

1. Betty Rollin, "Motherhood: Who Needs It?" *Look*, September 22, 1970, pp. 15–17.

2. Quoted in *ibid.*, p. 15.

3. Karl Menninger and Jeanetta Lyle Menninger, *Love Against Hate* (New York: Harcourt, Brace and World, 1942), p. 52.

4. Joseph C. Rheingold, *The Mother, Anxiety and Death* (Boston: Little, Brown and Co., 1967), p. 151.

5. Quoted in Rollin, *op. cit.*, p. 17.

6. Erich Fromm, *The Art of Loving* (New York: Harper & Row, 1956), pp. 42, 38.

7. Philip Wylie, *Generation of Vipers*, 2nd ed. (New York: Rinehart and Co., 1955), pp. 196–97.

8. Benjamin Spock, *Baby and Child Care* (New York: Pocket Books, 1957), p. 5.

9. Vivian Gornick, "Woman as Outsider," in *Woman in Sexist Society*, ed. Vivian Gornick and Barbara K. Moran (New York: New American Library, 1971), p. 138.

10. Erma Bombeck, *I Lost Everything in the Post-Natal Depression* (Garden City, N.Y.: Doubleday and Co., 1973).

11. Helene Deutsch, *The Psychology of Women*, Vols. I and II (New York: Bantam Books, 1945).

12. Nathan W. Ackerman, *The Psychodynamics of Family Life* (New York: Basic Books, 1958), pp. 76, 338.

13. Doris Lessing, *The Summer Before the Dark* (New York: Alfred A. Knopf, 1973), pp. 102, 110.

14. Quoted in "Argentina, Hoping to Double Her Population This Century, Is Taking Action to Restrict Birth Control" by Jonathan Kandell, *The New York Times*, March 17, 1974, p. 4.

15. Ellen Peck, "The Baby Trap," *Cosmopolitan*, June 1971.

16. Jean Libman Block, "The Betty Ford Nobody Knows," *Good Housekeeping*, May 1974, pp. 138, 141–42.

17. Angela Barron McBride, "Why Do You Really Want a Baby?" *Glamour*, October 1973, p. 180.

18. Mary Jane Sherfey, "The Evolution and Nature of Female Sexuality in Relation to Psychoanalytic Theory," *Journal of the American Psychoanalytic Association*, 14, 1 (January 1966), p. 90.

19. M. Esther Harding, *The Way of All Women* (New York: G. P. Putnam's Sons, 1970), p. 158.

20. Quoted in Menninger and Menninger, *op. cit.*, p. 33.

21. Philip Slater, *The Pursuit of Loneliness* (Boston: Beacon Press, 1970), p. 64. The sense of motherhood as "Mission Impossible" is developed here.

22. Shirley L. Radl, *Mother's Day Is Over* (New York: Charterhouse, 1973), p. 228.

23. Doris C. Sutterley and Gloria F. Donnelly, *Perspectives in Human Development: Nursing Throughout the Life Cycle* (Philadelphia: J. B. Lippincott Co., 1973), p. 39.

24. Judith M. Bardwick, *Psychology of Women: A Study of Bio-Cultural Conflicts* (New York: Harper & Row, 1971), p. 190.

25. Midge Decter, *The New Chastity* (New York: Berkley Medallion Books, 1972), p. 203.

26. *Ibid.*, p. 204.

27. Kirsten Amundsen, *The Silenced Majority* (Englewood Cliffs, N.J.: Prentice-Hall, Inc., 1971), p. 159. Claire Etaugh, "Effects of

Maternal Employment on Children: A Review of Recent Research," *Merrill-Palmer Quarterly*, 20, 2 (April 1974), pp. 71–98 writes that "satisfied" mothers, whether they work or not, have the best adjusted children.

28. Angela Barron McBride, *The Growth and Development of Mothers* (New York: Harper & Row, 1973), pp. 128–50.

29. Letty Cottin Pogrebin, "Motherhood," *Ms.*, May 1973, pp. 49–50.

30. Alice Abarbanel, "Redefining Motherhood," in *The Future of the Family*, ed. Louise Kapp Howe (New York: Simon and Schuster, 1972), p. 365.

31. Pogrebin, *op. cit.*, p. 97.

32. Margaret Mead, *Blackberry Winter* (New York: William Morrow and Co., 1972), p. 282.

33. Elizabeth Janeway, *Man's World, Woman's Place* (New York: William Morrow and Co., 1971), p. 150.

34. Robert Seidenberg, "Is Anatomy Destiny?" in *Psychoanalysis and Women*, ed. Jean Baker Miller (New York: Brunner/Mazel Publishers, 1973), p. 317.

35. Clara M. Thompson, *On Women*, ed. Maurice R. Green (New York: New American Library, 1971), p. 135.

36. McBride, *The Growth and Development of Mothers*, p. 6.

37. Jessie Bernard, *The Future of Motherhood* (New York: The Dial Press, 1974), p. 103.

38. Rochelle P. Wortis, "The Acceptance of the Concept of the Maternal Role by Behavioral Scientists: Its Effect on Women," *American Journal of Orthopsychiatry*, 41, 5 (October 1971), p. 741.

39. Joanne Koch and Lew Koch, "A Society Against Children," *Chicago Guide*, September 1974, p. 82.

40. Bennett M. Berger, Bruce M. Hackett, and R. Mervyn Millar, "Child Rearing in Communes," in *The Future of the Family*, pp. 162–63.

CHAPTER 5. THE HOME

1. Margaret Mead, *Blackberry Winter* (New York: William Morrow and Co., 1972), p. 12.

2. Robert Frost, "The Death of the Hired Man," *The Poetry of Robert Frost*, ed. Edward Connery Lathem (New York: Holt, Rinehart and Winston, 1969), p. 38.

3. Rudyard Kipling, "Our Lady of the Snows," *The Five Nations*, Vol. XXI (New York: Doubleday and Co.), p. 86.

4. Emmanuel Levinas, *Totality and Infinity*, trans. Alphonso Lingis (Pittsburgh, Pa.: Duquesne University Press, 1969), p. 155.

5. *Ibid.*, pp. 157–58.

6. Erik Erikson, "Inner and Outer Space: Reflections on Womanhood," *The Woman in America*, ed. Robert Jay Lifton (Boston: Beacon Press, 1965), p. 10.

7. *Ibid.*, p. 15.

8. Theodor Reik, *The Need to Be Loved* (New York: Bantam Books, 1963), p. 13.

9. Jessie Bernard, *The Future of Motherhood* (New York: The Dial Press, 1974), p. 125.

10. Thorstein Veblen, *The Theory of the Leisure Class* (Boston: Houghton Mifflin Co., 1973), p. 128.

11. John Kenneth Galbraith, *Economics and the Public Purpose* (Boston: Houghton Mifflin Co., 1973), p. 33. Chapter IV, "Consumption and the Concept of the Household," and Chapter XXIII, "The Equitable Household and Beyond," take an in-depth look at the economic structure of the household and what needs changing.

12. Simone de Beauvoir, *The Second Sex*, trans. and ed. H. M. Parshley (New York: Vintage Books, 1952), p. 480.

13. *Ibid.*, p. 504.

14. Quoted in "Fabric Softeners," *Consumer Reports*, May 1974, p. 419.

15. Ad in *The New York Times Magazine,* March 24, 1974, pp. 56–57.

16. Quoted in "Your Own Place in the Sun" by Daniel H. Yergin, *Harper's,* March 1974, p. 41.

17. Arthur Miller, "The Price," in *The Portable Arthur Miller,* ed. Harold Clurman (New York: The Viking Press, 1973), p. 378.

18. Arthur Asa Berger, "Sex and the Serpent on Madison Avenue," *Human Behavior,* 2, 6 (June 1973), p. 76. Such sentiments are well analyzed in this article.

19. "Happy Wedding Day!" Lafayette (Indiana) *Journal and Courier,* June 7, 1974, p. 18.

20. Carl G. Jung, "Approaching the Unconscious," in *Man and His Symbols,* ed. Carl G. Jung (New York: Dell Publishing Co., 1964), p. 67.

21. Doris Lessing, *The Summer Before the Dark* (New York: Alfred A. Knopf, 1973), p. 105.

22. Galbraith, *op. cit.,* p. 32.

23. Betty Friedan, *The Feminine Mystique* (New York: Dell Publishing Co., 1963), p. 231.

24. Susan Sands, "A Word for the Plastic and the Processed," *Ms.,* March 1974, p. 19.

25. Jean Kerr, *Please Don't Eat the Daisies* (Garden City, N.Y.: Doubleday and Co., 1957), p. 48.

26. Naomi Weisstein, "Why We Aren't Laughing . . . Any More," *Ms.,* November 1973, p. 88.

27. Erma Bombeck, "Mommy Makes Point with Her Needlepoint," Lafayette (Indiana) *Journal and Courier,* February 5, 1974, B-12.

28. Erma Bombeck, *I Lost Everything in the Post-Natal Depression,* (Garden City, N.Y.: Doubleday and Co., 1973), p. 141.

29. *Ibid.,* p. 141.

30. *Ibid.,* p. 15.

31. *Ibid.,* p. 93.

32. Friedan, *op. cit.,* pp. 11–27.

33. Robert Seidenberg, "The Trauma of Eventlessness," in *Psychoanalysis and Women,* ed. Jean Baker Miller (New York: Brunner/Mazel Publishers, 1973), p. 361.

34. Bombeck, *I Lost Everything in the Post-Natal Depression,* p. 126.

35. Mabel Blake Cohen, "Personal Identity and Sexual Identity," in *Psychoanalysis and Women,* p. 153.

36. Bombeck, *I Lost Everything in the Post-Natal Depression,* p. 159.

37. B. F. Skinner, *Walden Two* (New York: The Macmillan Co., 1948), p. 57.

38. Judy Syfers, "Why I Want a Wife," in *Radical Feminism,* ed. Anne Koedt, Ellen Levine, and Anita Rapone (New York: Quadrangle Books, 1973), pp. 60–62. This is a very funny, perceptive essay on why a wife would want a wife.

39. Skinner, *op. cit.,* p. 54.

40. Marge Piercy, *Small Changes* (Garden City, N.Y.: Doubleday and Co., 1973), pp. 351–52.

41. "Male and Female," *Time,* May 6, 1974, p. 81. There is a tendency on the part of professional women to deny their household help benefits they themselves take for granted.

42. Ann Crittenden Scott, "The Value of Housework," *Ms.,* July, 1972, p. 57. Housewives' services amount to one-fourth of the current GNP, or $250 billion.

CHAPTER 6. COOKING

1. Erich Neumann, *The Great Mother,* trans. Ralph Manheim (Princeton, N.J.: Princeton University Press, Bollingen Series XLVII, 1955), p. 283.

2. Jacquetta Hawkes and Sir Leonard Woolley, *Prehistory and the Beginning of Civilization* (New York: Harper & Row, 1963), p. 265.

3. Ruby R. Leavitt, "Women in Other Cultures," in *Woman in Sexist Society,* ed. Vivian Gornick and Barbara K. Moran (New York: New American Library, 1971), pp. 412–13.

4. Erich Fromm, *The Art of Loving* (New York: Harper & Row, 1956), p. 38.

5. Claude Lévi-Strauss, *The Raw and the Cooked,* trans. John Weightman and Doreen Weightman (New York: Harper & Row, 1969), pp. 269, 296.

6. Karl Menninger and Jeanetta Lyle Menninger, *Love Against Hate* (New York: Harcourt, Brace and World, 1942), p. 48.

7. Mary McGee Williams and Irene Kane, *On Becoming a Woman* (New York: Dell Publishing Co., 1959), pp. 67, 69, 131, 150.

8. Ernest Jones, *The Life and Work of Sigmund Freud,* Vol. I (New York: Basic Books, 1953), p. 104.

9. Lynn Young, "An Old-Fashioned Girl," *Newsweek,* June 24, 1974, p. 75. One woman who took Marabel Morgan's course on "The Total Woman" at a local Southern Baptist church welcomed her husband home dressed this way and he shouted "Praise the Lord!"

10. "J," *The Sensuous Woman* (New York: Dell Publishing Co., 1969), pp. 122, 116.

11. Neumann, *op. cit.,* p. 285.

12. Lévi-Strauss, *op. cit.,* pp. 335–36.

13. Neumann, *op. cit.,* p. 291.

14. *Ibid.,* p. 287.

15. John Guare, *The House of Blue Leaves* (New York: The Viking Press, 1972), p. 21.

16. Simone de Beauvoir, *Memoirs of a Dutiful Daughter,* trans. James Kirkup (Cleveland: World Publishing Co., 1959), p. 8.

17. Joyce Carol Oates, *Them* (New York: Vanguard Press, 1969), p. 208.

18. Hilde Bruch, *The Importance of Overweight* (New York: W. W. Norton and Co., 1957), p. 198.

19. Peg Bracken, *The I Hate To Cook Book* (New York: Fawcett World Library, 1960), p. 79.

20. Quoted in Natalie Shainess, "Images of Woman: Past and Present, Overt and Obscured," in *Psychoanalysis and Women,* ed. Jean Baker Miller (New York: Brunner/Mazel Publishers, 1973), p. 261.

21. "The Gourmet Murderer," *Newsweek,* December 3, 1973, p. 52.

22. "Mother's Day Death Investigated," Lafayette (Indiana) *Journal and Courier,* May 12, 1975, A-1.

CHAPTER 7. RELIGION

1. Quoted by Paula Hyman in "Is It Kosher to Be Feminist?" *Ms.,* July 1974, p. 77.

2. Quoted by Mary Ellmann in *Thinking About Women* (New York: Harcourt Brace Jovanovich, 1968), p. 11.

3. Quoted by Simone de Beauvoir in *The Second Sex,* trans. and ed. H. M. Parshley (New York: Vintage Books, 1952), p. 110.

4. Léon Joseph Cardinal Suenens, *Love and Control* (Westminster, Md.: The Newman Press, 1961), p. 67.

5. Quoted by Mary Daly in *The Church and the Second Sex,* 2nd ed. (New York: Harper Colophon Books, 1975), p. 91.

6. Quoted by Beauvoir in *The Second Sex,* p. 110.

7. Arlene Swidler, *Woman in a Man's Church* (New York: Paulist Press, 1972), p. 58.

8. "A Jewish Prayer," trans. Elsie Adams in *Up Against the Wall, Mother* . . . , ed. Elsie Adams and Mary Louise Briscoe (Beverly Hills, Calif.: Glencoe Press, 1971), p. 8.

9. Quoted by Una Stannard in "The Mask of Beauty," in *Woman in Sexist Society,* ed. Vivian Gornick and Barbara K. Moran (New York: New American Library, 1971), p. 197.

10. See "Obey Thy Husband," *Time,* May 20, 1974, p. 64, for a current statement of this philosophy by Rev. Bill Gothard, who advises the woman who is beaten by her husband to say, "God, thank you for this beating . . . Father, forgive them, for they know not what they do. But you know what you are doing through them to build character in me."

11. Eva Figes, *Patriarchal Attitudes* (Greenwich, Conn.: Fawcett Premier Books, 1970), p. 32.

12. St. Augustine, *The City of God,* trans. Gerald G. Walsh, Demetrius B. Zema, Grace Monahan, and Daniel J. Honan (Garden City, N.Y.: Image Books, 1958), pp. 306–7.

13. Garry Wills, *Bare Ruined Choirs: Doubt, Prophecy, and Radical Religion* (Garden City, N.Y.: Doubleday and Co., 1972), p. 227.

14. Bertrand Russell, *Marriage and Morals* (New York: Bantam Books, 1929), p. 41.

15. Vern L. Bullough and Bonnie Bullough, *The Subordinate Sex* (Baltimore: Penguin Books, 1973), p. 97.

16. *Ibid.,* p. 174.

17. *Ibid.,* p. 116.

18. *Ibid.,* p. 197.

19. Hyman, *op. cit.,* p. 77.

20. St. Francis de Sales, *Introduction to the Devout Life,* trans. and ed. John K. Ryan (Garden City, N.Y.: Image Books, 1950), pp. 222–23.

21. *Ibid.,* p. 217.

22. William F. McManus, *Marriage Guide for Engaged Catholics* (Glen Rock, N.J.: Deus Books, Paulist Press, 1961), p. 93.

23. Frederick Von Gagern, *Difficulties in Married Life,* trans. Meyrock Booth (New York: Deus Books, Paulist Press, 1953), p. 51.

24. *Ibid.,* p. 52.

25. Quoted of Pius XI by Daly, *op. cit.,* p. 110.

26. Wills, *op. cit.,* pp. 185–86.

27. Quoted by Thomas J. O'Donnell, *Morals in Medicine,* 2nd ed. (Westminster, Md.: The Newman Press, 1959), pp. 271–72.

28. Quoted by Daly, *op. cit.,* p. 114.

29. *Ibid.,* p. 113.

30. *Ibid.,* p. 98.

31. O'Donnell, *op. cit.,* p. 284.

32. *Ibid.,* p. 284.

33. *Ibid.,* p. 286.

34. Sally Cunneen, *Sex: Female; Religion: Catholic* (New York: Holt, Rinehart and Winston, 1968), p. 12.

35. Constance F. Parvey, "The Theology and Leadership of Women in the New Testament," *Religion and Sexism,* ed. Rosemary Radford Ruether (New York, Simon and Schuster, 1974), pp. 146–47.

36. Cunneen, *op. cit.,* p. 13.

37. F. J. Sheed, *Theology for Beginners* (New York: Sheed and Ward, 1957), p. 45.

38. Swidler, *op. cit.,* pp. 83–84.

39. Cunneen, *op. cit.,* p. 139.

40. Donald Gray, "On Patience: Human and Divine," *Cross Currents,* 24, 4 (Winter 1975), p. 416.

41. Erich Fromm, *The Crisis of Psychoanalysis* (Greenwich, Conn.: Fawcett Premier Books, 1970), p. 103.

42. Pierre Teilhard de Chardin, *Human Energy,* trans. J. M. Cohen (New York: Harcourt Brace Jovanovich, 1969), p. 73.

43. Kate Millett, *Sexual Politics* (New York: Avon Books, 1970), p. 37.

44. Quoted by Cunneen, *op. cit.,* p. 32.

45. Sheed, *op. cit.,* p. 169.

46. *Ibid.,* p. 169.

47. Quoted in W. B. Faherty, "Catholic Teaching on Women," in *Up Against the Wall, Mother . . . ,* ed. Elsie Adams and Mary Louise Briscoe (Beverly Hills, Calif.: Glencoe Press, 1971), p. 12.

48. Quoted by Frederick Franck, *Exploding Church* (New York: Delta Books, 1968), p. 68. Pope Paul VI also thinks woman "is a vision of virginal purity, which heals the highest emotive and ethical feelings of the human heart. . . . She is in the loneliness of man the emergence of companionship who knows the capacity of love, of value and cooperation and assistance, the power of faithfulness and industry, the most ordinary heroism of sacrifice." In this November 1966 speech to Italian gynecologists, woman is force-fed lethal compliments the way a fatted goose destined to be someone's pâté is force-fed grain.

49. Rosemary Haughton, "Beyond Women's Lib," *Catholic Digest,* January 1974, p. 24.

50. Sheed, *op. cit.,* p. 167.

51. Quoted by Julia O'Faolain and Lauro Martines, eds., *Not in God's Image* (New York: Harper Torchbooks, 1973), p. 138.

52. Louis Dupré, *Contraception and Catholics* (Baltimore: Helicon Press, 1964), p. 46.

53. *Ibid.,* p. 46.

54. Russell, *op. cit.,* p. 33.

55. Philip Rieff, *Freud: The Mind of the Moralist* (Garden City, N.Y.: Doubleday and Co., Inc., 1961), pp. 293, 301, 312.

56. George Bernard Shaw, *Joan of Arc*, in *The Bodley Head Bernard Shaw Collected Plays with Their Prefaces*, Vol. VI (London: Max Reinhardt, 1973), pp. 177–78.

57. Pierre Teilhard de Chardin, *The Divine Milieu* (New York: Harper Torchbooks, 1960), p. 96.

CHAPTER 8. THE JOB

1. Theodor Reik, *The Need to Be Loved* (New York: Bantam Books, 1963), p. 82.

2. Theodore Lidz, *The Person* (New York: Basic Books, 1968), p. 383.

3. "The Myth and the Reality" (Washington, D.C.: U.S. Government Printing Office, 1974, 0-550-115), pp. 1–2.

4. Lidz, *op. cit.*, p. 383.

5. Joan Acker, "Woman and Social Stratification: A Case of Intellectual Sexism," *Changing Women in a Changing Society*, ed. Joan Huber (Chicago: University of Chicago Press, 1973), p. 175.

6. Lidz, *op. cit.*, p. 384.

7. "The Myth and the Reality," p. 1.

8. *Dictionary of Occupational Titles*, 3rd ed. (Washington, D.C.: U.S. Government Printing Office, 1965), Vol. I.

9. Walter R. Gove and Jeannette F. Tudor, "Adult Sex Roles and Mental Illness," in *Changing Women in a Changing Society*, p. 53.

10. "The Myth and the Reality," p. 1.

11. *Ibid.*, p. 2.

12. Reported by Lenore J. Weitzman, "Legal Regulation of Marriage: Tradition and Change," *California Law Review*, 62, 4 (July-September 1974), p. 1219.

13. Lidz, *op. cit.*, p. 394.

14. Reported by Mirra Komarovsky, "Cultural Contradictions and Sex Roles: The Masculine Case," in *Changing Women in a Changing Society*, p. 116.

15. "1968—National Organization for Women (NOW) Bill of Rights," *Rebirth of Feminism*, ed. Judith Hole and Ellen Levine (New York: Quadrangle Books, 1971), p. 441.

16. Weitzman, *op. cit.*, p. 1191.

17. *Your Federal Income Tax*, 1974 ed. (Washington, D.C.: U.S. Government Printing Office, 1973), p. 97.

18. *Ibid.*, p. 98.

19. Hanna Papanek, "Men, Women, and Work: Reflections on the Two-Person Career," in *Changing Women in a Changing Society*, p. 90.

20. Frederick Von Gagern, *Difficulties in Married Life*, trans. Meyrock Booth (New York: Deus Books, Paulist Press, 1953), pp. 51–52.

21. Quoted by Alice Lake, "The Revolt of the Company Wife," *McCall's*, October 1973, p. 22.

22. *Ibid.*, p. 22.

23. Quoted by Phyllis Funke, "A Volunteer-Minded Grandmother," *The New York Times*, June 2, 1974, p. 15.

24. Phyllis McGinley, *The Province of the Heart* (New York: The Viking Press, 1959), p. 77.

25. Boyd C. Rollins and Harold Feldman, "Marital Satisfaction Over the Family Life Cycle," *Journal of Marriage and the Family*, 32, 1 (February 1970), p. 25.

26. Alice S. Rossi, "Equality Between the Sexes: An Immodest Proposal," in *The Woman in America*, ed. Robert Jay Lifton (Boston: Beacon Press, 1965), p. 114.

27. Sandra L. Bem and Daryl J. Bem, "Training the Woman to Know Her Place," in *The Future of the Family*, ed. Louise Kapp Howe (New York: Simon and Schuster, 1972) p. 222.

28. Jan E. Dizard, "The Price of Success," in *The Future of the Family*, p. 198.

29. Lynda Lytle Holmstrom, *The Two-Career Family* (Cambridge, Mass.: Schenkman Publishing Co., 1972), pp. 103–20.

30. Jessie Bernard, *The Future of Motherhood* (New York: The Dial Press, 1974), pp. 182–95.

31. *Ibid.*, p. 192.

32. Quoted by Myra MacPherson, "No More Mrs. Nice Guy," *New Times*, April 5, 1974, p. 42.

33. Quoted by Lyn Tornabene, "Cher's Own Story of Life Without Sonny," *Ladies' Home Journal*, July 1974, p. 50.

34. Boyce Rensberger, "The Face of Evolution," *The New York Times Magazine*, March 3, 1974, p. 44.

35. Quoted by Everett R. Holles, "Firemen's Wives Fight for Chauvinism on Job," *The New York Times*, July 28, 1974, p. 46.

36. Quoted by Marcia Slater Johnston, "Get a Job!" *Chicago Guide*, August 1974, p. 64.

37. Joan T. Roberts and Thetis M. Group, "The Women's Movement and Nursing," *Nursing Forum*, 12, 3 (1973), p. 315.

38. Barbara Ehrenreich and Deirdre English, *Witches, Midwives and Nurses*, 2nd ed. (Westbury, N.Y.: The Feminist Press, 1973), pp. 8–9.

39. Cynthia Krueger, "Do 'Bad Girls' Become Good Nurses?" in *The Professional Woman*, ed. Athena Theodore (Cambridge, Mass.: Schenkman Publishing Co., 1971), p. 689.

40. Lucretia Richter and Elizabeth Richter, "Nurses in Fiction," *American Journal of Nursing*, 74, 7 (July 1974), pp. 1280–81.

41. Ethel Bangert, *Nurse on Vacation* (New York: Thomas Bouregy and Co., 1970), p. 171.

42. Roberts and Group, *op. cit.*, p. 304.

43. Cynthia F. Epstein, "Encountering the Male Establishment: Sex-Status Limits on Women's Careers in the Professions," in *The Professional Woman,* p. 54.

44. "Progress Notes" (published by Pittsburgh Nurses NOW), March 1975, p. 3.

45. Quoted in Roberts and Group, *op. cit.,* p. 319.

46. Hildegard Peplau, "Principles of Psychiatric Nursing," in *American Handbook of Psychiatry,* Vol. II, ed. Silvano Arieti (New York: Basic Books, 1959), p. 1847.

47. Angela McBride, "Leadership: Problems and Possibilities in Nursing," *American Journal of Nursing,* 72, 8 (August 1972), pp. 1445–47.

48. Germaine Greer, *The Female Eunuch* (New York: McGraw-Hill Book Co., 1971), p. 147.

49. Lytton Strachey, *Eminent Victorians* (New York: Capricorn Books, 1963), pp. 129–96.

50. Eugenia Kennedy Spalding, *Professional Nursing: Trends and Relationships,* 5th ed. (Philadelphia: J. B. Lippincott Co., 1954), p. 86.

51. Bem and Bem, *op. cit.,* pp. 203–4.

CHAPTER 9. COLLISION COURSE OR . . .

1. Theodor Reik, *The Need to Be Loved* (New York: Bantam Books, 1963), p. 250.

2. Alice S. Rossi, "Maternalism, Sexuality, and the New Feminism," in *Contemporary Sexual Behavior: Critical Issues in the 1970s,* ed. Joseph Zubin and John Money (Baltimore: The Johns Hopkins University Press, 1973), pp. 162–63. Patriarchal values can also be looked at as "a masculine status compensation for the woman's biological ability to bear children."

3. Reported by Lenore J. Weitzman, "Legal Regulation of Marriage: Tradition and Change," *California Law Review*, 62, 4 (July-September 1974), p. 1223.

4. Roland Hall, "Dialectic," in *The Encyclopedia of Philosophy*, Vol. II, ed. Paul Edwards (New York: The Macmillan Company, 1967), p. 388.

5. Klaus F. Riegel, "Adult Life Crises: Toward a Dialectic Theory of Development," in *Life-Span Developmental Psychology: Normative Life Crises*, ed. N. Datan and L. H. Ginsberg (New York: Academic Press, 1975).

6. Ann Belford Ulanov, *The Feminine in Jungian Psychology and in Christian Theology* (Evanston, Ill.: Northwestern University Press, 1971), pp. 193–211.

7. Quoted in Simone de Beauvoir, *The Second Sex*, trans. and ed. H. M. Parshley (New York: Vintage Books, 1952), p. 99.

8. Ulanov, *op. cit.*, p. 191.

9. *Ibid.*, p. 337.

10. Sigmund Freud, "Some Psychological Consequences of the Anatomical Distinction Between the Sexes" (1925), *Collected Papers*, Vol. V, ed. James Strachey (New York: Basic Books, 1959), p. 196.

11. Meda Rebecca, Robert Hefner, and Barbara Oleshansky, "A Model of Sex-Role Transcendence," tentatively scheduled for *Journal of Social Issues*, issue on "Sex-Typed Roles: Persistence and Change," 1976.

12. Carole Offir, "What Are Little Girls Made Of? Puppy Dogs' Tails Too," *Psychology Today*, August 1974, pp. 43, 113.

13. Louisa May Alcott, *Little Women*, in *A House of Good Proportion*, ed. Michele Murray (New York: Simon and Schuster, 1973), pp. 81–82.

14. Robert C. Peck, "Psychological Developments in the Second Half of Life," in *Middle Age and Aging*, ed. Bernice L. Neugarten (Chicago: University of Chicago Press, 1968), p. 89.

15. Peter Blos, "Character Formation in Adolescence," *The Psychoanalytic Study of the Child,* Vol. XXIII, ed. Ruth Eissler *et al.* (New York: International Universities Press, 1968), pp. 257–58.

16. David Bakan, *The Duality of Human Existence* (Chicago: Rand McNally and Co., 1966), p. 236. Bakan, however, devotes more space to "agency" in his book than "communion."